The End of Multiculturalism?

Terrorism, integration and human rights

Derek McGhee

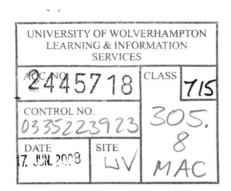

Open University Press

Open University Press
McGraw-Hill Education
McGraw-Hill House
Shoppenhangers Road
Maidenhead
Berkshire
England
SL6 2QL

email: enquiries@openup.co.uk
world wide web: www.openup.co.uk

and Two Penn Plaza, New York, NY 10121–2289, USA

First published 2008
Copyright © Derek McGhee 2008

A catalogue record of this book is available from the British Library

ISBN 978 0335 22391 6 (hb)
ISBN 978 0335 22392 3 (pb)

Library of Congress Cataloguing-in-Publication Data
CIP data applied for

Typeset by YHT Ltd, London
Printed in the UK by Bell and Bain Ltd, Glasgow

Fictitious names of companies, products, people, characters and/or data that may be used herein (in case studies or in examples) are not intended to represent any real individual, company, product or event.

The *McGraw-Hill* Companies

Contents

In memory of Jean Charles de Menezes

Acknowledgements

In many ways this book is a product of some very helpful advice I was given by Caroline Knowles and Claire Alexander when I had completed my previous book *Intolerant Britain?* In many ways this book is a product of the process of 'consolidation' that they advised.

I would also like to thank the Open University Press, especially Chris Cudmore for supporting the project. Various colleagues deserve a mention here for their support with regard to conversations held during the process of writing this book: Ed Bates for his careful reading of Chapter 1 and for our informative discussion on derogation; human rights and Conor Gearty's work; Silke Roth for pointing out that 'the new terrorism threat' should be examined in the context of previous terror threats; Sue Heath and Lee Price for putting up with my constant 'updates' on progress in the writing of this book; Kalwant Bhopal for being so enthusiastic about this book and for including me in a number of exciting projects while writing it; Milena Büchs for reading an earlier draft of the book and offering some insightful comments for its improvement; Traute Meyer for conversations on where the balance should be struck between individual rights and public protection and all the marvellous hospitality; Wendy Bottero for carefully reading a draft of this book and offering some extremely helpful suggestions as well as identifying potential 'awkward' passages; David Owen and Caroline Knowles for their careful reading of this book and their enthusiasm for the project; the members of the Runnymede Trust's Academic Forum for allowing me to share some of my views on integration, multiculturalism and human rights with them at a number of meetings.

I would like to thank the organizers of the War on Terror Seminar, School of Policy Studies, Bristol University, September 2007 for inviting me to speak and the participants of this seminar for their helpful comments on some of the book's themes. I would also like to extend my appreciation to the anonymous reviewers selected by the Open University Press to review the proposal for this book and the manuscript reviewer. Their constructive criticism and suggestions were incredibly helpful in the process of shaping my approach to writing this book.

I would also like to thank the editors of and anonymous reviewers selected by the *British Journal of Sociology* (for their comments on an article that included aspects of what has become Chapter 2) and *Critical Social Policy* (for their comments on an article that included aspects of what has become Chapter 3). I would also like to thank the editors and anonymous reviewers selected by *Ethnopolitics* (a version of Chapter 5 was published as 'The New Commission for Equality and Human Rights: building Community cohesion and revitalizing citizenship in contemporary Britain', *Ethnopolitics*, 2006, Vol. 5.2, 145–66) and the editors and anonymous reviewers selected by *Sociological Research Online* who offered suggestions on an article that includes aspects of Chapter 4 (which was published as Patriots of the Future? a critical examination of community cohesion strategies in contemporary Britain, *Sociological Research On-line*, September 2005, Vol. 10.3.)

I would also like to thank my family for all their support and affection during the writing of this book. I would like to thank my partner Andrew Cullis for being foolish enough to 'marry' me earlier this year. I would like to thank 'the in-laws', the Cullis family for all their support and affection, and finally, I would like to thank my parents John and Jeanette for a lifetime of unstinting love and support.

Preface

This book with its audacious title: *The End of Multiculturalism? Terrorism, Integration and Human Rights* can be described as a sequel to my last book *Intolerant Britain? Hate, Citizenship and Difference*. The latter was an exploration of the tension associated with the emergence of the reflexive 'intolerance of intolerance' in various areas of public policy (especially in relation to hate crimes) in contemporary Britain alongside the increasing hostility to multiculturalism that was expressed in the asylum and immigration policies dedicated to deterrence and integration policies that focused on assimilation. In *The End of Multiculturalism?* I continue to examine debates surrounding multiculturalism. However, in this book these debates are contextualized within the analysis of the new interrelated discourses of integration and security in contemporary Britain. The emphasis on securitization and integration in this book provides the critical framework for examining the shifting discourses on multiculturalism and human rights in contemporary British public policy.

Hostility to multiculturalism, if anything, has increased in contemporary British society since I wrote *Intolerant Britain?* This attack on multiculturalism is being led by opinion makers on both the left and the right of the political spectrum. It is important, however, to note that this hostility is being directed at a contested and multi-faceted concept. There are many multiculturalisms, for example, multiculturalism can be conservative, liberal, critical and reflexive (just to name a few). At the same time distinct versions of multiculturalisms emerge in different places, in that European multiculturalism is quite different from the American version and also different both again from the Indian version (Parekh 2000b: 349). According to Mason, whatever else it is, multiculturalism is an approach to cultural diversity (2007: 221). For Goldberg, multiculturalism, broadly conceived, 'is critical of and resistant to the necessarily reductive imperatives of monocultural assimilation' (1994: 7). Well yes and no. Some multiculturalisms advocate pluralism, some are closer in orientation to assimilation and some advocate a doctrine of cultural separation. Kivisto suggests that multiculturalism as a social policy ought to be viewed as a form of assimilation or incorporation that both valorizes ethnic diversity but also requires that newcomers embrace the core societal values of the 'host' country (2005b: 314). This is akin to the civic assimilation approach advocated by David Blunkett and others (see Chapter 4). However, others, for example Brian Barry, see multiculturalism as being socially divisive and based on the over-valorization of the distinctive cultural attributes of groups (2001: 304). Rather than attempting to forge unity, to establish shared values between groups, some multiculturalists, according to Barry, 'view a single set of rules applying to all its members is bound to be oppressive to cultural minorities, because the rules will simply reflect the culture of the majority' (2001: 300). The various Government-derived projects for attempting to find shared values that reflect the values of all social groups in Britain will be examined in Chapters 4, 5 and 6.

The debates on multiculturalism that are examined in this book focus on the primary accusation against multiculturalism from the left and the right of the political spectrum in contemporary British society: that multiculturalism is associated with (1) the lack of integration between different communities, (2) the preferential treatment of some groups over others, and (3) a patriotic deficit in certain communities. Rather than launching into a normative examination of the concept, this book examines contemporary debates about multiculturalism (see Introduction). These debates are in turn examined in the context of particular discourses: integration, security and human rights in various chapters of this book.

As well as examining the often ambivalent hostility to multiculturalism in contemporary Britain, a number of chapters in this book are devoted to examining the impact of anti-terrorism legislation and the new security discourses that justify them on Muslim communities. By so doing Britain's relationship with Muslim communities is brought to the fore in the examination of multiculturalism, citizenship, integration and human rights in various chapters.

Introduction

This book adopts the approach to examining 'multiculturalism' found in Schuster and Solomos's (2001) introduction to the special issue of *Patterns of Prejudice*, that is, they set out to examine 'what debates about multiculturalism tell us about the changing nature of states, citizenship and political identity' (2001: 4). In this special issue Schuster and Solomos focused on globalization and migration patterns to explore these debates. In this book, the subtitle: *Terrorism, Integration and Human Rights* indicates a different (but related) focus in order to explore the unfolding debates on multiculturalism in contemporary Britain and what these debates can tell us about not only the changing nature of Britain, British citizenship and British identities; but what these (and related debates, on for example, human rights) can tell us about the reflexive business of governing. Rather than the 'civil rights movement multiculturalism', that emerged, for example, in the USA associated with identity politics (Modood 2007: 2), what is explored here is the political idea of multiculturalism that emerges in the response to immigration. That is, a variety of multiculturalism associated with Britain and Europe that 'focuses on the consequences of immigration' (Modood 2007: 2) from this perspective, multiculturalism can be defined as 'the political accommodation of minorities formed by immigration to western countries from outside the prosperous west' (2007: 5).

Chapters 4, 5 and 6 focus most directly on the debates on multiculturalism. These chapters map an emergent consensus (on the right and the left of the political spectrum) that suggests that multiculturalism has become a divisive force in British society. Chapters 4, 5 and 6, therefore, are dedicated to examining how multiculturalism is presented in political discourse and what is being suggested to replace it (for example, 'integration with diversity', a 'proper human rights culture' and Britishness based on 'shared values'). Chapters 1, 2 and 3 do not explore debates on multiculturalism directly; rather, the focus of these chapters is on security, human rights and citizenship. The location of these chapters before the chapters that examine multiculturalism, assimilation and integration is deliberate. By ordering the chapters in this way, a clear message is being relayed to readers; that is, the debates on multiculturalism (especially debates on the alleged failure of multiculturalism) should be examined in the context of wider debates on human rights, citizenship and security in contemporary British society.

It should be noted that the particularly 'British debates' that are examined here have developed in the context of a European Union (EU) wide backlash against 'multiculturalism' post-9/11. According to Fekete, after 9/11 many European states including Britain began steering their 'race relations' policies away from 'multiculturalism' towards monoculturalism and cultural homogenization (2004: 18). Fekete observed that in many European countries 'national identity debates' have coalesced around a pattern of events[1] and themes specific to that country (2004: 18). In Britain the recent debates on national identity and the alleged failure of multiculturalism have coalesced around the social disorder in Oldham, Burnley and Bradford in the summer of 2001[2] (see Chapter 4) and the bombings and attempted bombings in London in July 2005 (see Chapters 2 and 3). It is suggested that these events, including the events that have occurred outside Britain, especially the attacks on the USA on 11 September 2001, have resulted in the introduction of a number of high-profile debates in Britain with regard to immigration, integration, citizenship, 'race' inequality and human rights. At the same time, these debates have often included concerns and accusations against 'the Muslim community'[3] resulting in a number of related 'questions' clustering around Muslim communities in Britain. According to Modood, Muslims in western Europe (estimated at over 15 million) are larger than the combined populations of Finland, Denmark and Ireland:

> For this, if for no other reason, Muslims have become central to the merits and demerits of multiculturalism as a public policy in western Europe, though, it is to state the obvious that, at least since the attacks of 11 September 2001, Muslim migrants and settlers have come under new political and security scrutiny.
>
> (Modood 2007: 4)

The Islamophobic flavour of debates on multiculturalism and terrorism is examined in the context of the enduring questions regarding 'Muslim integration' and 'Muslim loyalty' in contemporary Britain (see Chapters 2 and 3). It is suggested that these questions are central to the debates that have ensued in response to the social disorder in 2001, the 9/11 attacks and especially the involvement of 'home-grown' suicide bombers in the 7/7 attacks. However, these events, especially 9/11 and 7/7, have also introduced parallel debates on human rights that have led to calls by certain sections of the media and senior politicians (Government and Opposition) for a rebalancing of human rights in contemporary Britain. Human rights are at a crossroads, in the same year as the Equality Act of 2006 established the new Commission on Equality and Human Rights, senior members of the Government and the Opposition began to attack human rights in earnest. For example, in 2006 there were calls from David Cameron (Leader of the Opposition) to repel the Human Rights Act and replace it with a Bill of Rights. In 2006 Tony Blair, Lord Falconer (the Lord

Chancellor) and the Department for Constitutional Affairs all called for the rebalancing of human rights that would put the rights of the law-abiding majority and the exigencies of security before the rights of 'the individual' (see Chapter 6). At the heart of these debates are the citizenship, residence and human rights and freedoms of terror suspects and the communities that they are associated with in contemporary Britain.

This book is an examination of the debates on multiculturalism, Britishness (citizenship, values and patriotism) and human rights in the context of the tabloid and the Government's presentation of a critical mass of side-effects (Beck et al. 2003: 2) associated with, for example, 'failed' immigration policies that allegedly have not integrated migrant communities sufficiently enough (Chapter 4); the alienation and perceived grievances of young British people that result in them being 'susceptible' to being recruited into extremist networks (Chapter 3); the Human Rights Act of 1998 being perceived as a terrorist's or criminal's charter by 'the law-abiding majority' rather than as a set of values that ensures the rights and establishes the responsibilities of all (Chapter 6). This reflexivity on the side-effects of previous immigration policies and the presentation of the current terrorism threat as being unprecedented have resulted in a number of institutional reorientations (Grin 2005: 48); for example, many Government departments are being reorganized in line with security requirements[4] and a number of Parliamentary or quasi-Parliamentary investigations have been introduced into the failures of past integration policies (Fekete 2004: 19).[5] The outcome of the latter is that immigration and asylum policy now focuses on managed integration strategies (McGhee 2005a) including citizenship classes and ceremonies, English language tests and managed migration strategies have been introduced in order to 'cherry-pick' the migrant workers 'Britain needs' (see Chapter 4). At the same time, this reflexivity is associated with the development of anti-terrorism legislation (see Chapters 1 and 2) that have in turn unleashed conflicts between the executive and the judiciary with regard to the interpretation and implementation of these laws in accordance with human rights (in particular, precedents established by the European Court of Human Rights). This reflexivity is associated with the perceived failures of previous policies and with regard to responding to 'unprecedented threats' (especially from extremist organizations such as Al-Qaeda) have in turn resulted in the tension between what Parekh describes as the two conflicting demands in multicultural[6] societies; that is, to foster unity and to respect diversity (2000b: 196) reaching new heights.

Post-7/7 the respect for diversity has become conditional on a new duty to integrate at the level of shared values (see Chapter 6). In a speech made in 2002, David Blunkett, the then Home Secretary, suggested: 'We need a new relationship between governed and governing, which reflects the profound changes that have taken place in our society' (2002: 4). This book includes an examination of a number of attempted introductions of 'new relationships' between those who govern and the governed. The most explicit of these is the call for a new relationship between the Government and Muslim communities made by Ruth Kelly and Tony Blair in 2006 (see Chapter 3). In most cases these new relationships are expressed in terms of a need to rebalance the emphasis of previous policies.

Two further 'rebalancing activities', already mentioned above, are found in various chapters in the book, that is, a de-emphasizing of the respect for diversity in favour of emphasizing shared values (Chapters 4, 5 and 6); and the rebalancing of the human rights in favour of the law-abiding majority over the rights of 'the individual' (Chapters 1 and 6). For Zedner, Government discourses associated with 'rebalancing' usually take two forms: (1) rebalancing can presuppose a prior imbalance in the form of an existing disequilibrium; or (2) can be introduced in response to external factors 'that can be said to tip the balance out of kilter' (Zedner 2005: 511). The internal imbalance in the form of an existing disequilibrium that is central to Government 'rebalancing' discourses in this book is multiculturalism. The external threat that is tipping the balance of precarious multiculturalism and human rights in contemporary Britain is the perceived threat from Al-Qaeda. In many ways the threat from Al-Qaeda has been turned inwards, to focus on the eradication of the threat of extremism in the form of undesirable 'foreign' influences in Britain (see Chapters 1 and 2).

In this book the accepted wisdom associated with the suggestion that multiculturalism is now a divisive force, and that Britain (and the rest of the world) is facing unprecedented threats from Al-Qaeda is critically examined. Multiculturalism, to say the least, is a highly contested term, and as noted in the Preface, there are many different types of multiculturalism, and multiculturalism means different things in different countries (Bonnett 2000: 90). More than this multiculturalism means different things, and is interpreted very differently within the same country. To illustrate this point the opinions of three leading British academics who are all broadly on the centre left of the political spectrum are compared. For example, Paul Gilroy refuses to use the term 'multiculturalism' in relation to diversity and race relations in contemporary Britain. Gilroy prefers the term 'conviviality' rather than multiculturalism (Gilroy 2004, 2005) 'for, in Britain at least, there has been no such ideology for at least two decades' (2005: 438). According to Gilroy, 'convivial culture sprouted spontaneously and unappreciated from the detritus of the failed social experiment of the mid-60s' (2005: 438). However, Anthony Giddens voiced some concern about what he saw as the suddenness of the backlash against multiculturalism when he said 'everyone seemed suddenly to be dismissive of the notion – not only the traditional critics on the far right but nowadays most of the liberal left too' (2006: 1).[7] For Giddens these new critics of multiculturalism, for example, Trevor Phillips (see Chapter 4):

risk contributing to the processes they decry, since they are so dismissive of the achievements that mark this country out from others, particularly in Europe. I can't think of any other EU State that has been more successful than the UK in managing cultural diversity.

(Giddens 2006: 1)

Other high-profile academics, for example Tariq Modood, think that 'multiculturalism is still an attractive and worthwhile political project; and that we need more of it rather than less' (2005: 2). Modood qualifies this statement by saying:

> this, however, does not mean that those calling for integration do not have a point; multiculturalism and integration are complementary ideas. What it does mean is that integration should take a multicultural rather than assimilative form.
>
> (Modood 2005: 2)

Therefore, according to Gilroy, multiculturalism was a failed 1960s experiment that has not really influenced British policy-making for a number of decades. Giddens seems to be pro-multiculturalism, suggesting that it has been a successful policy for managing diversity. Modood is also pro-multiculturalism but wants multiculturalism to complement the new integration strategies in order to avoid falling back into assimilation. Multiculturalism is presented rather benignly above as being merely outdated or as a positive means of managing diversity and as a guiding principle for integration strategies. This is hardly the stuff of nightmares. This begs the question, why is this concept consistently presented as such a threat to British values by media and political commentators of the right and the left in contemporary Britain? Is multiculturalism really the problem? Moreover, will its 'replacements', for example, Modood's multiculturalist integration or David Blunkett's civic assimilation (see Chapter 4) or Gordon Brown's civic nationalism (see Chapter 6) be more successful in promoting unity in diversity in twenty-first-century Britain?

At the same time questions have been raised by numerous commentators on the actual threat from Al-Qaeda together with question marks over the alleged 'unprecedented nature' of this alleged threat (see Chapter 2). According to Burnett and Whyte (2005), the presentation of terrorism in this way amounts to a new terrorism discourse that legitimizes the emergence of 'the security State' replete with an armoury of new legislation (see Chapters 1 and 2).

The extent of the influence of multiculturalism in British policy-making is disputed, as are the claims that the threat from Al-Qaeda is unprecedented. However, both 'integration' and the new terrorism threat are extremely important 'governing issues' that must be critically examined. Kooiman's analysis of contemporary governance (2005: 9) is helpful in navigating these questions. According to Kooiman, governing bodies, for example, Govern-ments, make systematic use of images, instruments and action in their gov-erning practices (2005: 9). For example, Governments generate or exploit images (for example, of dangerous terrorists, segregated communities, of human rights exploited by 'criminals') that in turn generate 'instrumenta-tions' in the form of formal instruments (for example, Green Papers, White Papers, Parliamentary and quasi-Parliamentary reviews, legislation, Select Committee reports) and associated informal activities (for example, in the form of speeches made by politicians accompanying formal actions). According to Kooiman, the action level of governance relies upon the 'con-vincing and socially penetrating images' and sufficient social-political will or support enlisted through agenda-setting work of formal and informal instrumentation (2005: 62). Kooiman suggests that governing 'action' usually takes the form of governing 'reaction' (2005: 63). Governing is often reflexive in that it takes the form of reacting to the actions and policies introduced by previous administrations (Kooiman 2005: 63).

In many ways this book is dedicated to examining the reflexive business of governing as patterns of chains of action and reaction with regard to the balance-tipping 'phenomena' of multiculturalism and terrorism. This is cer-tainly not a straightforward process, for as will become evident the business of governing is often inconsistent and contradictory. For example, in the chapters that follow the Government will be seen to be both champion and attack human rights; at the same time multiculturalism is attacked but the ideals of multiculturalism including respect for diversity remain prominent in Government discourses; at the same time, Muslim communities in Britain are presented as partners against terrorism and as suspect communities that harbour extremists. Throughout this book the array of formal and informal instruments that set out 'the problem' to be investigated (for example, the lack of community cohesion, the exploitation of human rights by terrorists, the weakness of British citizenship) are examined in order to explore how they are being deployed in order to move Britain from what is presented by the Government as a problematic state of affairs to a less problematic state of affairs (in which, for example, shared values are established, everyone can speak English, terrorist suspects can be deported).

In this book an array of what Nikolas Rose calls 'strategic texts'[8] are analysed in order to examine 'certain rationalities of politics' and the specific ways of rationalizing how government 'is to be exercised' (1999: xxii) in the context of multiple circuits of power that connect a diversity of authorities and forces within a variety of complex assemblages (Rose 1999: xxi), for example, in the form of Parliamentary debates (House of Commons and House of Lords), Government departments (the Home Office, the

Communities and Local Government Department), Commissions (Commission for Racial Equality, Commission on Integration and Community Cohesion, Commission on Equality and Human Rights) and Select Committees (Home Affairs Committee, Joint Committee on Human Rights). This book is a sustained investigation of specific technologies of government, which are imbued with aspirations for the shaping of conduct in the hope of producing certain desired effects and averting certain undesired events (Rose 1999: 52). Muslim communities in particular are caught up in the intersecting technologies of integration and security. These technologies are dedicated to inculcating particular forms of life through reshaping relationships and 'reshaping of various roles' (Rose 1999: 52). When it comes to Muslim communities the desired effects of these technologies are: docility, moderation, patriotism, participation, responsibility and obedience. In many ways this book is dedicated to mapping the emergent discourses of security, integration and human rights in contemporary Britain. At the same time this book attempts to examine the convergence of these discourses in the form of increasingly authoritarian declarations on the necessity of establishing shared 'British' values.

Chapter summaries

Chapter 1 is an examination of the anti-terrorism legislation introduced in Britain since 2000. The major focus of this chapter is on the provisions in the Anti-terrorism, Crime and Security Act 2001 (associated with the internment of foreign national terror suspects) and Prevention of Terrorism Act 2005 (associated with placing terror suspects under control orders, when the provisions of the 2001 Act were found to infringe on detainees' human rights). It explores the Government's thwarted intentions of deporting foreign-born terror suspects (because of human rights protections) to their countries of origin. The Government's latest strategy for deporting foreign-born terror suspects is examined here, that is, the development of 'memoranda of understanding' with receiving countries, who promise not to subject returned terror suspects to ill-treatment. Diplomatic assurances such as these are described as torture by proxy and as the exporting of extremism by various select Committees and NGOs. It is suggested that the development of the memoranda of understanding with habitually torturing states illustrates the tension between human rights and citizenship that is being revealed in the 'war on terror'.

Chapter 2 follows on from Chapter 1 in that citizenship and 'the right to have rights' is examined with regard to 'the war terror' in Britain associated with restrictions of the freedom of speech. Rather than focusing on the terrorist and terrorist acts, the Terrorism Act 2006 is presented here as legislation dedicated to clamping down on extremist influences and the introduction of a vague list of unacceptable activities. It also examines the extension of the powers of the Home Secretary to deport not only foreign national terror suspects but also naturalized and dual-national terror suspects. In both Chapters 1 and 2 the impact of these anti-terrorism laws and expanded immigration provisions (associated with deportation) on Muslim communities are examined. It suggests that the debates concerning 'Muslim loyalty' that were ignited during the Rushdie affair went into overdrive after 9/11. In post-7/7 Britain the chilling effect associated with the introduction of ill-defined 'unacceptable behaviour' prohibitions have resulted in a limited repertoire of subject positions (with an emphasis on moderation) for Muslim communities. Chapters 1 and 2 include an examination of the emergence of what some commentators have called 'the security State', the emergence of which has been legitimized by the 'new terrorism' hegemony that simplifies the 'war on terror' to a 'war against evil'.

In Chapter 3, themes introduced in Chapters 1 and 2 associated with the questioning of 'Muslim loyalty' are developed in the examination of the other side of anti-terrorism legislation, that is, a 'community relations' approach to fighting terrorism. It examines the central problematic associated with presenting Muslim communities in Britain as being suspect communities in the war on terror. Various pre-7/7 and post-7/7 initiatives and consultation exercises are examined to ascertain the extent of the 'broader' (community relations) counter-terrorism strategy in Britain. In many ways this chapter can be described as an exploration of the discursive battle between those who are willing and those who are unwilling to recognize the relationship between 'Muslim' grievances and radicalization. It suggests that the Government's marginalization of 'Muslim grievances', for example, with regard to poverty, and the perceptions that British and American foreign policies are anti-Islamic, are decreasing the chances of developing a much needed community relations approach to counter-terrorism that could result in increasing flows of intelligence from Muslim communities about extremist activities to the security forces. It also introduces the concept of community cohesion into considerations of anti-terrorism strategies.

Chapter 4 examines various Government and quasi-Government reviews, strategies and consultations strategies that have been introduced since the riots in Oldham, Burnley and Bradford since 2001 including the *Community Cohesion Review* led by Ted Cantle to the *Strength in Diversity* and *Improving Opportunities* strategies of 2004 and 2005, respectively. In this chapter the explicit attack on multiculturalism as being a divisive force in British society in these texts is explored. The policies that will replace 'multiculturalism', that is, 'integration with diversity' and 'active citizenship' are explored here, as are the shifting emphases (from cultural explanations associated with the 'parallel lives hypothesis' associated with Cantle) to the more holistic approaches that emphasize material factors as well as cultural factors in strategies introduced in 2004 and 2005. This chapter ends with an examination of the remit and findings of the Commission for Integration and Community Cohesion in 2006 and 2007. It is suggested here that many of the strategies and reviews included in this chapter reiterate Blunkett's problematization of, and solutions, to the alleged weakness of British citizenship. It suggests that the 'integration with diversity' discourses common to all of these strategies and reviews are an example of a civic assimilationist model that demands that everyone in Britain, regardless of ethnicity, religion or culture share a set of common values.

Chapter 5 takes the themes developed in Chapter 4 into debates about human rights. In particular it examines the White Paper introduced in 2004 (and related reports) for consultation on the proposed Commission on Equality and Human Rights. It suggests that this new Commission can be seen as a parallel strategy to the wider community cohesion and integration strategies (explored in Chapter 4), in that the new Commission will include a community relations function, ensure equality of service between groups and provide the shared values (enshrined in the European Convention on Human Rights and Fundamental Freedoms) that will unite Britain in its diversity. The new Commission has one other similarity with the community cohesion and integration strategies analysed in Chapter 4; like them, the new Commission is promoted as an antidote to 'divisive' multiculturalism. It also suggests that the major threat to the promises found in the White Paper with regard to establishing a 'proper human rights culture' in Britain is the retreat from human rights associated with anti-terrorism legislation.

Chapter 6 develops themes introduced in the previous chapters through focusing on contemporary debates on 'Britishness'. The civic assimilationist model found in the consultation strategies and reviews examined in Chapter 4 is expanded in this chapter into the civic nationalist emphasis of Gordon Brown and Tony Blair's discourses on Britishness. Shared values are once again the focus of this chapter. However, the emphasis on shared values takes on a rather more authoritarian tone whereby the expectation associated with the sharing of British values is transformed into a patriotic duty that becomes the basis from which an individual can call themselves British. At the same time the second part of this chapter notes the absence of human rights in Gordon Brown and Tony Blair's detailed speeches in 2006 on Britishness and the quest for establishing common values for all in Britain. It suggests, following on from the conclusions made in Chapter 5, that human rights are competing with and losing out to 'security' in public debates. However, this is not the retreat from human rights suggested in previous chapters. Rather, human rights are being co-opted (albeit a 'rebalanced' interpretation of human rights) into the discourses of security. The new terrorism hegemony, as introduced in Chapters 1 and 2, has co-opted human rights discourse through de-emphasizing the rights of the individual in order to emphasize 'the right to life' of the law-abiding majority thus introducing the possibility for the emergence of a very different type of human rights culture in Britain.

The book ends with an Afterword that brings the numerous strands of the debates examined in previous chapters together. The convergence between the new security, integration and human rights discourses that have emerged since 7/7 is explored as is the effect of this convergence on the initial discussion on a British Bill of Rights and Duties in the first few months of Gordon Brown's premiership.

1 Deportation, detention and torture by proxy: foreign national terror suspects in Britain

> The evil of torture lies elsewhere, it denies its victims the minimum recognition offered by a liberal social and legal system and, in so doing, it destroys the respect people routinely expect from others.
>
> (Douzinas 2000: 293)

Introduction

Anti-terrorism legislation, to say the least, is one of the most controversial areas of public policy in contemporary Britain. This chapter maps out the Government's fixation on a particular solution to 'the terrorist threat' since 9/11, that is, the territorial exclusion (deportation) of terror suspects from Britain. It explores the Government's often frustrated attempts to rid Britain of the 'terror threat' through deportation and examines the creation of the legislative alternatives to deportation in the form of the internment without charge and control orders. The overall intention of this chapter, and the next two chapters, is to emphasize the relationship between the new security discourse associated with the 'terror threat' and the simultaneous emergence of a new authoritarian integration discourse and draconian legislation in the areas of anti-terrorism and in asylum and immigration that are being introduced under the pernicious remit of 'minimizing insecurity' (Lash 1994a: 116).

As such this chapter examines the Government's derogation from Article 5 of the ECHR[1] in order to indefinitely detain terror suspects that they have selected for deportation; the introduction of control orders (when indefinite detention was deemed unlawful by the House of Lords); and, the development of memoranda of understanding with 'receiving countries' (many with a poor human rights record, and a history of resorting to torture) in order to deport terror suspects.

In order to secure the deportation of terror suspects, the Government has had to chart a rather ignoble course through numerous Articles of the ECHR through the introduction of various terrorism and related immigration laws since 2000; the result being that Britain, one of the world's champions of human rights, is fast becoming one of the world's notorious abusers of human rights (Fekete 2005a: 25). These new powers are going to leave the Government with blood on their hands, whether through not admitting would-be asylum seekers and leaving them to their plight or through deporting terror suspects to an uncertain future in receiving countries with poor human rights records. The chapter is organized in four parts. In the first part Britain and the USA's legislative response to terrorism since 9/11 are explored. At the same time Britain's post-9/11 anti-terrorism laws are contextualized within its response to previous 'terror threats' and political violence in Northern Ireland. This section critically examines literatures that suggest that post-9/11 anti-terrorism legislation will have an impact on all of our human rights and have repercussions beyond terrorism through some of the provisions becoming normalized into the criminal law. This section concludes that it is not all of 'our' human rights that are under threat here, rather anti-terrorism laws on both sides of the Atlantic are fundamentally an attack on foreign nationals, in particular Muslim foreign nationals.

Part two examines how the Government has attempted to circumvent some of the restrictions imposed by ECHR case law on the deportation of foreign national terror suspects. It will be suggested here that many of the controversial anti-terrorism provisions such as indefinite detention without trial and control orders are related to the Government's frustrated attempts to remove foreign national terror suspects from Britain.

In the third part of the chapter the emphasis is on the controversial 'memoranda of understanding' and diplomatic assurances that Britain has been developing with those countries who will receive deported foreign national terror suspects from Britain. The Government's attempts to circumvent ECHR case law and other international obligations prohibiting inhuman or ill-treatment and torture through developing diplomatic assurances with receiving countries that have poor human rights records (including systematic torture) are examined.

The fourth part of the chapter examines the implications of this course of action through the work of Herzfeld, Agamben and Dworkin. The diplomatic assurances established by the Government and 'torturing states' are described as the materialization of a state of exception in which the rights of the few are sacrificed in the name of the many. The extreme violence of the bureaucratic exclusion of deportees are described as a project of distinguishing between those whose rights are respected and those whose rights are contingent, that is, between citizens and what Agamben calls *Homo sacer*, those radically excluded from the political community of rights-bearing citizens. In this part and in the conclusion, the impact of these provisions on Muslim communities in Britain are considered.

The anti-terrorism threat?

Much of what has been written in Britain and the USA about the post-9/11 anti-terrorism laws focuses on the erosion of human rights or on finding the balance between civil liberties and security. Ronald Dworkin has suggested that in the post-9/11 context Americans face two types of danger in which further terrorist attacks are the most obvious danger. Dworkin also suggests that there is another less obvious danger that should be recognized, which takes the form of the Bush administration's violation of many fundamental individual rights (2003: 1). Dworkin is not alone when he states that the latter violations, if they survive the state of emergency, will result in the character of American society changing for the worse (2003: 1). There is already evidence of the expanded use of the provisions of the Patriot Act in relation to offences unrelated to terrorism. According to Lichtblau, writing in the *The New York Times*, the Bush Administration has been using its expanded authority under these far-reaching laws to investigate suspected drug traffickers, white-collar criminals, blackmailers, child pornographers, money launderers, spies and even corrupt foreign leaders (2003: 1).

Breathtakingly broad definitions of terrorism (Dworkin 2003: 2) have been introduced on both sides of the Atlantic alongside sweeping open-ended pernicious powers. For example, in the USA the Patriot Act has been used as a catch-all to harass and prosecute environmental protesters (Huck 2005: 1). In Britain, due to the wide remit of the definition of terrorism included in the pre-9/11 Terrorism Act of 2000,[2] many activities, for example, anti-globalization protests and other forms of protest, could be criminalized (Hyland 2001: 4). In Europe, according to Fekete (2004), there were two options for European Union (EU) Member States with regard to the incorporation of the EU Common Position and Framework Decision issued by the European Commission after 9/11. Some, Britain in particular, introduced state of emergency legislation and new anti-terrorist laws. Other EU Member States amended existing public order, criminal justice and aliens' legislation and extended police powers (Fekete 2004: 6). Regardless of the approach taken, according to Fekete, the result in all cases was the creation of 'a shadow criminal justice system for foreign nationals' (2004: 6) that has resulted in the recasting of citizenship laws according to security considerations (2004: 4).

The development of a separate 'executive' justice system for dealing with terror suspects in post-9/11 (and post-7/7) Britain is examined below. These developments are not unique to the threat from Al-Qaeda. Hillyard (2006) has mapped out the similarities between the responses to the IRA threat and 'the' Al-Qaeda threat. In both cases legislation was developed to introduce internment, shoot-to-kill policies, expanded 'stop and search', restrictions on the freedom of expression, turning a blind eye to torture,[3] territorial restrictions,[4] as well as developing a separate executive justice system. Hill-yard suggests that all the Government's anti-terrorism measures introduced since 2000 have already been tried and failed in Northern Ireland and that all these special measures were ultimately counterproductive (2006: 5) as they exacerbated rather than ameliorated 'the troubles'.

The problem, as identified by Zedner, is that 'special powers' introduced to fight terrorism become normalized (2005: 525). For example, these special anti-terrorism laws have a habit of being extended, of developing a life of their own independent of the 'transitory panic' that gave birth to them (Ewing and Gearty 1990: 213) and despite the 'sunset clauses' requiring them to be time-limited 'experience suggests that such powers tend to be repeatedly extended into de facto permanence' (Zedner 2005: 525). As a result the security measures 'we' welcome today may in turn be turned against 'us', Zedner cautions that 'we need not join al Qaeda to find ourselves subject to them' (2005: 515, 516).

The erosion of human rights and civil liberties as the 'war on terror' measures become normalized into the 'war on crime' is certainly something 'we' should all be concerned about as Britain and the USA take further, potentially irreversible steps, towards becoming much less liberal States (Dworkin 2003: 4). It is undeniable that certain sections of the population, namely Muslims in the USA and Britain are at the head of the queue when it comes to the risk of having their human rights violated. According to Dworkin, the reality is:

> with hardly any exceptions, no American who is not a Muslim and has no Muslim connections actually runs any risk of being labelled an enemy combatant and being locked up in a military jail.
>
> (Dworkin 2003: 4)

It is not only Muslims who are at the head of the queue when it comes to the potential violations of human rights: it is Muslim foreign nationals who are the clear front-runners. At the same time we need to further differentiate the Muslim foreign nationals who are being targeted by this legislation, that is, those individuals who are repeatedly represented as the primary threat to Britain through the political process of folk-devil construction (Burnett and Whyte 2005: 1). Burnett and Whyte, following Jefferson and Holloway (1997), suggest that fear of the outsider represents a powerful political tool in the reproduction of social order (2005: 1, 2). According to Burnett and Whyte, the *other* in the 'war on terrorism' is not as readily knowable, accountable and controllable as the various other 'enemies' in the wars on crime (2005: 2) as a result:

the terrorist must be ideologically represented as knowable, action-able and controllable in a particular form. The construction of 'ter-rorism' as something that the State can do something about is central to the justification for the expansion of it juridical and military reach.

(Burnett and Whyte 2005: 2)

The Bush administration's 'war on terrorism' in the USA has been recalibrated in Britain to that of a 'war on extremism', or more accurately (which is further developed in the next chapter) a war on those individuals who promote, glorify, support and encourage extremism in Britain. Foreign national terror suspects, especially (but not exclusively) foreign nationals terror suspects, who have entered Britain as asylum seekers, are central to the Government's war on extremism.[5] In many ways the Government's response to the post-9/11 terrorist threat was justified 'less on the basis of a threat to the United Kingdom as such and more by the Government's intention to prevent the country being used as a base for international terrorists' (Bates 2006: 259).[6]

In the rest of this chapter the most controversial aspects of the Government's anti-terrorism strategy is examined, in particular the Government's strategy for eradicating those individuals who are increasingly presented in the following terms: as those individuals 'who are not British nationals, who are here as guests in our country but are abusing that hospitality' (Blunkett, in Bates 2006: 253).

Deportation, torture and foreign national terrorist suspects

In the post-9/11 context, as revealed below, the Government's primary objective is the removal of foreign national terror suspects and foreign nationals engaging in unacceptable behaviour (for example, promoting or glorifying terrorism) from Britain. This is to be achieved by grafting anti-terrorist laws onto immigration law in order to avoid the normal checks and balances of the criminal law (Fekete 2006: 76). Deportation, exclusion and exile are not new practices introduced in the post-9/11 context. Between 1976 and 1987 the British Police applied for 390 exclusion orders (353 of these were granted) against British citizens and Irish residents in Britain on the basis that these individuals were suspected of being involved in the commissioning, preparation or instigation of acts of terrorism 'connected to Northern Ireland' (Ewing and Gearty 1990: 217). Exclusion orders were granted by the Home Secretary, in the absence of a judicial review and often based on 'secret intelligence' (1990: 217). Ewing and Gearty described these exclusion orders as 'the most widely disliked, illiberal and controversial part of the whole anti-

terrorism legislation' (1990: 217). One could say that the anti-terrorism legislation that has been introduced since 9/11 has been primarily concerned
with making the Government's desire to deport foreign national terror suspects a reality.[7] The major obstacle to the Government achieving its ambitions in this area are the protections afforded by Articles 3 (prohibition of
torture and inhumane or degrading treatment or punishment) and 5 (right to
liberty and security) of the ECHR. In many ways the *Chahal* v. *UK* case[8] heard
in the European Court of Human Rights in 1996 has been the Government's
major obstacle in its attempts to deport foreign national terror suspects from
Britain. The Chahal ruling resulted in the Conservative Government at the
time being confronted by a dilemma in respect to persons who are suspected
of being international terrorists. They wanted to remove terror suspects from
Britain through deportation; however, they were prevented from doing so
because there were grounds to think that they would be subjected to torture
or inhumane and degrading treatment in the receiving country (Fenwick
2002: 731).

The *Chahal* v. *UK* ruling raised two problems for the Government. The
first problem the Government faced was that it could not deport a foreign
national who posed a security risk if there was any possibility of them being
subjected to torture or inhumane treatment in the country they were being
returned to. The second problem facing the Government was the issue of the
disclosure of the information that led to the arrest and deportation of a foreign national terror suspect. The unwillingness of the Government to satisfy a
terror suspect's right under Article 5 of the ECHR to challenge their detention
(pending deportation) in open court was also highlighted by the European
Court in the Chahal case. The first of these problems resulted in the Government derogating from Article 5 (1) of the ECHR on 18 December 2001
(Bates 2006: 258) in order to introduce indefinite detention without trial of
foreign nationals suspected of involvement in terrorism (Nellis 2007: 264)
who had been certified by the Home Secretary under section 21 of the Anti-
terrorism, Crime and Security Act of 2001. The second problem in relation to
the Government's desire to avoid the disclosure of intelligence that led to the
Home Secretary's certification of a terrorist suspect was addressed by setting
up a special court to hear closed material. It should be noted that closed
material is often not admissible in a court of law, for example, telephone
intercepts, which if used in court would infringe the privacy provisions of
Article 8 of the ECHR. At the same time under the Regulation of Investigatory
Powers Act 2000, the evidential use of intercept material is not permitted in
Britain (Home Office 2004a: Para. 35). Moreover, this closed material could be
the product of covert surveillance that the security services are not prepared
to disclose (Lord Phillips 2006: 7).

In order to allow certificated suspects to appeal against their detention
and have the 'closed' evidence held against them tested (but not in open

court) the Government set up the Special Immigration Appeals Commission (SIAC). The SIAC was described by BBC News as the most controversial and secretive court within English Law (2004: 1). The SIAC was established in 1997 in the Special Immigration Appeals Commission Act 1997 after the Government lost the Chahal case at the European Court of Human Rights in 1996.[9] The SIAC Act 1997 provided for an independent judicial tribunal to hear appeals against immigration decisions, thus replacing the internal Home Office advisory panel that had scrutinized the Chahal appeal (House of Commons Constitutional Affairs Committee 2005: Para. 48). Moreover the SIAC Act 1997 was amended by the Anti-terrorism, Crime and Security Act of 2001 that introduced the use of special advocates (security cleared lawyers) to represent appellants,[10] thus addressing one of the Chahal complaints which was upheld by the European Court of Human Rights, that he was not allowed legal representation.

According to the Government in its statement to the Constitutional Affairs Committee's inquiry, the Special Advocate system ensured the non-disclosure of sensitive material (to the appellant) while allowing for the independent scrutiny of that sensitive material by an advocate appointed to represent the interests of the appellant (2005: Para. 48). Although the Special Advocate system is an improvement in that appellants are now provided with legal representation, there are a number of limitations in this system when compared to the classic lawyer/client relationship. The main limitation is that the Special Advocate is precluded from communicating highly pertinent information (the closed case) to the appellant and as a result, the scope of the Special Advocate to receive meaningful instruction from the appellant is limited. At the same time the Special Advocate has limited access to outside support in that they are prohibited from calling in witnesses, including expert witnesses and have limited access to the support enjoyed by 'ordinary lawyers' (for example, solicitors, barristers, experts and administrative support) (House of Commons Constitutional Affairs Committee 2005: Para. 62). This raises a number of ethical problems as:

> since a lawyer who cannot take full instructions from his client, nor report to his client, who is not responsible to his client and whose relationship with the client lacks the quality of confidence inherent in any ordinary lawyer-client relationship, is acting in a way hitherto unknown to the legal profession.
>
> (Lord Bingham, in House of Commons Constitutional Affairs Committee 2005: Para. 63)

This is an example of bureaucratic obstructionism in which 'classified information' is linked to bureaucratic (or executive) control. Here secrecy is represented as knowledge (Herzfeld 1992: 158) in a parallel justice system legitimized by what Burnett and Whyte describe as 'the new terrorism hegemony' (2005: 6) associated with 'unprecedented threats' and equally unprecedented security responses (this is further developed in the next chapter).

The indefinite detention without charge of foreign national terror suspects introduced in part 4 of the Anti-terrorism, Crime and Security Act of 2001 has been subjected to numerous appeals. Initially the SIAC upheld the appeal on the ground that the order was discriminatory and contrary to Article 14 of the ECHR (see below). In response to this the Home Secretary appealed to the Court of Appeal. The Court of Appeal allowed the judicial challenge, holding that the discrimination was justified because the detainees had no right to be in the country in the first place, and furthermore, they were free to leave if they wished. However, this reasoning did not stand in the House of Lords (Lord Phillips 2006: 4). The Law Lords ruled, following the SIAC, that the indefinite detention without trial of foreign terrorist suspects was deemed to be contrary to Article 14 of the ECHR. The result of the latter was that the Home Secretary had to come up with an alternative to indefinite detention for the foreign national terror suspects held in Belmarsh Prison. It should be noted that Lord Phillips, the Lord Chief Justice of England and Wales, described this reassertion of the judiciary against executive detention, in the House of Lords in the case of *A and others* v. *Secretary of State* for the Home Department [2004] UKHL 56 to be ' ... one of the most dramatic to have been given in my time in the law' (2006: 4). This is a landmark ruling regarding the balance to be struck between the protection of human rights and national security (Bates 2006: 247). First, the major grounds of appeal was that the provisions of part 4 of the Anti-terrorism, Crime and Security Act 2001 were deemed by the majority of Law Lords hearing the case to be disproportionate to the risk of international terrorism facing Britain, and second, these provisions were found to be discriminatory and thus an infringement of Article 14 (prohibition of discrimination) of the ECHR as they focused on foreign national terror suspects and not on British national terror suspects too (Lord Bingham, in *A and others* v. *Secretary of State* 2004: Paras. 31, 32 and 46).

In response to the above, the Home Secretary introduced a system of control orders that were introduced in the Prevention of Terrorism Act 2005 to replace indefinite detention. This Act introduced two types of control orders: derogating control orders and non-derogating control orders (Lord Phillips 2006: 7) that will apply to all persons on British soil, whether foreigners or British nationals (Gil-Robles 2005: 7), thus addressing the discriminatory (foreign national) focus of the Anti-terrorism, Crime and Security Act 2001 (however, in reality, control orders have only been used on foreign nationals). According to Lord Phillips, derogating control orders (derogating from Article 5 of the ECHR) amount to a deprivation of liberty. Non-derogating control orders fall short of depriving the suspect of their liberty and therefore fall short of derogating from Convention rights. The latter necessitates terror suspects to be required to remain in a residence, and location decided by the Home Office on the understanding that they would remain inside the residence for 18 out of every 24 hours. After losing an appeal, where it was ruled that the non-derogating control orders introduced in the Prevention of Terrorism Act 2005 amounted to a severe restriction on movement and a deprivation of liberty contrary to Article 5 of the ECHR, the Home Secretary has been forced to reduce house arrest from 18 to 14 hours a day (Lord Phillips 2006: 7). The detainees formally held at Belmarsh Prison were released and placed under non-derogating control orders (Mantouvalou 2006: 163).

Currently, 18 non-derogating control orders have been served on individuals in Britain. Four individuals have absconded since being served with control orders. In response to the disappearance of three men on control orders in May 2007, John Reid announced that the Home Office would be proposing further measures to combat terror in the form of a new counter-terrorism Bill. Reid had the following to say about control orders: 'control orders are far from the best option ... they are not even the second best option for tackling terror suspects' (Reid, House of Commons [Hansard] 24 May 2007: Column 1428). Reid stated that under the constraints imposed upon him by Parliament, the courts and the law, it is difficult to prevent 'determined individuals' from absconding. Reid announced that he will consider other options including derogation 'if we have exhausted ways of overturning previous judgments on the issues' (Reid, House of Commons (Hansard) 24 May 2007: Column 1428).

Control orders and previous to them, indefinite detention, have been temporary measures introduced while the Government devised a more permanent solution. With the introduction of the Terrorism Act 2006 and the Immigration, Asylum and Nationality Act 2006 in conjunction with the development of memoranda of understanding between the Government and certain 'receiving' states, the deportation of foreign national terror suspects (even when the receiving states have a poor human rights record and resort to ill-treatment and torture) is fast becoming a reality in Britain. Just as with indefinite detention and later control orders, deportation of foreign and dual-national terror suspects to countries where they have a reasonable fear of being tortured will result from the Home Secretary acting on evidence that would often be deemed inadmissible in court.

The history of anti-terrorism legislation in Britain, especially since the 1970s, has involved some conflict between the executive and the judiciary, between those elected to democratic institutions, who are answerable to Parliament and those 'independent judges charged to interpret and apply the law' (Lord Bingham, in *A and others* v. *Secretary of State* 2004: 42). In relation to the waves of anti-terrorism legislation introduced since 9/11 in Britain, a number of commentators have once again pointed out that 'executive detention' followed by 'executive control orders' (Mantouvalou 2006: 165) have substituted the 'ordinary criminal justice system' with exceptional measures in the form of a parallel system run by the executive (Gil-Robles 2005: 10). At the same time many commentators, among them senior judges, have questioned the Government's resort to 'immigration powers' to respond to matters of national security. For example, the Privy Counsellor Review Committee was concerned about the risk of exporting terrorism in the Government's decision to employ immigration powers to respond to matters of national security.

> Seeking to deport terrorist suspects does not seem to us to be a satisfactory response, given the risk of exporting terrorism ... While deporting such people might free up the British police, intelligence, security and prison service resources, it would not necessarily reduce the threat to British interests abroad, or make the world a safer place more generally. Indeed there is a risk that the suspects might even return without the authorities being aware of it.
>
> (Privy Counsellor Review Committee 2003: Para. 95)

The Home Office highlighted its impotence in the 'war against terrorism' when they defended their deportation and voluntary departure policies (in response to the Privy Counsellor Review Committee report) in the Discussion Paper: *Counter-terrorism Powers: Reconciling Security and Liberty in an Open Society*, when it stated that: 'deportation has the advantage of disrupting the activities of suspected terrorist' (Home Office 2004a: Para. 32). Perhaps the Government's deportation plans are a little more sinister than merely disrupting terrorist activities through deporting suspected terrorists from Britain. This is explored in the next section.

Exporting torture

> Under the spell of the terrorist threat, a lawless space has opened up which permits what was until recently forbidden, a double *carte blanche* in interstate relations. Each state can combat its domestic enemies as 'terrorists' with the blessing of the international community and the human rights violations of allies are treated with discretion and thereby facilitated.
>
> (Beck 2006: 140)

In many ways the Government's strategy of continuing to problematize the restrictions imposed by the Chahal ruling might lead them, like the Bush administration, to selectively abandon multilateral, international human rights institutions (Ashby Wilson 2005: 6). At the very heart of these reorientations from human rights on both sides of the Atlantic is the torture and potential torture of 'enemy combatants' and terror suspects. For example, in the USA approval from senior-level officials has been granted for techniques for 'softening up' detainees in Guantánamo and Iraq, these are in breach of the Geneva Conventions of 1949 that ban all use of 'mutilations, cruel treatment and torture' of prisoners of war and detained civilians during all armed conflicts (Ross 2005: 15). The Bush administration tried to get round this by making a distinction between interrogation techniques involving inhuman and degrading treatment (called 'augmented techniques of coercive interrogation'), which were justifiable in the context of the 'war on terror' and those that amounted to actual 'torture'(Robertson 2005: xiv). Both varieties of techniques are prohibited under various multilateral conventions, for example, Article 5 of the Universal Declaration of Human Rights, Article 3 of the ECHR, other conventions such as the 1966 International Convention on Civil and Political Rights and the 1984 Convention Against Torture and Other Cruel, Inhuman or Degrading Treatment or Punishment also ban such activities unequivocally (Robertson 2005: xiv).

Human Rights Watch has suggested that a permissive culture of torture has been allowed to take root among policy-makers in the USA, and that this is a culture that Britain has been unwilling to confront (House of Commons Foreign Affairs Committee 2005: Para. 85). In Britain Amnesty International has observed a 'creeping acceptance of the practice of torture' with regard to the Court of Appeal ruling in a case in August 2004[11] that evidence obtained under torture would be deemed admissible in court unless it had been directly procured by British agents or if the British agent had connived in its procurement (House of Commons Foreign Affairs Committee 2005: Para. 95). At the same time Liberty and Justice (in their joint report on Human Rights) are deeply concerned that some of the closed material scrutinized in appeals by the SIAC does not allow for the consideration of whether evidence was obtained by way of torture (2005: Para. 37). That is:

> Quite simply, there is no way for SIAC to determine whether any material received by the UK Government from countries such as Algeria have been obtained under torture because the UK Government itself does not know and is not about to ask.
>
> (Liberty and Justice 2005: Para. 37)

For a time evidence produced during torture was being accepted by British courts. Lord Justice David Neuberger took an impassioned stand against the majority decision in the Court of Appeal to allow the consideration of evidence produced through torture when he stated that:

Democratic societies, faced with terrorist threats, should not readily accept that the threat justifies the use of torture, or that the end justifies the means. It can be said that, by using torture, or even by adopting the fruits of torture, a democratic state is weakening its case against terrorists by adopting their methods.

(Berlins 2007: 2)

The Law Lords supported Neuberger's minority position in the Court of Appeal. Lord Bingham stated that this was not an argument about the law of evidence; rather, this was an issue of constitutional principle (Lord Bingham, in *A and others* v. *Secretary of State* 2005: Para. 51). Despite the House of Lords upholding the appeal, the Home Office Minister, Tony McNulty, later admitted to Channel 4 News that the Government could only establish 'as far as possible' that evidence had not been gathered under torture (BBC News 2005b: 1), thus leaving the possibility that the fruits of torture could still have influence in identifying and certifying terror suspects.

It seems that Britain has at least learned some of the lessons from the past with regard to the degradation and treatment of detainees, in relation to cases brought before the European Court of Human Rights by the Republic of Ireland against Britain, over 'the in-depth interrogations' to which internees in Belfast were subjected to in the 1970s at the hands of the British Army (Robertson 2005: xx). However, the lesson Britain might have learned is how to avoid getting their own hands dirty when it comes to inflicting inhuman treatment and torture on terror suspects in order to extract intelligence or to exact vengeful punishment (more on this below). Perhaps one could go as far as to say that the possibility of deporting both foreign and dual-national terror suspects from Britain could be a salutary measure, designed to make 'potential' terrorists, and those involved in promoting (or glorifying) terrorism, think twice about their activities.

The Government's ambition that has been thwarted by European Court rulings with regard to deporting terror suspects to countries where there is a reasonable chance that they will be subjected to degrading, inhuman treatment and perhaps even torture, is now a possibility.[12] This has been made possible through the development of diplomatic assurances with receiving countries. The Government's deportation plans for foreign and dual-national terror suspects have been described as a diplomatic mechanism for circumventing ECHR protections and 1951 Geneva Convention prohibitions (see below) by exporting or what the Islamic Human Rights Commission have described as 'outsourcing' torture, degrading and inhuman treatment to receiving countries abroad (2005: 4). At the same time Britain has also become implicated in the USA's practice of exporting, or, outsourcing torture in the practice of 'extraordinary renditions' in which one State surrenders fugitives to another (Pattenden 2006: 2). Extraordinary renditions are associated with the CIA sending detainees to countries in the Middle East, including Egypt and Syria, known to practice torture routinely (Brody 2005: 149). The USA is rendering recalcitrant detainees to these countries where torture is routine for questioning, to extract intelligence from them (Dworkin 2003: 2; Pattenden 2006: 2). Britain and other EU Member States' complicity in this activity was exposed by a report published by the European Parliament in November 2006. This report suggested that the air territory or airspace of certain EU Member States had been used in the cases of 'extraordinary renditions' and that agents or officials of Member States have been involved in acts of extraordinary rendition, in the form of assistance with transport, the communication of information to facilitate arbitrary arrests and participation in interrogation (European Parliament 2006: 2).

It has not been established whether the Government is attempting to export terror suspects for interrogation to a third country, although given the creeping acceptance of 'the fruits of torture' in recent tribunals and Court of Appeal decisions in Britain, the event of this happening remains a possibility. Rather, the Government has embarked upon a specific strategy whereby it is attempting to get round the restrictions of the Chahal ruling with regard to Article 3 of the ECHR and the 'principle of non-refoulement' established in Article 33(1) of the 1951 Geneva Convention Relating to the Status of Refugees that prohibits contracting States to expel or return a refugee to the frontiers of territories where their life or freedom would be threatened on account of their race, religion, nationality, membership of a particular social group or political opinion (Fekete 2005a: 25). A number of the terror suspects who were detained and are now on control orders came to Britain as asylum seekers and are therefore protected by the non-refoulement principle. Fenwick has pointed out that the non-refoulement principle could be 'abused' by asylum-seeking terror suspects who could present themselves as 'a terrorist' in order to be eligible for refugee status and thus protection under Article 33 (1) (2002: 741). To prevent this from happening the Government introduced Section 54 of the Immigration, Asylum and Nationality Act 2006 that allows the Home Secretary to automatically refuse asylum in Britain to anyone who has participated in 'terrorism' (HM Government 2006: Annex A). Thus, the Government is attempting to use bilateral diplomatic assurances with particular receiving countries in order to circumvent one of the absolute rights within the ECHR: Article 3 (Kennedy 2005: 304) and one of the most important principles of the 1951 Geneva Convention: the principle of non-refoulement (Fekete 2005a: 25).

The diplomatic assurances that Britain has developed in various forms with a number of potential receiving countries (for example, Libya, Algeria, Jordan, Egypt, Lebanon and Morocco) have been described as empty promises that are not worth the paper they are written on, and as being unenforceable (Human Rights Watch, in Joint Committee on Human Rights 2006a: Para.

113). According to Human Rights Watch it would be impossible for the Government to honour a diplomatic assurance made in good faith because there would not be sufficient control of the actors on the ground to ensure that torture did not take place, since, when the practice is systematic, it means that it is routine in the conduct of the operations of the security forces; it is not that an order is given that a particular person should be subjected to ill-treatment (Joint Committee on Human Rights 2006a: Para. 113). The Immigration Law Practitioners' Association statement to the Committee echoed the above by stating that: 'the reality is that reliable assurances are simply not within the gift of highly placed officials where security services and those charged with the day to day care of those detained are able in practice to perpetrate torture with impunity' (Joint Committee on Human Rights 2006a: Para. 113).

Diplomatic Assurances, especially with States such as Jordan, Egypt and Algeria, is tantamount to Britain trusting 'habitual torturing states' not to torture (Immigration Law Practitioners' Association, in Joint Committee on Human Rights 2006a: Para. 110). The Council of Europe's Commissioner for Human Rights suggests that the weakness inherent in the practice of diplomatic assurances lies in the fact that where there is a need for such assurances, there is clearly an acknowledged risk of torture or ill-treatment. He concludes that 'due to the absolute prohibition of torture or inhuman or degrading treatment, formal assurances cannot be sufficient to permit exclusions where risk is nonetheless considered to remain' (Gil-Robles 2005: Para. 29). Similarly, the European Court of Human Rights (in their ruling in the case of *Ramzy* v. *The Netherlands*) suggested that the process of seeking diplomatic assurances or memoranda of understanding 'amounts to an admission that the person would be at risk of torture or ill-treatment in the receiving state if returned' (2005: Para. 39).

It has also become clear that the Government has been attempting to refine its position with regard to balancing the risk to national security on one hand and the risk of a deported terror suspect being subjected to inhuman and degrading treatment on the other hand. According to the Joint Committee on Human Rights:

> inhuman and degrading treatment, the Government argues, is a much broader bracket than torture, and the Government says that it is wholly unreasonable not to allow public safety considerations to be taken into account even where Article 3 ECHR is engaged because of a real risk of inhuman or degrading treatment.
>
> (2006a: Para 119)

The Committee described the Government's attempt to distinguish between inhuman and degrading treatment on one hand and torture on the other hand as a 'deeply unattractive' practice (2006a: Para. 121), which they dismissed with the following statement:

> Inhuman and degrading treatment at the lower end of the Article 3 ECHR spectrum is not the sort of treatment of which those individuals are likely to be at risk. They are more likely to face a real risk of either torture or death.
>
> (Joint Committee on Human Rights 2006a: Para. 121)

Perhaps the Government is falling back on what Žižek describes as the pragmatic utilitarianism of those commentators who are willing to talk about the place of torture in contemporary society (2002: 102).[13] According to Gearty, Michael Ignatieff's book *The Lesser Evil: Political Ethics in an Age of Terror* (2005), is the best example of this genre that depicts the dilemma of contemporary North America as one in which we fight evil with evil or we succumb (Gearty 2006: 132–3). The logic that this 'evilization' process (see Chapter 2) introduces is that western democracies are indeed entitled 'to do some wrong in their struggle for survival' (Gearty 2006: 133). This is a different variety of wrong-doing or 'evil' because, unlike the terrorists, the defenders of democracy know what they are doing is wrong even when they are doing it; however, they are safe in the knowledge that they have a set of democratic values to hand to stop things getting out of control (Gearty 2006: 133). This 'necessary evil' is thus construed as being a better variety of evil than the terrorists' evil as the former protect 'us' from evil itself (Gearty 2006: 134).

Muslim disquiet and right to have rights

> We have heard evidence that the existence of these powers, and uncertainty about them, has led to understandable disquiet amongst some parts of the Muslim population. It is important that legislation against terrorism should attract wide public acceptance to maximise its effectiveness.
>
> (Privy Counsellor Review Committee 2003: Para. 196)

There are a number of problems with the Government's fixation on the expulsion of foreign national terror suspects. There is the concern, as mentioned above, that by granting terror suspects who have been subject to certification by the Home Secretary the right to voluntary departure, or by forcefully deporting others, Britain could be exporting terrorism in the form of allowing those suspected of terrorism to regroup in order to carry on their alleged activities abroad. This has led to the conclusion that 'deportation is a remarkably short sighted response to international terrorism' (Fitzpatrick

2003: 256). Not only is deportation a short-sighted response to international terrorism, the foreign national, or more accurately Muslim foreign national focus of deportation and measures associated with the thwarted intention to deport (for example, executive detention and control orders) is counter-productive, as it could alienate public opinion and potentially damage the flow of intelligence that could come from Muslim communities in Britain. The last thing that the Government should be doing is further alienating Muslim communities by launching strategies that target them in dis-criminatory ways (see Chapter 3). According to Waldron, if information is key in the 'war on terrorism', Governments cannot alienate Muslim communities (Waldron 2003: 206). Moreover, the Government could be adding to the 'reservoir of discontent' among Muslim communities in Britain (Human Rights Watch, in House of Commons Foreign Affairs Committee 2005: Para. 69) while simultaneously increasing the sympathy for terrorist and terror suspects in otherwise law-abiding Muslim communities (Freeman 2005: 48; Hayes 2006: 57; Waldron 2003: 200–04). According to the Council of Europe's Commissioner for Human Rights, the application of the Anti-terrorism, Crime and Security Act of 2001 and the Prevention of Terrorism Act 2005 to high-profile Muslim cases:

> has had a negative affect on both the perceptions of Muslims by the rest of the population and the confidence of many Muslims in the fairness of the executive ... human rights abuses in the context of anti-terrorism measures have repercussions extending beyond their impact on the individual persons to entire communities. This in itself argues for considerable caution in the adoption of measures in this area.
>
> (Gil-Robles 2005: Para. 32)

Indefinite detention, control orders and now the deportation of terror sus-pects undoubtedly have an impact on Muslim communities. To date, these new powers have been used exclusively on the members of Muslim com-munities. The application of some of these anti-terrorism measures on foreign national terror suspects, to the neglect of 'British national' terror suspects, are applied in explicit defiance of human rights. In place of the equality of esteem at the core of human rights such terrorism laws often offer 'inequality of esteem, judging people ... by where they are from and by which culture or faith it is to which they belong' (Gearty 2006: 103). This in turn introduces a new distinction with regard to 'the right to have rights' (Arendt 1979: 226) in contemporary Britain. The creeping acceptance of torture, whether in the form of the inclusion of 'torture evidence' as part of the Home Secretary's certification decision-making process and as part of the closed material in SIAC appeals; or in the Government's seeming 'conscious denial' (Cohen

2001: 4) about the actual plight of the terror suspects they are willing to deport to an uncertain future is evidence that their intentions are more than just trying to find the balance between human rights and security and more about sacrificing the rights of 'the few' (that is, Muslim foreign nationals) to allegedly safeguard the rights of the many (Dworkin 2003: 4; Ignatieff 2005: 32; Zedner 2005: 514).

This leads to a corrosive indifference, in the form of a rejection of our common humanity (Herzfeld 1992: 1), which results in certain individuals' right to have rights being fundamentally undermined. According to Herzfeld, it is through the actions of the protectors of 'our' interests that makes the indifference to the fate of others morally acceptable (1992: 166). When 'we' place the majority's security over other people's rights, we put in jeopardy the most fundamental of all moral principles: the principle of shared humanity (Dworkin 2003: 4). Žižek suggests that such projects throw into high relief the distinction Agamben makes between the full citizen and *Homo sacer*, that is, individuals who are alive as human beings but who are not deemed to be part of the political community (Žižek 2002: 91). These individuals are the radically excluded; those who are no longer recognized as human, and who are denied the recognition of human dignity (Balibar 2004: 119). For Agamben, the *Homo sacer* is an outcast, a banned man; he is tabooed and dangerous (1998: 79). The inequality of esteem, the denial of shared humanity and the dehumanization associated with the activity of stripping certain individuals of their rights (and their right to have rights) are fast becoming a reality in contemporary Britain. Agamben urges us to be vigilant for the metamorphoses of 'the structure of the camp' in the 'hidden matrix of the politics in which we are living' (1998: 175).

According to Dean, Agamben's metaphor of the camp has no essential form, 'it has a history of transformations and mutations and is a site invested with different political purposes' (2007: 178). Some examples of the camps many forms are transit camps, collection camps, processing centres, labour camps, concentration camps, gulags and ghettos. Throughout history these camps have been associated with the subjugation of different populations (for example, POWs, refugees, political prisoners, forced labourers) through different treatments and regimes (forced labour, discipline, torture, mass murder) (Dean 2007: 178). The essence of the camp consists in the materialization of the state of exception and in the subsequent creation of a space in which the bare life and the judicial rule enter into a threshold of indistinction (Agamben 1998: 174). Those denied citizenship are also denied their humanity through the denial of their elementary 'human' rights concerning survival (Balibar 2004: 119); they are alive as human beings yet have been radically excluded from the political community. Those so excluded, according to Balibar, force 'us' to address the reality of extreme violence in contemporary political societies and in the very heart of everyday life (2004: 120).

Conclusion

Post-9/11 British anti-terrorism legislation, especially key aspects of it – indefinite detention, control orders, derogating from the ECHR, and finally the development of the memoranda of understanding with receiving countries – are the by-products of the original intention of deportation. The diplomatic assurances included within these memoranda of understanding are not a falsification or a cover-up; by their very existence, they are an acknowledgement of the potential for inhuman or ill-treatment and torture.

More than that, according to the European Court of Human Rights, the reliance on diplomatic assurances will open up 'a dangerous loophole in the non-refoulement obligation' and will ultimately 'erode the prohibition of torture and other ill treatment' (House of Commons Constitutional Affairs Committee 2005: Para. 41). Stable democracies, such as the USA and Britain 'make the weather', according to Gearty; where they go with human rights, other countries willingly follow (2006: 107). As Žižek reminds us, the pragmatic utilitarianism evident in the 'war on terror' that prioritizes the rights of the many while sacrificing the rights of the few with impunity is like letting the genie out of the bottle (2002: 104). It crosses a line; it could lead to ever more innovative circumventions of fundamental rights and principles resulting in further episodes of selective indifference to the rights of others.

In the next chapter many of the themes developed above, in relation to Muslim disquiet and uncertainty, are examined in the context of the introduction of a list of vaguely defined 'unacceptable behaviours' under the Terrorism Act 2006 which, when combined with the very broad definition of 'terrorism' introduced in the Terrorism Act 2000, are set to have a significant impact on Muslim contestation, debate and dissent against the war on terrorism.

2 In between allegiance and evilization: *the* Muslim question post-7/7

> How we defeat terrorism, for defeat it we must, I believe will be the defining challenge, not of this Government but of this generation.
>
> (Lord Falconer 2007: 2)

Introduction

Across Europe immigration reforms are being introduced that build into citizenship and residence rights measures that constrain freedom of speech (Fekete 2005b: 1). This chapter examines the British version of these European-wide 'reforms' in the post-7/7 context. In particular the chapter focuses on the new deportation and deprivation of citizenship provisions proposed in the Immigration, Asylum and Nationality Act 2006, and their relationship with the list of 'unacceptable behaviours' introduced in the Terrorism Act 2006. Two discourses are explored in this chapter, both of which are related to Muslims in Britain. The first is the discourse associated with 'Muslim loyalty' to Britain. The second is associated with the new terrorist threat, especially the suggestion that this threat is unprecedented and that the perpetrators of it are 'evil'. Questions in the West regarding Muslim loyalty are not unique to the post-9/11 world. The issue of Muslim loyalty in Britain entered the political stage during the Rushdie affair in 1989. It was in the aftermath of the 9/11 attacks on the USA in 2001 that the issue of Muslim disloyalty was reignited in Britain. The response to 9/11 was the introduction of states of emergency on both sides of the Atlantic complete with a range of anti-terrorism laws, for example, the Patriot Act 2001 in the USA. In Britain the new powers described in the previous chapter associated with the Anti-Terrorism, Crime and Security Act 2001 and the Prevention of Terrorism Act 2005 have resulted, according to the House of Commons Home Affairs Committee, in Muslim communities being transformed into 'suspect communities' (2005: 47). This suspicion, which is examined in the next chapter, is not just directed at a minority of Muslims who are suspected of being directly involved in terrorist activities (or indirectly involved in terrorist activities through incitement); this suspicion, it is argued, has the potential for being extended to include all members of Muslim communities in Britain in that a new order of hospitality (Honig 2006: 112), as noted in the previous chapter, has been established.

The events that took place in July 2005 in London, especially the fact that those involved were 'British' Muslims, has resulted in the introduction of anti-terrorism laws in Britain that attempt to silence, exile and marginalize 'extremist' voices. In particular it is the impact of the undifferentiated use of 'extremism' in this context that is examined in order to explore the potential impact of the introduction of the list of prohibited unacceptable behaviours in the Terrorism Act 2006 on Muslim communities, especially since 'extremism' in Government discourse is undifferentiated from 'radicalism'.

The chapter is comprised of two parts. Part one briefly examines the politicization of Muslim disloyalty in Britain from the Rushdie affair to the aftermath of 9/11 and 7/7 before moving on to examine the impact of the 'war on terrorism' on Muslims. In part two the focus is on specific provisions within the Terrorism Act 2006 and the Immigration, Asylum and Nationality Act 2006 that increases the Home Secretary's powers for revoking citizenship from dual nationals. These developments in the British anti-terrorism legislation is critically examined through employing the political philosophies of Mouffe, Buck-Morss and Žižek. The chapter concludes, following Beck, by suggesting that the Government's fixation on rectifying the alleged side-effects associated with Britain's immigration and asylum policies (which it is alleged have allowed 'extremists' to enter Britain) and human rights protections (which have protected the rights of 'foreign national' extremists residing in Britain over the 'law-abiding majority') will result in further unintended and counterproductive side-effects. These side-effects include the increased alienation (and potentially the radicalization) of members of Muslim communities. At the very least this legislation will have a 'chilling effect' that is likely to restrict the avenues of political contestation and political dissent among the members of Muslim communities in Britain, which will thus restrict the freedom of expression of sections of the population in Britain. It is suggested that this legislation will in turn introduce a limited repertoire of moderate subject positions for Muslims in Britain in the foreseeable future.

Part one: War on terror or war on Islam?

Muslim communities in the West are suspected of numerous shortcomings. For example, many in the West, according to Beck, suspect that Muslims cannot be 'real democrats' (2006: 167); others suspect Muslims as being 'sleepers', 'fifth columnists', 'enemies within' who are working clandestinely to undermine 'our' way of life (Allen 2005: 51). In the context of the post-9/11 global war on terrorism these suspicions, and this othering of Muslim communities, have become exacerbated by activities related to Al-Qaeda in Britain, Spain, Indonesia and in the Middle East. In response to these activities, concepts that seem to belong to the past, for example, loyalty, treason and patriotism (Werbner 2000: 310), have resurfaced in recent years to question the place and intentions of Muslims living in the West. Although this has intensified since 9/11, commentators and academics such as Edward Said reminded us that there is nothing new about this ambivalence to Islam in the West. This ambivalence, according to Said, has been woven into the fabric of European life for centuries (1978: 59, 60).

Tahir Abbas suggests that before the events of 9/11, the Rushdie affair of 1989 highlighted to the world 'that there were issues pertaining to the South Asian Muslim community' that were regarded as relatively innocuous until then (2007: 5). According to Parekh (2000b), British Muslims had three objections to Rushdie's book *The Satanic Verses*. First, the book gave an inaccurate account of Islam prompting Muslims to stand up for the honour of their faith and the integrity of their cultural heritage. Second, Muslims argued that the book was 'abusive', 'insulting' and 'scurrilous' in its treatment of men and women whom they consider to be holy and whose sacred memories they consider themselves to be custodians of. In particular it was Rushdie's use of 'indecent', 'filthy' and 'abominably foul' language that insulted Mohammed (for Muslims this is an unforgivable capital crime) that infuriated Muslim leaders. The third complaint listed by Parekh was that the book had demeaned and degraded Muslims in their own, and especially in others' eyes. It reinforced stereotypes and added a few more; 'it presented them as barbarians following a fraudulent religion created by a cunning manipulator and devoid of a sound system of morality' (Parekh 2000b: 299).

It was during the Rushdie affair that the question of Muslim loyalty was brought to the political fore in Britain. At this time, according to Werbner, British Muslims were perceived as coming close to denying the jurisdiction of British law when they supported Ayatollah Khomeini's death sentence on Rushdie (2000: 310). For Silvestri, the *fatwa* had the effect of projecting a distant Islamic world into the western world (2007: 59). As a result of the Rushdie affair, Muslims in Britain were seen as harbouring ambiguous loyalties or diasporic disloyalty to their 'host' country (Werbner 2000: 309, 311). At the same time British Muslims felt a degree of shame and responsibility that Rushdie, a Muslim author living in Britain, had offended the transnational Muslim *ummah*[1] through his 'act of perfidy' (Werbner 2000: 309, 311).

There are multiple layers of accusations of disloyalty and 'outrage' here; for example, Rushdie was accused of disloyalty to the *ummah*. At the same time Modood suggests that the anger and shame generated by Rushdie's actions was associated with the elevated position Rushdie enjoyed in Muslim communities in Britain, that is: 'virtually every practicing Muslim was offended by passages from the book and shocked that it was written by a

Muslim of whom till then the Asian community were proud' (Modood 1992: 269). This anger and shame was translated into action in the form of public protests, which in Bradford took the form of mass book-burning events (Greaves 2005: 69) against the publication of the novel, which in turn caused widespread animosity among the British public as a result of the associations of book-burning events to Nazism (Greaves 2005: 69) and concerns that Muslims in Britain were incapable of submitting to British law.[2] At the very heart of the latter was the growing concern in Britain that Muslims were susceptible to fundamentalism and therefore could be conceived as being undemocratic in orientation.

According to Parekh, Muslim extraterritorial loyalty to *ummah* is neither unique to Muslims nor amounts to much in practice; he suggests that 'Jews press the cause of Israel, Indians of India, and blacks of Africa. Loyalty to *ummah* has rarely led to disloyalty to their country of settlement' (Parekh 2006a: 182).

The results of the 1990 Trust's survey, *Muslim Views: Foreign Policy and its Effects*, suggests that Parekh's account of the power of the *ummah* over Muslims in Britain is accurate. For example, the 1990 Trust reported that 89 per cent of the 1213 Muslims who responded to their online survey said that although they felt included in the global concept of *ummah*, they did not experience a contradiction between being loyal to *ummah* and being British; in fact, 92.7 per cent of respondents to the survey said that their loyalty towards *ummah* did not contradict their roles as a citizen of a nation (The 1990 Trust 2006: 5). The perceptions of international *ummatic* attachments as being problematic (see Chapter 3) is associated with the categorization of Muslim communities in Britain in primarily religious terms after the Rushdie affair, the result being that 'groups previously known by national or regional origin – Pakistani, Mirpuri, Bengali, and Punjabi, for example – are now all seen as part of a single Muslim community' (Yuval-Davis 1992: 284). By categorizing diverse Muslim communities in religious terms, the Government and security services are susceptible in the current climate of viewing diverse Muslim communities through the lens of Islamophobia (Fekete 2004: 10). The Runnymede Trust was the first to define Islamophobia. The Trust suggested that the word Islamophobia has been introduced by the Muslim community to describe this new social reality:

> [Islamophobia is] an unfounded hostility towards Islam. It refers also to the practical consequences of such hostility in unfair discrimination against Muslim individuals and communities, and exclusion of Muslims from mainstream political and social affairs.
> (Runnymede Trust 1997)

Abbas describes seven features of Islamophobia:

1. Muslim cultures are seen as monolithic.
2. Islamic cultures are significantly different from other cultures.
3. Islam is perceived as being implacably threatening.
4. Islam's adherents use their faith to political or military advantage.
5. Muslim criticism of western cultures and societies are rejected out of hand.
6. The fear of Islam is mixed with racist hostility to immigration.
7. Islamophobia is assumed to be natural and unproblematic.

(Abbas 2005: 12)

A number of these 'features' are evident in the West's perceptions of the threat from 'Islamist' terrorists since 9/11. These can often take the form of raised suspicions with regard to Muslim disloyalty to 'the West', which is exacerbated by the fear that this disloyalty could shade into acts of violence against the British public. This is a greater level of 'concern' than that generated during the Rushdie affair and more than a suspicion that Muslim transnational *ummatic* attachments (Birt 2005: 106) could overrule respect for British laws. In the post-9/11 and especially post-7/7 context this 'loyalty paranoia' (Marranci 2006: 100) in Britain has become a burning issue articulated in tabloid and Government discourses fixated with alleged 'enemies-within' in the war on terrorism (Abbas 2007: 7).

In the USA President Bush's immediate post-9/11 references to a new 'crusade' eventually shifted, according to Mamdani, to the project of attempting to differentiate between 'good Muslims' and 'bad Muslims' (2005: 15). President Bush attempted to achieve this by suggesting that 'bad Muslims' were clearly responsible for terrorism; and by assuring the American people that 'good Muslims' were anxious to 'clear their names' and conscience after 9/11 (Mamdani 2005: 15). The problem with this clumsy attempt at differentiating between Muslims was it suggested that the transition from 'bad' to 'good' was to be achieved through the obligation placed on all Muslims to prove their credentials 'by joining in a war against "bad Muslims"' (Mamdani 2005: 15). Patel suggests that Bush and Blair's attempts to be politically correct with regard to their 'two Islam's' discourse in which a bad or distorted Islam is blamed for the political violence is profoundly dangerous and misleading (2007: 47). Patel suggests that these discourses serve to alienate Muslim citizens in the USA and Britain (2007: 47). In post-9/11 Britain the question of Muslim loyalty has evolved into accusations of treason especially in relation to the activities of British-born Muslims or Muslims residing in Britain who have been involved in activities that are deemed to be in opposition to the interests of the British State.

In this climate Islamophobia in Britain, according to a report published by the Commission on British Muslims and Islamophobia (CBMI), is becoming increasingly institutionalized (Doward and Hinsliff 2004: 1). The

Terrorism Act 2000 and Anti-terrorism, Crime and Security Act 2001 were singled out in this report as creating a climate of fear among Muslims in Britain. Sadiq Khan (Chair of the Muslim Council of Britain's Legal Affairs Committee) told the CBMI that this legislation has 'led to the internment in the UK of Muslim men, respectable charities having their funds seized, and charities suffering because Muslims are reluctant to donate for fear of being accused of funding "terrorists"' (Doward and Hinsliff 2004: 2). Police stop and search practices were singled out as a key indication of institutionalized Islamophobia in the post-9/11 context in the CBMI report. At the same time a number of sources cited a 300 per cent increase in police stop and search techniques against 'Asians' in Britain between July 2003–July 2004 (Aaronovitch 2004: 5; Tempest 2004: 1). According to Alexander, the emergent spectres of religious 'fundamentalism' and the threat of terrorism now mean that young Muslim men are becoming increasingly inseparable from the image of violence associated with the disturbances in 2001 and fears that further violence is being fermented in the extremist Islamic schoolrooms of the preachers of racial hatred (Alexander 2003: 1, 2).

In my previous book, *Intolerant Britain? Hate, Citizenship and Difference*, I examined some of the political fall-out associated with the 9/11 attacks and reports that young British men have been volunteering to fight with the Taliban against Anglo-American forces in Afghanistan. The latter were singled out as being particularly problematic. For example, this prompted calls for these individuals to be charged with 'treasonable acts' by the former Home Office Minister, Anne Widdecombe, and Baroness Thatcher called on all Muslims to declare the attacks on the twin towers as disgraceful and 'not the way of Islam' (see McGhee 2005a: 99–101).

The post-9/11 climate is both a culture of fear (Furedi 1997), and a culture of indignation in which Muslims in Britain are viewed with suspicion. In this context, the tabloids have suggested that the benevolence of Britain's immigration and asylum policies and championing of human rights and multiculturalism is being thrown back in the taxpayers' faces. This is clearly fertile ground for the far right political manipulation of the 'cluster of resentments' (Hewitt 2005: 2) among the socially excluded white working class. As I observed in *Intolerant Britain?*, the questioning of Muslim loyalty to Britain is not a far right preserve. For example, David Blunkett, when Home Secretary, nailed his colours to the mast of the new common-sense 'social' risk sensibility in relation to Muslims in Britain when he stated in the post-Bradford riots, post-9/11 but pre-Afghanistan war context of November 2001, that:

> We could live in a world which is airy-fairy, libertarian, where everyone does precisely what they like and we believe the best of everybody and then they destroy us.
>
> (Blunkett, in Hillyard 2002: 107)

This statement from a former Home Secretary could be seen as a precursor to the post-7/7 cross-party attack on human rights and the Human Rights Act 1998 and the introduction of the 'rule-changing' legislation that would reform citizenship, asylum and residence rights in Britain for foreign nationals deemed to have been involved in or associated with terrorist activities (see below).

It is increasingly difficult to work out in the post-9/11 world just who 'we' are supposed to be at 'war' with: a network (Al-Qaeda), an individual (Osama Bin Laden), a State (Afghanistan) or States (the 'axis of evil'), a tyrant (the late Saddam Hussain), or are we at war with 'terror' in general? In contrast to the nation-state terrorism (of which ETA in Spain and the IRA in Northern Ireland are examples), the activities of Al-Qaeda are transnationally oriented and organized, networked by satellites, laptops and websites (Beck 2006: 113). For Beck, Al-Qaeda's mode of organization can be described as a type of transnational communication action network for which we use the term 'multinational' in the economic sphere and the term 'non-governmental organization' in the sphere of civil society (2006: 113). Al-Qaeda is therefore not guided or restricted by territorial jurisdictions; it is the first multinational terrorist organization capable of functioning from Latin America to Japan and all the continents in between (Beck 2006: 113). As a result of this, according to Žižek, the 'war on terrorism' has introduced a new era of paranoiac warfare in which the greatest task will be to identify the enemy and his weapons (2002: 37). At the same time the deterritorialized and spectral nature of Al-Qaeda, an enemy who could be anywhere and nowhere, has resulted in the fear of this enemy being subsequently turned inwards in a Macarthyite declaration of war on 'inner enemies'.

A number of commentators have suggested that the 'new' post-9/11 terrorism threat has been dramatically overstated (Ashby-Wilson 2005: 6; Freeman 2005: 38). Gearson has suggested that although the 9/11 attack was unprecedented, the excessive novelty attributed to this event has led to 'confused policy responses' (Gearson 2002: 12) in that the problem of 'terrorism' that emerged in the post-9/11 world became conflated with that of 'rogue states' and weapons of mass destruction (2002: 20–3). Rather than describe a 'new terror threat', a number of commentators and academics have begun to examine the proliferation of 'new terrorism discourse' that organizes how 'we' in the West talk, think about and understand the 'new' terrorism threat. For Zedner, this new discourse is premised on the construction of a vague or ill-defined threat, in which 'the more ill-defined the threat, the greater its potential to tip the balance in favour of tougher security measures' (Zedner 2005: 512). For Burnett and Whyte, the paradigm shift from the old to the new in terms of terrorism is not really substantiated with systematic analysis of empirical data; the new terrorism discourse is for them a concoction of theories associated with the alleged belief systems of the protagonists, and their alleged access to weapons of mass destruction (2005: 3). The discursive work of the new terrorism discourse is that it brings together, as David Blunkett does in his Foreword to the discussion paper *Counter-terrorism Powers: Reconciling Security and Liberty in an Open Society* (quoted in the next section), a number of bombings, which Burnett and Whyte describe as 'events and non-events', into a cohesive framework (2005: 6). According to Burnett and Whyte, the new terrorism threat is made 'knowable' through the construction and reiteration of this unity among diverse events in which:

> the capacity to inflict attacks upon unsuspecting populations and access to weapons of mass destruction are generalised across all groups labelled 'terrorist' . . . it is the universality of the new terrorism thesis; its utility as a grand narrative which provides a basis for making the terrorist 'knowable'.
>
> (Burnett and Whyte 2005: 6)

Beck suggests that in the new war on terror it is neither judges, nor international courts, but powerful Governments, who define and identify transnational terrorists, and by so doing, they empower themselves by defining who is *their* enemy (2002a: 44). The 'terrorist enemy images' generated by Governments, according to Beck, are deterritorialized, denationalized and flexible constructions that legitimize the global interventions of military powers as self-defence (2002a: 44). Žižek reminds us of the central irony of the contemporary war against terrorism that this is a war where 'freedom' is increasingly being forsaken in order to defend 'freedom' (2002: 83).[3] We are constantly told that 9/11 changed everything. The result is that the states of emergency that were introduced in the USA and in Britain have resulted in fundamental changes with regard to the respect for human, asylum, citizenship and residence rights as well as expanded surveillance and police powers. In this context, according to Gearty, terrorism laws are presented to the public as 'the essential saviours of our society, safeguards against an otherwise inevitable barbarism: in short the new common sense of our age' (Gearty 2006: 102). The logic associated with this new common sense is that because terrorists use the USA and Britain's freedoms as a weapon against 'us', then in order to defend 'us' 'our' freedoms need to be limited. This is achieved, according to Žižek, through liberating the State from 'excessive' legal constraints (2002: 107). As a result 9/11 has ushered in a permanent state of emergency, which for the foreseeable future will be the normal state in the USA. Since the 7/7 attacks in Britain there is some evidence (this is further developed below) of Britain making a partial transition to a similar socio-political formation.

Buck-Morss suggests that since 9/11 there are two Americas; one America that is a voting citizen and that is institutionally a democratic republic. However, there is another America (as described by Žižek above) that she describes as the national security State in a permanent state of emergency (2003: 29). This other America, for Buck-Morss, is increasingly undemocratic, barbaric and violent. This other America operates in a 'wild zone of power' (2003: 29). In foreign policy terms the American national security State is a war machine positioned within a geopolitical landscape and it must have a localized enemy for its powers to appear legitimate (Buck-Morss 2003: 30). In domestic policy terms the American state of emergency provides justification for totalitarian practices against its citizens (Buck-Morss 2003: 31).

In the previous chapter, the negative impact of Britain's emergent anti-terrorism legislation on Muslim communities was noted. According to Abbas, British and American foreign policy and the introduction of a state of emergency in both countries in the name of the 'war on terror' is perceived by many Muslims across the world as a war on Islam (Abbas 2005: 4; Malik 2006: 17).[4] Despite clumsy attempts to distinguish between, for example, 'the two Islams' (George Bush) and true and 'distorted' Islam (Tony Blair) since 9/11 Muslims have been characterized as barbaric, ignorant, blinkered semi-citizens prone to terrorism and fundamentalism (Abbas 2005: 11). Arguably, Muslims have not just been 'characterized' as semi-citizens; they have also been treated like semi-citizens (or more accurately 'conditional citizens') in the USA and Britain since 2001. As revealed below, domestic policy, including the introduction of anti-terrorism legislation on both sides of the Atlantic have resulted in the 'old distinction between citizenship and human rights' being reborn (Žižek 2002: 95).

Universal citizenship, according to an Islamic Human Rights Commission (IHRC) report, has become contested by the spectre of conditionality in the recent debates in the media and by politicians (2004: 7). The conditionality of rights is an established component of Third-Way politics in Britain. The Giddensian-inspired mantra 'no rights without responsibilities' is associated with the widening of democracy in the ethos of participatory democracy. There is evidence that this mantra is a significant component in Britain's most recent anti-terrorism legislation. The conditions of the right to remain in Britain (for foreign nationals) and the revoking of citizenship rights (for dual nationals) is that they have not and will not be involved in behaviours defined as being 'unacceptable'. In the same year that the Equalities Act 2006 established the new Commission for Equality and Human Rights (introduced in October 2007, see Chapter 5) in Britain, the Government and the Opposition are intent on modifying and/or repealing the Human Rights Act 1998 in the name of striking a better balance between the rights of criminals (including terrorists) and the public (see Chapter 6). In Chapter 1, it was argued, following Dworkin, Waldron and Zedner, that it was not really the rights of the general public that were under threat in the context of the 'war on terrorism'; rather, it was the rights of foreign nationals, or more accurately Muslim foreign nationals that were most in jeopardy.

According to Dworkin, the post-7/7 'balancing' metaphor with regard to human rights in Britain is dangerous as there is little indication of the principle basis for deciding exactly where the balance between competing rights is to be struck. Tony Blair is clear where the balance should be struck by stating in his 'Let's talk' speech that 'the demands of the majority of the law abiding community have to take precedence' (Blair, in Dworkin 2006: 28). The problem is that the plight of Muslim foreign nationals comes down to whether the Home Secretary suspects (often based on evidence that would be inadmissible in court) their involvement in terrorist activities. But 'terrorist activities' since the introduction of the Terrorism Act 2000 are very loosely defined and very broad (Fenwick 2002: 733). In Britain's war on extremism, the human rights of individuals are seen as at best conditional, and at worst something to be abandoned just because they prove to be an 'inconvenience' (Dworkin 2006: 28). This is especially the case if 'individual rights' get in the way of the Government's ambition of protecting the law-abiding majority (see Chapter 6).

Part two: Breaking free from irksome restrictions

Various Home Secretaries (Straw, Blunkett, Clarke and Reid) have all emphasized the need to strengthen legislation, strengthen democracy and balance rights in 'the new war on terrorism' since 1999. For example, when Jack Straw introduced the new powers in the Terrorism Act 2000, he said that he was 'simply protecting democracy'. He suggested that extensive measures were needed since 'by its nature terrorism is designed to strike at the heart of our democratic values' (Straw, in Fenwick 2002: 724). Since 9/11, Home Secretaries' pronouncements have become increasingly reflexive in tone;[5] for example, David Blunkett, in the Foreword of the discussion paper, *Counter-terrorism Powers: Reconciling Security and Liberty in an Open Society,* said:

> My first responsibility as Home Secretary is to do everything I can to ensure our common security but is this security worth having if the price is a series of unacceptable restrictions on our hard-won freedoms? ... How can we preserve effective judicial scrutiny of any restrictions on our freedom, while increasing our capacity to forestall the types of terrorist atrocity we have seen in New York, Washington, Bali, Casablanca, Jakarta and Istanbul?
>
> (Blunkett, in Home Office 2004a: Foreword)

Since the bombings and attempted bombings during July 2005, the reflexivity of the Home Secretary has gone up a gear or two. For example, Charles Clarke, talking of the restrictions placed on Governments by the ECHR (some of which were explored in Chapter 1), stated in a speech to the European Parliament in September 2005:

> The view of my Government is that this balance is not right for the circumstances we now face – circumstances very different from those faced by the founding fathers of the European Convention on Human Rights – and that it needs to be closely examined in that context.
>
> (Clarke 2005: 4)

John Reid joined Clarke in his attack of fundamental standards and principles with regard to the 'laws of war' and the Geneva Convention. Reid (while still Secretary of State for Defence), in his speech to the Royal United Services Institute for Defence and Security in April 2006, stated that Governments fighting the contemporary war on terrorism, which he describes as '21st century conflict' are restricted by '20th century rules' (2006). Reid suggests that 'we' have entered into an 'age of uncertainty' in which national security is being jeopardized because institutions and legal frameworks are not adapting as fast as needed (Home Office 2006a: 1). He argued that Britain's security apparatus was created during the Cold War in response to the threat of fascism, but that the threat was now from 'fascist individuals' (Reid, in McLaren 2006: 1). In many ways, John Reid's overt attack on international and domestic legislative restrictions has the most in common with the Bush administration's attitude to what Berman refers to as 'the restrictions and timidities of the past' (2003: 192). According to Berman, for the Bush administration, laws, formal treaties, the customs of civilized nations and the legitimacy of international institutions were deemed 'the dross of the past, and Bush was plunging into the future' (2003: 193). The overwhelming desire of the Labour Government, post-7/7, seems to be rather similar; they too seem to desire freedom from 'irksome restrictions' (Berman 2003: 192).

The bombings in London on 7 July 2005 and the attempted bombings on the 21 July 2005 have had a significant impact on Britain's counter-terrorism policies. A few weeks after these incidents Tony Blair stated in a press conference that he had been set up to unveil what has become known as his 12-point plan to tackle terrorism: 'Let there be no doubt, the rules of the game are changing' (Blair, in Brown and Woolf 2005: 4). The overwhelming focus of these 12 points (many of which are included in the Terrorism Act 2006) is to attack what the Government views as the fertile ground of radicalization in contemporary Britain. Blair declared at the press conference that the new anti-terror laws would aim to 'pull up this evil ideology by its roots' (Blair, in

Jeffrey 2006: 1). This legislation allows the Government to deport 'preachers of hate', close down 'extremist mosques' and put 'radicals' under house arrest. The Terrorism Act also introduced an ill-defined list of 'unacceptable behaviours' that makes it an offence to condone or glorify terrorism (anywhere, not only in Britain).

According to a Home Office press release, the list of unacceptable behaviours covers any non-British citizen whether in Britain or abroad who uses any means or medium, including:

- Writing, producing, publishing or distributing material;
- Public speaking including preaching;
- Running a website; or
- Using a position of responsibility such as teacher, community or youth leader

To express views which:

- Foment, justify or glorify terrorist violence in furtherance of particular beliefs;
- Seek to provoke others to terrorist acts;
- Foment other serious criminal activity or seek to provoke others to serious criminal acts; or
- Foster hatred which might lead to inter-community violence in the UK

(Home Office 2005a)

As noted in the previous chapter, non-British nationals who indulge in such behaviours will be deported, and individuals who are suspected of engaging in these prohibited behaviours who attempt to make a claim for asylum in Britain will be excluded (Brown and Woolf 2005: 4). All these provisions are controversial. Perhaps the most controversial aspects of the post-7/7 counter-terrorism proposals have been those targeting incitement, glorification and condoning terrorism. These provisions are dedicated to silencing the 'vocal' tip of the radical Islamist 'iceberg' in Britain.[6] According to Shami Chakrabarti (Director of Liberty), many of the post-7/7 counter-terrorism provisions are a knee-jerk political response that will result in people being stripped of basic rights and freedoms in the name of fighting terror (2005: 15). There is little doubt at the target of this legislation: the tabloid coined 'hate clerics', for example, Abu Qatada, Abu Hamza al-Masri, Sheik Abdullah el-Faisal, Omar Bakri Mohammed) and other 'Muslim' radicals, for example, Mohammed al-Massari who runs the Tajeed website (Johnston 2005: 1), Abu Izzadeen of the al-Ghurabaa (the strangers) and Abu Uzair, formerly of the al-Muhajiroun (the Emigrants) now believed to belong to 'the Saviour Sect' (Graham 2005:

1). By targeting these individuals to such an extent, the Government's assumptions regarding what the main cause of radicalization in Muslim young people is, is exposed. It seems that it all comes down to removing 'undesirable influences' from British soil.

The Terrorism Act 2006 is a very good example of the collision between the forces of the 'post-political', 'third-way' centre-left consensual politics (Mouffe 2005) and what Buck-Morss has described above as the emerging national security State (2003). This Act taken together with the Immigration, Asylum and Nationality Act 2006, as revealed below, are the most recent examples of the political manoeuvrings of a State 'at war' against a foreigner/ enemy group within its own territory. This convergence is perhaps most evident with regard to these laws in relation to the drawing of the frontier of 'the political' at the moral level (Mouffe 2005: 73). Mouffe (2005) defines post-political politics as the collapse of adversarial politics represented by the distinctions between left-wing and right-wing political parties and associated constituents of supporters within the electorate. By 'the political' Mouffe means the dimension of antagonism that she takes to be constitutive of human societies, while by 'politics' she means the set of practices and institutions through which an order is created, organizing human coexistence in the context of conflictuality provided by the political (Mouffe 2005: 9). According to Mouffe, the pronouncements of the eclipse of adversarial politics (between left and right) has resulted in the moralization of contemporary politics (2005: 75). In political terms this means the 'we'/'they' opposition constitutive of politics is now constructed according to moral categories of 'good' versus 'evil' (Mouffe 2005: 75) 'freedom' versus 'fundamentalism'.

Fundamentalists, according to Mouffe, are the only radical opponents of the post-political consensus in that they, in reaction to the development of the post-traditional society, attempt to reassert the old certainties of tradition (2005: 49). By rejecting the advances in reflexive modernization, fundamentalists place themselves against the course of history and as a result they cannot be allowed to participate in the dialogical discussions so central to centre-left politics. Mouffe suggests that 'this type of opponent is not an adversary but an enemy, that is, one whose demands are not recognized as legitimate and who must be excluded from democratic debate' (2005: 49–50). Žižek concurs with this position when he declares that what is emerging in the guise of 'the terrorist' on whom 'the war on terrorism' has been declared is precisely the figure of the political enemy, foreclosed from the political space proper (2002: 93). According to Žižek, tolerant liberal democracies remain deeply Schmittian in their 'friend/enemy' recognition and construction processes, although this process does involve a reflexive 'twist' post-9/11 in the form of defining 'the enemy'; in this instance Al-Qaeda, as a fundamentalist opponent of pluralistic tolerance (2002: 110). In the 'war on terrorism' the activities of 'the enemy' are defined in cultural (as being pre-modern, savage and barbaric) and often in theological terms (as being evil), outside of historical time and therefore abstracted from context (Mamdani 2005: 4). For Mamdani, it is no longer the market (capitalism), nor the State (democracy), but rather culture (modernity) itself that is said to be the dividing line ' . . . between those in favour of a peaceful, civic existence and those inclined to terror. It is said that our world is divided between those who are modern and those who are premodern' (2005: 18). Mamdani makes a further distinction, that is, between the pre-modern (those not modern yet) and the anti-modern. The former encourages relations based on philanthropy; the latter is productive of fear and pre-emptive police and military action (2005: 18).

Fundamentalists, especially if their opposition is violent or extremist, can be defined (and have been defined by Bush and Blair) as 'enemies of freedom', 'enemies of our way of life'. Al-Qaeda organizations have been conceptualized as being ideologically (as opposed to 'politically') driven. This has contributed to the assumption in the West that Al-Qaeda are beyond the boundaries of negotiation or reasoning (Burnett and Whyte 2005: 5). This in turn supports the thesis that Al-Qaeda symbolizes a broader threat to global order and civility than previous terrorist groups which in turn 'leads to a fundamental reassessment in the methods and aims of counter-terrorism measures, and in a broader sense, foreign policy goals' (Burnett and Whyte 2005: 6). Mouffe suggests that in this process, whereby fundamentalists are presented as the constitutive outside of the 'the we' of the post-political 'dialogical' consensus, is in fact achieved through labelling them 'evil extremists' (2005: 55). Evilization, for Mouffe, is highly problematic from a political point of view because it forecloses debate and it outlaws contestation (2005: 55). Parekh suggests that this response, although understandable, is deeply flawed as:

> It makes no attempt to understand the agents and the wider context of their actions, and all too easily dismisses them as inhuman monsters. Once they are so perceived, it becomes easier to argue that the only way to deal with them is to terrorize them . . . this reduces us to their level and weakens our moral authority to condemn them.
> (Parekh 2002: 271)

In terms of domestic policy, evilization has particular consequences. For example, in post-9/11 North America, 'one mandate for all seems non-negotiable: to be against terrorism means to accept the legitimacy of the US deployment of its military power globally to fight terrorists as it alone, secretly, defines them' (Buck-Morss 2003: 28). What is at stake for Muslims in this context, according to Buck-Morss, is not their right to practise their religion, rather 'it is their right to challenge collectively, in Islam's name, the terrorist actions of States' (2003: 28). The Muslim critique of the West (Islamism), according to Buck-Morss, is not always militant, traditionalist and fundamentalist (2003: 3). There are many different varieties of Islamisms, from extremist varieties to modern critical discourses, focusing on the undemocratic imposition of a new world order by the USA. Buck-Morss suggests that by dismissing all Islamisms as extremist, the West has silenced:

> a contemporary political discourse of opposition and debate, dealing with issues of social justice, legitimate power, and ethical life in a way that challenges the hegemony of Western political and cultural norms.
>
> (Buck-Morss 2003: 2)

Buck-Morss, like Mouffe, believes (and this is further examined in the next chapter) that in the post-9/11 context there is little discursive space in the USA and Britain for criticism, dissent and contestation originating from Muslim communities with regard to foreign policy and domestic policy. According to Elsworthy and Rifkind, the International Crisis Group report published in 2005 offers a similar warning to the current American (and European) approaches that refuses to differentiate between 'modernist' and 'fundamentalist' varieties of Islamism. According to the report, in adopting such a strategy:

> American and European policy makers risk provoking one of two equally undesirable outcomes: either encouraging the different strands of Islamic activism to band together in reaction, attenuating differences that might otherwise be fruitfully developed, or causing the non-violent and modernist tendencies to be eclipsed by the *jihadis.*
>
> (Elsworthy and Rifkind 2006: 29)

In Britain, with the introduction of a list of unacceptable behaviours in the Terrorism Act 2006, the State's suppression of alternative and critical discourses has intensified. This legislation is concerned with silencing the outspoken and public inciters of terrorist activities in Britain, for example, the radicals and 'hate' clerics. The provisions are so vague yet so clearly targeted at Muslim communities that they could be described as introducing an attack on the freedom of expression and freedom of opposition of a minority group in Britain. In this climate there are concerns that extremist and radical Muslim activities are becoming increasingly conflated. It is unclear, for example, where radical, yet still lawful political opposition would end and where activities deemed to be extremist and therefore unlawful would begin. For example, the Muslim Council of Britain were quick to voice their concerns with regard to the list of unacceptable behaviours included in the

Terrorism Act 2006; they describe the lists as 'too wide and unclear' (BBC News 2005c). At the same time, in a press release, Liberty stated: 'we are deeply concerned that the criminal offence of condoning, glorifying, or justifying terrorism is broad enough to catch moderate as well as ranting politicians and religious spokespeople' (Liberty Press Release 2005). Hayla Gowan of Amnesty International has also suggested that:

> The vagueness and breadth of the definition of 'unacceptable behaviour' and 'terrorism' can lead to further injustices and risk further undermining human rights protection in the UK. Instead of strengthening security, they will further alienate vulnerable sections of society.
>
> (Amnesty International Press Release 2005: 1)

By labelling these behaviours as 'unacceptable', the Government is constructing the 'us' of law-abiding communities as opposed to 'them' the unacceptable, extremist enemies of 'our' freedom. The vagueness and breadth of these behaviours could leave, or might have the effect of leaving, many members of especially Muslim communities in Britain, unsure as to whether their activities could be defined as 'unacceptable' or not. The result of this legislation will be a chilling effect in the form of a suppression of debate, which, according to Gilroy, will allow minimal scope for active dissent (2004: 65).

DEMOS have suggested in their *Bringing it Home* report that a 'lazy parlance' exists in British society where the words 'extremist' and 'radical' have become interchangeable, the result being, especially with the introduction of 'unacceptable behaviours' in the Terrorism Act 2006 ' ... that any Muslim expressing anything other than unremitting support for the Government is under suspicion' (DEMOS 2006: 41–2). DEMOS suggest that in order to counter the chilling effect of this legislation in the form of the closing down of 'the space of important debates' (2006: 42), the Government needs to recognize the distinction between radicalization that DEMOS describe as community anger and frustration and the related, yet far more serious activities associated with 'violent extremism' (2006: 42).

According to a number of recent opinion polls, there is wide-scale 'radicalized' dissatisfaction among Muslims in Britain and there is a history of Muslims in Britain forging links with Muslims in other countries, especially where Muslims are an oppressed minority group (see Chapter 3). There are concerns that the provisions of the Terrorism Act 2006 could cover a number of previously unremarkable activities, for instance British Muslim support for 'struggles for self determination in the Muslim world' (Birt 2006a: 8).

Through the conflation of the activities of extremist and non-extremist Muslims, this legislation could result in the creation of a very limited repertoire of subject positions available for Muslims in Britain, especially when these unacceptable behaviours are linked with deportation rules, set out in the Immigration, Asylum and Nationality Act 2006 (which extends the powers introduced in the Nationality, Immigration and Asylum Act 2002) in which those engaging in unacceptable behaviours who are foreign nationals (even those who have been granted asylum in Britain), or who hold dual citizenship, could find themselves deported and/or have their British citizenship revoked, on the grounds that their activities are not conducive to the public good.[7] The problem with this, according to the Joint Committee on Human Rights, is that the Home Secretary's power to exclude or deport on the grounds that a person's presence in Britain is not conducive to the public good is an extremely broad power that will introduce a considerable sense of unease throughout Muslim communities in Britain (House of Commons Home Affairs Committee 2005: Para. 112).

At the same time the unacceptable behaviour provisions within the Terrorism Act 2006, coupled with the deportation and deprivation of citizenship provisions in the Immigration, Asylum and Nationality Act 2006, can also be described as an attempt by the Government to formalize the distinction between 'moderate' and 'extreme' Muslims in Britain. This legislation is clearly a solution to the indignation aroused by media reports that certain preachers, radicals and terror suspects who have been granted asylum in Britain have subsequently plotted and incited violence against Britain while enjoying the benefits (health, education, welfare and human rights protections) of living in Britain. There is more to these provisions than the above. The list of unacceptable behaviours in conjunction with the new deportation rules for foreign and dual nationals is more than just a chipping away at the exposed (visible and high-profile) tip of 'Muslim extremism'. These provisions are an extremely territorial response to fighting an invisible, virtual, multinational and deterritorialized network. By removing the visible and vocal inciters of extremism in the name of security, the Government is exposing its powerlessness, as argued in the last chapter, in the fight against actual terrorists and future terrorists. The actual and future terrorists in this war on terrorism occupy a spectral dimension in that they are invisible 'enemies'. As Elworthy and Rifkind remind us, the 7/7 bombers did not incite, contest or advertise their intentions; they were, on the whole, unremarkable (2006: 36). It was their unremarkableness, their invisibility and ability to exist, organize and carry out their suicide mission on 7 July 2005 'under the radar' that haunts the provisions associated with the Terrorism Act 2006.[8] These provisions desperately focus on 'the marked' (the indirect inciters of extremism). They are less effective against the unmarked, the unremarkable individuals (Phelan 1993), who are able to live double lives and who present ordinariness to the outside world while planning terrorist attacks (Elsworthy and Rifkind 2006: 36).

The major casualty of the war on terrorism on both sides of the Atlantic, as alluded to earlier, is human rights. In this war 'we' are encouraged to forsake 'freedom' to fight the enemies of freedom and we are urged to forsake the fundamental values of democracy to fight the enemies of democracy. In response to Tony Blair's announcement that the rules of the game are changing after 7/7, the Director of Liberty, Shami Chakrabarti, stated in a press release that 'public safety has never been a game. The fundamental values of a democracy cannot be changed because we are provoked by terrorists' (2005). Hayla Gowan of Amnesty International stated: 'security and human rights are not alternatives; they go hand in hand. Respect for human rights is the route to security not the obstacle to it' (Amnesty International Press Release 2005: 1). The Government's fixation on deporting foreign nationals and depriving individuals with dual citizenship of their British citizenship who the Home Secretary (not a court) decides have been engaging in 'unacceptable behaviours' is not unprecedented in the West. History has shown us that even birthright citizenship or naturalization may provide little protection of human rights for groups who are turned into foreigners by the threat of 'war' (Bauböck 1997: 4). The treatment of aliens, foreigners and others in our midst, according to Benhabib, is a crucial test case for the moral conscience as well as political reflexivity of liberal democracies (2002: 177). She elaborates:

> The rights of foreigners and aliens, whether they be refugees or guest workers, asylum seekers or adventurers, indicates the threshold, that boundary, at the site of which identity of the 'we, the people', is defined and renegotiated, bounded and unravelled, circumscribed or rendered fluid.
>
> (Benhabib 2002: 177)

In the context of the war on terrorism, Muslims in general, rather than a specific State, become suspects due to the virtual, multinational and invisible nature of the Al-Qaeda network. In Britain the legacy of the Terrorism Act and the Immigration, Asylum and Nationality Act will be the eradication of the minority of 'hard-core' fundamentalists in Britain who are already known to the Government. The wider social costs of scratching the 'itch' of this extremist minority through this legislation will be the silencing of dissent, political contestation and much needed debate through the pressures of compulsory moderation that will impact on all Muslims in Britain (this is further developed in the next chapter). This legislation, and the persuasive discourse of the new terrorism threat, complete with the 'new' enemy in the form of the 'fascist individual' (Reid 2006) beyond negotiation and reason, throws 'the threshold' of citizenship, belonging and loyalty into very high relief indeed.

According to the Commission for Racial Equality (CRE) the deprivation of citizenship provisions in the Immigration, Asylum and Nationality Act 2006 are sources of concern for certain communities as they are much wider than existing provisions of this kind in the British Nationality Act 1981 and in the Nationality, Immigration and Asylum Act 2002. One of the concerns raised by the CRE is that one person (the Home Secretary) under the provision of this Act takes the ultimate decision to deprive a person of their citizenship. This is particularly worrying for established minority ethnic communities, because this introduces what Bonnie Honig describes as a 'conditional order of hospitality' (2006: 112) in which 'the host', for example, Britain, can strip British citizenship from those who consider themselves to be British. That is, this legislation introduces the possibility of British citizenship being stripped from dual nationals 'who were born in the UK and who have never lived in the country of their other nationality ... where they do not speak the language, and where they have no links' (CRE 2006a: 11).[9]

The Joint Committee on Human Rights state that deporting dual nationals (including individuals who are British nationals, but have dual nationality) especially the second and third generation of established minority ethnic communities, as a result of the Home Secretary harbouring suspicions, could be a disproportionate interference with family life under Article 8 of the ECHR, especially if these individuals 'had lived most of their life in this country, all of their family and other connections were in this country and they had no family or other connections in the receiving state' (Joint Committee on Human Rights 2006a: Para. 25). The Committee were concerned that there are inadequate safeguards against the arbitrary exercise of executive power with regard to the deprivation of citizenship given the serious consequences of the latter for individuals that entails the loss of the right to a British passport, loss of British diplomatic protection, loss of status, loss of right to participate in the democratic processes of Britain, as well as serious damage to their reputation and dignity (Joint Committee on Human Rights 2006a: Para. 159).

Thus, British citizens, based on intelligence they will never be party to, could face expulsion, become separated from their family, have their links with Britain severed, all of which has been justified by 'a pressing social need' proportionate to a legitimate aim 'such as protecting national security or prevention of crime or disorder' (Fekete 2006: 87). What these new powers amount to is a recalibration of what it means to be a citizen, of the rights of the citizen. This drives a wedge between communities of 'full' and communities of naturalized, foreign and 'dual' citizens. It shatters the sociologically inadequate binarisms between nationals and foreigners, citizens and migrants 'as many citizens are of migrant origin and many nationals are foreign born' (Benhabib 2006a: 68). As a result these laws could potentially have a devastating impact on communities, neighbours and families. It establishes new membership norms (Benhabib 2006b: 18) that lowers the threshold of 'Britishness' to questions of allegiance, loyalty and moderation that in the contemporary climate seem to be exclusively directed at Muslim communities (this is further developed in Chapter 6).

The indifference to the rights of the few is created, according to Herzfeld, through the selective deployment of a kin-based discrimination between selves and others (1992: 172). Herzfeld reminds us that an attitude of indifference is only justifiable if directed outside the reference group – at those who are 'other' (1992: 172). In this case, 'the other' is undoubtedly Muslim, the selves (to be protected from the other) are 'the we', the law-abiding British public, which includes moderate, law-abiding Muslims, on the condition that they remain so.

Conclusion

The post-9/11 state of emergency in Britain and the laws that have been passed that make up Britain's recent, Al-Qaeda-focused, anti-terrorism strategy since 2001 have proven to be highly controversial. In many ways these laws are examples of the practices of the post-political (in the Mouffian sense) national security State (as described by Buck-Morss and Žižek) marking the boundary of the political through constructing an enemy figure as the constitutive outside of the law-abiding 'we'. These laws in combination make lawful the eradication of the fundamentalist/extremist activities of 'foreigners' (including dual nationals). 'Evil extremists', it seems, deserve no better. They are excluded from dialogue, negotiation or rehabilitation. Their plight is assumed eradication through deportation that amounts to an attempted 'malicide', which Mamdani describes as 'the annihilation of evil' (2005: 26).

The problem, as raised by the CRE, Amnesty International and Liberty is that the unacceptable behaviour provisions and the new rules for deportation will not just have an impact upon those high-profile radicals and clerics so fascinating to the tabloids and broadsheets alike, but also have an adverse effect upon race relations and community cohesion in Britain (which is explored in the next chapter). At the same time, these laws will undoubtedly have a chilling effect upon legitimate contestation and debate with regard to the fear that even 'moderates' who have become naturalized or are dual nationals could be caught by the Terrorism Act and be deported under the criteria of the Immigration, Asylum and Nationality Act if their activities are deemed by the Home Secretary to be the wrong side of radical, that is, they have shaded into extremism.

The problem with these laws is that the Government is attempting to use them to wage a war on the most obvious vocal and public figures of 'Muslim' extremism in Britain; individuals whose activities could be controlled and monitored in Britain. The intention of the laws is certainly salutary. The warning is clear; Britain will no longer play the human rights observing 'host' to individuals who would plot against 'us'. In fact, this legislation could be perceived as yet another example of the institutionalization of Islamophobia. Legislation such as the Terrorism Act and the Immigration, Asylum and Nationality Act that blatantly targets 'Muslim extremism' in this way, has the potential to construct all Muslims as potential extremist/enemies unless proven differently and that renders their human rights, citizenship and right to remain in Britain conditional. This brings the 'war on terrorism' very close to home. These laws have the potential to foster insecurity among the members of Muslim communities in Britain that might in the long run prove to be counter-productive, as it could intensify the identificational impasse (Gilliat-Ray 1998) that many young Muslims in the West allegedly experience, which could lead to their increasing alienation. According to Elsworthy and Rifkind, an analysis of the root causes of political violence reveals 'the persistent influence of powerlessness, exclusion, trauma and humiliation' (2006: 10). Perhaps what Britain needs in the aftermath of 7/7 are not salutary provisions that force all members of the Muslim community into compulsory moderation by limiting their avenues of potential political contestation but rather strategies that foster respect, dialogue and shared understandings, as championed by the House of Commons Home Affairs Committee (which is examined in the next chapter), which promote legitimate protest as a healthy manifestation of democracy. This legislation has implications for all (Muslims and non-Muslims). Even though these laws are 'Muslim-focused', and will predominantly impact on foreign nationals, according to Gareth Crossman (Liberty's Policy Director), their effect could be much wider: 'These new powers make us not only less free, we are also less safe when we drive dissent underground and alienate minorities ... ' (Liberty Press Release 2006: 1).

3 Counter-terrorism, community relations, radicalization and 'Muslim grievances'

> Attempts by Government to deny the legitimacy of Muslim grievances serve to deny space for democratic protest and blur the distinction between radical dissent and extremism.
>
> (Yaqoob 2007: 288)

Introduction

This chapter can be described as an exploration of the following question: is there a 'community-relations' focused counter-terrorism strategy in Britain? In response to this question the chapter attempts to do two things. First, I attempt to map the extent of what can be described as a 'community-relations' approach to counter-terrorism in Britain. Second, I explore the potential and actual obstacles in developing such a community-relations approach to counter-terrorism. With regard to the former, it examines, for example, the recommendations made by the Home Affairs Committee for combining some of the approaches associated with community cohesion with counter-terrorism strategies to create a 'broader' counter-terrorism strategy in Britain. With regard to the latter, this chapter is dedicated to examining, for example, the relationship between grievances associated with Muslim communities (for example, Islamophobia, social exclusion and perceptions of anti-Muslim foreign policy) and radicalization in the recommendations for the introduction of a broader community-relations counter-terrorism strategy. In many ways these two interrelated explorations are intertwined throughout this chapter as it moves from the critical analysis of the recommendations for developing a 'broader' community-relations approach to counter-terrorism made by the Home Affairs Committee, to an overtly critical examination of the Government's selective take-up of recommendations made by the Preventing Extremism Working Groups and the Government's own recommendations in its Counter International Terrorism Strategy.

One could be forgiven for thinking that Britain already has a wider or 'broader' counter-terrorism that includes a 'community-relations' approach.

Indeed, the Government has had a long-term strategy for countering international terrorism in place since 2003 called CONTEST. CONTEST has four principal strands: prevent, pursue, protect and prepare (HM Government 2006: 1). According to Blick et al. there are two interconnected aims in this strategy: 'first, gaining vital intelligence that will expose the terrorists; and secondly, engaging with the Muslim communities to obtain that intelligence' (2006: 31). The CONTEST strategy has all the hallmarks of a well-rounded counter-terrorism strategy. Unfortunately, according to Blick et al., the Government has given prominence to 'the hard end of the strategy' such as legislation, measures against 'preachers of hate' and the pursuit and disruption of potential terrorist activities (2006: 31–2). As a result the hard-edged approach to counter-terrorism is not complemented with equal vigour with a counter-terrorism strategy that focuses on positive engagement and building trust between Government and targeted communities.

In many ways, as indicated above, this chapter is dedicated to uncovering groups of recommendations for striking a better balance between 'tough' or 'hard-edged' legislative and coercive counter-terrorism strategies and approaches that include more positive engagement with 'targeted' communities. In order to do this a number of strategic texts that focus on how a broader, community-relations counter-terrorism strategy could be developed in Britain is examined; for example, the House of Commons Home Affairs Committee[1] report, *Terrorism and Community Relations* (2005), the *Preventing Extremism Together* Working Groups' report of 2005 and HM Government's *Countering International Terrorism* strategy report of 2006. These documents are examined with regard to what they have to say about the relationship between counter-terrorism legislation and the more community-relations and social justice approaches to counter-terrorism in order to map the potential for a 'broader' counter-terrorism strategy in Britain.

The central theme that this chapter develops across the documents under analysis is that, in combination, the draconian anti-terrorism laws (see Chapters 1 and 2) and the official denial of the relationship between Muslim grievances and radicalization is antithetical to the establishment of effective partnerships with Muslim communities in the war on extremism. At the same time the Government's binary thinking with regard to good and bad Muslims comes back to haunt it here. The Blair Government's discourse of evilization (see Chapter 2) in which extremists are deemed to be deranged fanatics leaves little room for understanding the wider context of radicalization in the form of grievances and perceptions felt and experienced by Muslim communities in Britain and abroad with regard to, for example, social justice and foreign policy.

This chapter expands the analysis in Chapter 2 in that it is a critical statement on the power of discourse and the marginalization of alternative discourses in the context of a Government (the Blair Government) in crisis. As a result post-9/11 counter-terrorism policy in Britain has developed in the main at the expense of the appreciation of the wider contexts of radicalization. At the same time the Government's subordination of alternative discourses on radicalization and extremism (including the potential link between British foreign policy and radicalization) has resulted in their development of 'partnership approaches' on terrorism with Muslim communities being viewed as ineffective paper exercises. The major obstacle to create an effective partnership with Muslim communities in Britain is the Government's contradictory approach to Muslim communities as both suspect communities harbouring terrorists and as *the* communities they most need work with against extremism.

This chapter comprises of seven parts. Parts one and two examine the Home Affairs Committee's attempts to develop a broader counter-terrorism strategy through combining recommendations that have emerged in relation to improving community cohesion with a counter-terrorism strategy. Parts three and four examine the relationship between social injustice, British foreign policy and radicalization – through examining what the Home Affairs Committee, Gordon Brown and a number of academics have to say about the relationship between 'Muslim' social exclusion and radicalization. Here the marginalization of the relationship between foreign policy and radicalization by members of the Cabinet under Tony Blair is also explored. Parts five, six and seven examine the place of 'grievances' and consultation with Muslim communities in the war on terror in Britain.

Suspect communities and community cohesion

9/11 has been described as a global watershed moment, as an event that ushered in a new world order, and new ways of governing, which has included the erosion and suspension of civil liberties and human rights on both sides of the Atlantic (Buck-Morss 2003; Ignatieff 2005; Gearty 2005a). As already suggested in earlier chapters, 9/11 prompted a swift response in terms of anti-terrorism measures in both the USA and Britain. It was the emergency anti-terrorism legislation introduced in Britain, and its explicit focus on Muslim terror suspects that led the House of Commons Home Affairs Committee to suggest that Muslim communities on both sides of the Atlantic were being treated like 'suspect communities' by Governments, the media and the general public alike (2005: 47). According to the Committee, this treatment of Muslim communities in Britain is problematic and ultimately counter-productive in 'fighting' terrorism. The Committee set out to do something about this; the challenge that they set themselves was to ensure that:

the new terrorism legislation cannot and must not simply be a set of police and judicial powers. It must be part of an explicit broader anti-terrorism strategy.

(House of Commons Home Affairs Committee 2005: 49)

One of the recommendations made by the House of Commons Home Affairs Committee was that the Home Office should review the links between its work on community cohesion and anti-terrorism (2005: 33).[2] The Committee suggested that the Home Office 'does not yet appreciate that the implementation of its community cohesion strategy is central to its ability to deal with the community impact of international terrorism' (2005: 33). In the next part of the chapter the Home Affairs Committee's recommendations for combining recommendations for improving community cohesion with *the* counter-terrorism strategy is critically examined. Before that however, it is important to include a brief introduction to the origins and the place of 'community cohesion' in recent Home Office strategies.

There is a large and growing collection of reports, reviews and guidance on community cohesion that attempt to account for the lack of community cohesion and offer recommendations for building greater community cohesion between community groups in some of Britain's most 'culturally' disharmonious areas, especially with regard to the disturbances that occurred in Oldham, Burnley and Bradford in 2001 (McGhee 2005a). The lack of community cohesion in these areas was described in the Cantle-chaired *Community Cohesion* report as being the result of community groups living 'parallel lives' (Home Office 2001). It was suggested in these reports that segregation between antagonized community groups in these areas (mostly white and Pakistani-Muslim communities) reached deep into every aspect of social life including housing, employment and cultural activities (Home Office 2001). This segregation occurred in areas associated with multiple levels of deprivation (Denham Communities 2002; Allen 2003) where the competition for scarce resources was intensified by myths of 'preferential treatment' on both sides of the community divide (Home Office 2001). Community cohesion has been defined in a range of different ways since the publication of the Cantle report in 2001. Recent reports have settled upon the definition devised by the Local Government Association in their *Guidance on Community Cohesion* that was published in 2002. This is not a definition of community cohesion *per se,* rather, this is a definition of a cohesive community. In this definition a cohesive community is a community where:

- There is a common vision and a sense of belonging for all communities.
- The diversity of people's different backgrounds and circumstances is appreciated and positively valued.

- Those from different backgrounds have similar life opportunities.
- Strong and positive relationships are being developed between people from different backgrounds in the workplace, in schools and within neighborhoods.

(Local Government Association 2002: 6)

Despite the range of issues included in this definition, the Cantle report (and the Local Government Association) focuses almost exclusively on increasing contact and opening up the channels of communication between community groups in local areas in order to overcome segregation. Thus, poor integration, ineffective communication and lack of contact between community groups was deemed to be the overwhelming problem behind the segregation of these communities in these areas above all other related problems such as deprivation, targeted far right activities and alleged institutional racism and Islamophobia in the police (McGhee 2003, 2005a; Harrison 2005b; Werbner 2005). As a result of this the Cantle and related reports have attracted a great deal of criticism especially with regard to the emphasis on segregation and their main recommendations for overcoming segregation: increasing contact between culturally different yet spatially proximate communities. According to Kalra, 'segregation' discourse in the Cantle report is tantamount to a drastic simplification of the problems being experienced in towns like Oldham and Burnley and in the city of Bradford. Kalra suggests that the 'comically simple' thesis proffered by Cantle and others amounts to something of the order of: 'these people do not live together and therefore this is the reason they do not get on and therefore riot' (Kalra 2002: 25). Other commentators such as Kundnani (2001a, 2001b) and Amin (2002) have also noted that in the local reports, for example, the Bradford District Race Review (2001) and in the national reports such as the Cantle report that 'segregation discourse' has focused too much on 'Asians' as segregated from whites, rather than the process of whites segregating from racialized groups (Kalra 2002: 24). 'White flight' and the fear of racial harassment (Kundnani 2001a: 107) are two dynamics in the 'segregation discourse' that are de-emphasized in these policy reviews.

It is not only social scientists who have criticized community cohesion discourse. Organizations representing ethnic and religious minority groups have also criticized the community cohesion agenda. For example, the Commission on British Muslims and Islamophobia (CBMI) was critical of the over-emphasis of 'the contact hypothesis' in the Cantle report. According to the CBMI, the contact hypothesis is grounded in the ' ... naïve faith that if only there were more contact between different communities all would be well' (2004: 62). The CBMI suggest that the community cohesion agenda got off to a poor start, for it appeared unambiguously to be based on negative views and stereotypes of British Muslim communities and to be proposing mere assimilation rather than genuine inclusion (2004: 63).

Despite these criticisms directed at the Cantle report recommendations, the Home Affairs Committee viewed the Cantle recommendations on community cohesion as valid and decided that these recommendations should become a major component of their proposals for the development of a broader counter-terrorism strategy in Britain.

Community cohesion and counter-terrorism

The challenge facing Britain, according to the House of Commons Home Affairs Committee, is that it needs to act effectively against terror suspects within particular communities without being seen as targeting or stigmatizing that community (2005: 47). As noted above, the Committee suggested that the Home Office does not yet appreciate that the implementation of its community cohesion strategy is central to its ability to deal with the community impact of international terrorism' (2005: 33). The Committee considered the Cantle report to be a blueprint for improving community relations, especially between Muslim communities and the rest of Britain in the context of the war on terror.

The Committee made specific statements regarding the focus of their inquiry, that is, that their concern was to attempt to reduce the negative impact of counter-terrorism provisions on the members of Muslim communities in Britain. The Committee was not alone in their concern about the negative impact of 9/11 (including the introduction of counter-terrorism legislation) on British Muslim communities. The Council of Europe's Commissioner for Human Rights, Alvaro Gil-Robles (see Chapter 1), suggested in his report that exclusive application of the derogating provisions of the Anti-terrorism, Crime and Security Act 2001, and the application of non-derogating control orders in the Prevention of Terrorism Act 2005 to high-profile Muslim cases, has had a negative effect on both the perception of Muslims by the rest of the population and the confidence of many Muslims on the executive (Gil-Robles 2005: 12). Gil-Robles suggested that although strong measures may prove necessary to counter serious terrorist threats their impact on certain communities should be considered (2005: 12).

The Home Affairs Committee was well aware of this problem and was at pains to include a consideration of 'community relations' alongside the Government's emphasis on national security. In many ways the Committee had the best of intentions; however, their over-reliance on the Cantle report resulted in the development of a rather limited set of recommendations. In particular, the Committee seemed to be fixated (following Cantle) on the role community leaders should be playing in building and maintaining community cohesion. Faith leaders, according to the Committee's vision for a 'broader' counter-terrorism strategy, had a crucial role to play:

> faith leaders, can make an important contribution: we call on them to build bridges to other communities, including by dropping defensive and reactive stances to create a climate of tolerance and mutual respect.
>
> (House of Commons Home Affairs Committee 2005: 3)

This statement has some of the hallmarks of the Cantle approach to community cohesion, for example, increasing contact; opening up channels of communication and encouraging effective dialogue in local areas between 'community leaders'. This approach has attracted significant criticisms (see, Kundnani 2001a; Kalra 2002; CBMI 2004; McGhee 2005a) in relation to both Cantle's diagnosis of the problem, that is, Muslims have not integrated with their white neighbours and Cantle's solution to this problem: increase contact between Muslim and white neighbours. The former is associated with the 'parallel lives' theory and the latter is associated with the much derided 'contact hypothesis' (CBMI 2004).

It is not only the role that Muslim faith leaders might play in creating 'a healthy public life' through their bridge-building and dialogic role (more on this below) that is being recommended here. The Committee also suggested that the Government introduce mechanisms for assisting and supporting Muslim leaders to take a stand against terrorism. That is:

> In the context of international terrorism, it must be explicitly and specifically set out how British Muslim leaders will be supported in assisting British Muslims in resisting extremist views.
>
> (House of Commons Home Affairs Committee 2005: 49)

The first step in this process, according to the Committee, is to ensure that Central Government and Local Government engage directly with Muslim communities in the discussion of 'difficult issues', especially terrorism.[3] The Committee noticed that it would be impossible for the Government to support Muslim communities to resist terrorism if those representing Government departments were uncomfortable talking about terrorism with Muslims. The outcome of the Committee's inquiry was that there seemed to be greater confidence at local levels than nationally with regard to tackling 'difficult issues' such as terrorism. The 'task', as the Committee saw it, was 'to create an infrastructure for dialogue that will enable that confidence and that experience of tackling difficult problems together ... on a national scale' (2005: 60) and this was to be achieved through implementing the Government's proposals for action on community cohesion ' ... with vigor ... ' (2005: 60).

It is through engagement, and the 'open and honest' discussion between communities and between communities and Government that the Home Affairs Committee ran up against the second obstacle to support Muslim communities in Britain to become involved in the 'fight' against terrorism. This is associated with the Committee's ambition of encouraging ' ... the overwhelmingly law-abiding members of the Muslim community' to take a stand against extreme views and terrorism (2005: 20). This ambition is associated with the intention of mobilizing and hopefully cultivating 'moderation' through building the capacity of what O'Malley and other 'Governmentality' scholars refer to as 'indigenous mechanisms' (1996) whether they be 'communities', cultural groups, neighbourhoods or associations (Dean 1999: 195). This is described by the Committee in terms of the Government strengthening already existing practices within Muslim communities:

> It is clear that extreme views are challenged everyday of the week within Muslim communities. Nonetheless, this work needs to be developed in the years to come and it is important that public policy supports those people who will shoulder the responsibility of doing so.
>
> (House of Commons Home Affairs Committee 2005: 57)

The problem, according to the Committee, was that these practices do not amount to a 'coherent strategy' across Muslim communities in Britain (House of Commons Home Affairs Committee 2005: 65). Once again, this Committee turned its attention on faith leaders by suggesting that in order to build this coherent strategy, the Government should instruct 'faith leaders' to ' ... condemn, without equivocation, those of their co-religionists who advocate violence ... ' (2005: 48). It is worthwhile spending some time unpacking this. There are two main problems with the Committee's recommendations here: first, their use of language, or implied meanings and second, the Committee's presentations of Muslim faith leaders (especially 'foreign' faith leaders) as being *the* weak points in this strategy.

One of the main problems with attempting to build a 'coherent' strategy against terrorism in this way is that the Home Affairs Committee is relying on a discursive repertoire already employed by the Government in their statements justifying the 'war on extremism'. As a result, the broader counter-terrorism discourse introduced by the Home Affairs Committee seems indistinguishable from the war on extremism discourse associated with various Home Secretaries over the years. Both the broader counter-terrorism strategy and the war on extremism are founded on unstable binary oppositions, for example, violence (good violence/bad violence) and Muslim identity (moderate/extremist; law-abiding/criminal). There is a danger in setting up the 'coherent strategy' against terrorism in this way as it could result, as the war on terrorism has, on offering only a limited role to only some Muslims who would be invited to a highly circumscribed debate (see Chapter 2). The assumption here is that the Government would be able to unproblematically cultivate a 'moderate' majority to work with them on *their* counter-terrorism strategy. As revealed below, this could be a problematic process since the Government's counter-terrorism strategy (regardless of their attempts to keep these issues separate, see below) is closely connected to their foreign policies, especially in relation to the war in Iraq and the continuing conflict in Afghanistan.

According to Modood, bridge-building between Governments and Muslim communities ' ... does not simply mean asking moderate Muslims to join and support the new project against terrorism' (2002: 116). There is a risk that this strategy could shade into the 'you are either with us or against us' stance associated with the Bush administration's brutal simplifications and clear distinctions between two Islams: good Islam and bad Islam that was examined in the previous chapter. The Home Affairs Committee tried to negotiate the problems associated with approaches such as this by attempting to make clearer the distinction between lawful and unlawful acts. For example, they stipulated that Muslims expressing anti-western ' ... reactionary social views ... ' were lawful acts that fall within the bounds of free speech. However, they stipulated that Muslims who advocated terrorism or other forms of violence were engaging in unlawful activities (2005: 48). In the post-7/7 context, these distinctions between legitimate 'radical' political dissent and violent extremism have become potentially even more blurred in relation to the vague terms that prohibit activities deemed 'unacceptable behaviours' introduced in the Terrorism Act 2006 (see Chapter 2).

Another issue that was not adequately considered by the Home Affairs Committee was that by advocating an infrastructure of engagement and dialogue be set up between the Government and 'the Muslim community' the binary oppositions that structure the Government's discourse on the global war on terrorism could be troubled by critical counter-discourses that present a less clear-cut definition of 'law-abiding' and criminal violence in relation to terrorism, the global war on terrorism and the continuing war in Iraq from various perspectives, including Muslim perspectives. The Committee give no space in its report and recommendations as to how these types of discourse will be co-opted into their broader counter-terrorism strategy. In fact, the Blair Government's refusal to co-opt these oppositional discourses that emphasize, for example, the links between foreign policy and radicalization of young Muslims in Britain, see below, is a major stumbling block for the development of an effective 'broader' counter-terrorism strategy in the form of partnerships between Government and Muslim communities.

Modood suggests that Muslims in the West can be a critical source of dialogue, understanding and bridge-building (2002: 115). However, Modood's emphasis is on the 'critical' here, as he certainly does not see the role that the Muslim diaspora in the West are supposed to play with regard to dialogue as being simply a matter of supporting, for example, *the* counter-terrorism strategy and British foreign policy. Muslim groups are likely to combine their condemnation of terrorist acts of violence, as noted above, along with a troubling critique of the Government's foreign policy and domestic counter-terrorism legislation in their 'consultation' with Government.

The second major problem with regard to the Committee's suggestion for a coherent strategy related to the nation-wide condemnation of terrorism in Muslim communities in Britain is their over-emphasis on 'foreign' faith leaders. It is here where the Home Affairs Committee's attempt to combine community cohesion and counter-terrorism discourses become closely aligned to the Government's 'war' on extremist or unacceptable ideas, especially when these ideas are suspected of being disseminated by foreign nationals (see Chapters 1 and 2). However, the Committee's fixation on 'foreign' faith leaders can also be connected to developments within recent immigration and asylum policy, especially the introduction of English language and citizenship classes and ceremonies synonymous with the 'managed migration' policies introduced under the Nationality, Immigration and Asylum Act 2002 (see Chapter 4). The Home Office Home Affairs Committee was concerned that ' ... preachers from other countries, who have a reputation for extremist views can, during their visits to Britain, harm community relations' during their stay (2005: 49). It was not only the extremist views of these 'foreign-born Imams' that was a source of concern for the Home Office Home Affairs Committee; these faith leaders were also viewed as being inadequately skilled with regard to the role they were expected to play in relation to wider community cohesion strategies because it was assumed ' ... they were unlikely to have much understanding of the host country ... ' (2005: 52).

The Home Office Home Affairs Committee believed that foreign faith leaders' lack of familiarity and their potential lack of sensitivity to the challenges of building community cohesion in twenty-first-century Britain could lead to ' ... increasing segregations ... ' between Muslim communities and other community groups (2005: 52). The Home Office in its evidence to the Home Affairs Committee stated that existing regulations with regard to 'foreign ministers of religion' focus on English language proficiency. These current regulations stipulate that foreign ministers of religion who wish to minister in Britain have to demonstrate spoken English at IELT level 4 (described as limited user level). The Home Office intended to raise this requirement to IELTs level 6 by 2007 (in, Home Affairs Committee 2005: 52). A second stage of consultation (with faith communities) was launched by the Home Office in March 2005; according to their evidence presented to the Committee, with regard to further tightening regulations, the Home Office would:

> try and ensure ministers of religion from abroad can play a full role in the community ... it includes things like civic knowledge,

> engagement in communities, pre-entry qualifications, and we want to explore with the faith communities what ought to be the range of skills and abilities that people who want to come into this country as ministers of religion should possess.
>
> (Home Office Home Affairs Committee 2005: 52)[4]

The Home Affairs Committee commended the Home Office's efforts with regard to the above. It would continue to review the success of these efforts, but suggested that the ideas 'from other countries' should also be studied (2005: 52). The ideas from other countries (mostly the Netherlands) that proved to be particularly appealing to this Committee were the 'targeted courses in citizenship' for Imams; and, providing funding for the education of 'local-born' Imams (2005: 49, 52). The assumption was that British-born (or home-grown) Imams could be better conduits of community cohesion initiatives in their local areas than 'foreigners'.

Despite the best of intentions, the Home Affairs Committee's attempts to convince the Government to launch a broader counter-terrorism strategy that would combine anti-terrorism legislation with a wider community cohesion strategy was limited from the start. The main reason for this was that the Committee adopted rather than problematized the legacies of Cantle's community cohesion strategy and Government discourses associated with the war on extremism. The influence of the former resulted in the Committee's attention being too focused on local leadership, especially Muslim faith leaders; this resulted in the Committee being as fixated as the Government on eradicating 'undesirable influences'. By examining the recommendations and concerns made by the Home Affairs Committee with regard to community and faith leaders, the problems associated with trying to build an infrastructure of dialogue, and a unified (Government and Muslim community and faith leadership) stance against extremism is particularly revealing.

In many ways, the weakness of 'Muslim community leadership' with regard to, for example, how representative they are, and how in touch with young people they are, has resulted in the Blair Government losing faith in the usual business of governing through communities (that is, governing through community leaders). As a result (see below), new indigenous mechanisms in the form of alternative Muslim organizations that allegedly better represent Muslims, including young people and women, are being consulted by the Government in its attempts to 'work with' organizations who are better able (and willing) to take an effective stance on extremism. According to Nikolas Rose, 'the community' emerged as the ideal territory for the administration of the individual and collective existence in the second half of the twentieth century (1999b: 136, 189).

New Labour's communitarianism is most evident, according to Rose, in their strategy of 'Government through community' (1999b: 136). Governing through community requires a respatialization of Government (for example, joined-up Government, see McGhee 2005a) and a conceptualization of community as a 'valorized political zone' (Rose 1999b: 189). Conceived in this way, community links the individual (who identifies with his or her community) to Government (especially a valorized Local Government) through the latter's engagement with 'community leaders' or local representatives. According to Rose, 'for to govern communities, it seems one must first of all link oneself up with those who, or claim, moral authority in 'the black community' or 'the local community' (1999b: 189). In many ways, Government through community, or more accurately Government through engagement with community leaders and representatives has been a staple component of what has become known as multiculturalism at the level in the context of Local Government. The Blair Government's lack of faith in governing through existing or traditional 'community' channels to create a uniform stance against extremism is particularly revealing with regard to the impact of security on what Alibhai-Brown describes as the non-interference pact under multiculturalism (2000: 7) in which the Government is being more selective with regard to the community 'representatives' it is willing to consult. This is further developed in the last section of the chapter.

The link between poverty, young Muslims and radicalization

Reaching deep into faith communities, in order to engage so-called 'harder to reach groups' (especially young people), in debates on British identity, British citizenship and on issues such as terrorism is a central concern of many Government departments and committees.[5] The Home Affairs Committee's concern in this regard is no exception to the general trend. The Committee's insistence that Central and Local Government should reach out to and engage young people, in order to increase the representativeness of faith-based organizations (more on this below) is only half the story. This is very much a 'kill two birds with one stone' strategy associated with, on the one hand, increasing the presence and influence of young people in 'Muslim organizations' for Government consultation purposes. However, on the other hand, this strategy is also dedicated to 'engaging' young people, especially Muslim young people, before extremists do. This is a proactive strategy that is not unique to the Home Affairs Committee. For example, in October 2003 the former American Defense Secretary, Donald Rumsfeld, reflecting on two years of waging 'the global war on terrorism', asked his advisers:

> Are we capturing, killing or deterring and dissuading more terrorists everyday than the madarassas and the radical clerics are recruiting,

> training and deploying against us? Does the US need to fashion a
> broad, integrated plan to stop the next generation of terrorists?
> (The National Commission on the Terrorist Attacks Upon
> the United States 2004: 374–5)

The National Commission declared Rumsfeld's questions to be 'the right
questions' and they called for the invigoration of American foreign policy,
with an emphasis on helping ' ... moderate Muslims combat extremist
ideas ... ' (2004: 376). Thus, the intention was to undermine extremism and
anti-American hostility through promoting ' ... America's message of
opportunity to the Arab and Muslim world ... ' (2004: 376). This is clearly not
an easy task and one that the Americans have not adequately invested in
during the war on terror. The situation in Britain is obviously different to say
the least. However, it is clear that reaching out to young Muslims, through
strategies that would include them and engage them (before extremists do), is
limited by the restricted dialogue that these young people are being invited to
participate in. Now, the Home Affairs Committee has rejected explanations
that linked terrorism to social exclusion in their report. Instead the Committee, following the Cantle Report, emphasized the importance of cultural
factors (this is further developed in the next chapter), especially the weak
sense of British citizenship, the detachment of British Muslims from the social
mainstream and the relative lack of Muslim political participation in Britain
as being the central 'social problems' to be addressed. By so doing, the Home
Office Home Affairs Committee managed to de-emphasize material factors
such as poverty and high unemployment among, for example, Pakistani and
Bangladeshi communities,[6] as contributing to radicalization.

The Home Office Affairs Committee suggested that explanations such as
social exclusion were simplistic and mono-causal when employed to explain
why a small number of young Muslim people are 'drawn into terrorism'
(2005: 49).[7] The Home Affairs Committee was dismissive of the necessity of a
parallel 'social justice' strategy:

> our discussions in the United Kingdom, France and the Netherlands
> leads us to reject simplistic, mono-causal explanations like social
> exclusion. Whilst the economic disadvantage and social deprivation
> of Muslim communities is well documented, active terrorists are at
> least likely to come from prosperous families or be personally well-
> educated and successful.[8]
> (Home Office Home Affairs Committee 2005: 49)

This stance on social exclusion is to the neglect of what Abbas describes as the
'sense of dislocation and alienation' that many young Muslims feel (2007:
10). According to Abbas, they 'live in poverty, in overcrowded homes,

segregated areas, declining inner city zones, face educational under-achievement, high unemployment, low graduate employment, and experi-ence poor health' (2007: 10). At the same time the Home Affairs Committee de-emphasize the links between deprivation and discrimination with regard to the lack of community cohesion, and the rise of extremism and funda-mentalism is out of step with some of the other programmes and consultation exercises that have emerged from the Home Office in 2004–5.

For example, this is a departure from the emphasis of the Home Office's *Strength in Diversity* consultation strategy and *Improving Opportunities* strategy introduced in 2004 and 2005 (see Chapter 4) in which the focus was on both enhancing the 'sense' of citizenship and increasing the participation and engagement of ethnic and religious minority groups within a 'race equality strategy' designed to improve the opportunities and increase the social inclusion of ethnic and religious minority groups (MacTaggart, in Home Office 2004b: 1–2). These strategies, which primarily focus upon ethnic and religious minority youth, were also promoted as an antidote to what the then Home Secretary described as the rise of extremism and fundamentalism in Britain (Blunkett 2004: 2). The first major failing of the Home Affairs Com-mittee with regard to the above is once again its over-reliance on the Cantle report and a relative lack of familiarity with subsequent Home Office initia-tives that have modified, developed and expanded 'the community cohesion agenda' beyond the recommendations made in the Cantle report with regard to creating dialogue, increasing contact and involving young people.[9]

The Home Office Home Affairs Committee was adamant, from its analysis of witness statements and submissions to the Committee, that it was a sense of rejection by British society that has led young people to turn to Islam, and which has in turn led a few individuals to move to extremism (2005: 49). The overwhelming conclusion that the Home Office Home Affairs Committee came to was that 'questions of identity' were linked to a small number of 'well-educated and apparently integrated young British people' turning to religion (2005: 52). It was, however, the problematic subsequent step that a small number of young people take, that is, 'the move to extremism' after turning to Islam[10] that the Committee was eager to interrupt.

Another problem associated with the Home Affairs Committee's rejection of social exclusion as a significant factor in the biography of terrorists and potential terrorists (because of high 'educational attainment' and 'affluence' of some individuals suspected of being involved in terrorist activities) is its unfamiliarity with social movement theories. Certain aspects of social movement theory can adequately explain why some members of 'elite' groups[11] can prove to be more prone to insurgent activities than the members of less powerful and less educated groups. Social movement theories, espe-cially in the form of resource mobilization theories, are capable of connecting the activities, activism and 'insurgent consciousness' of individuals (especially affluent or elite individuals) with those of oppressed groups. In fact, resource mobilization theories offers explanations as to why elite, affluent and 'educated' individuals or groups might be the first to develop an insurgent consciousness, as they, in advance of less powerful, oppressed individuals and groups, will be able to ' ... attribute their grievances to ... ' what they might see as ' ... changeable aspects of the social world ... ' from their privileged position (Crossley 2002: 114).[12] Crossley suggests that Tarrow's 'grievance interpretation' schema is crucial for understanding social movement activism and engagement (2002: 137). According to Crossley ' ... it is because agents feel injustices and feel wronged – or that others are wronged – that they are moved to action' (2002: 137).

Thus, felt injury and solidarity with others, especially oppressed groups, can arise regardless if individuals come from 'well-off families' or not. In fact, it is almost expected in social movement theory that elite, educated and privileged individuals lead the way. Why should this be any different with regard to the 'turn to extremism' in relation to young Muslim people? Can the relative deprivation facing Muslims at home and abroad[13] and their perceptions of 'anti-Muslim' foreign policies of western regimes towards Muslim States really be de-emphasized just because some who have turned to terrorism are thought to have come from prosperous families? There is little attempt here to understand *ummatic* attachments (see Chapter 2); that is, the experience of the *ummah* as a 'community of emotions' (Marranci 2006: 107) expressed by many western-born Muslims as solidarity with oppressed Muslims (in the domestic context but also internationally). The Home Affairs Committee repeatedly referred to the multiple factors attributed to the radicalization of young Muslims in Britain, yet it failed to fully develop and fully engage with the wider causes of malcontent among Muslim youths. In the next part, yet another obstacle to developing a broader community-relations counter-terrorism strategy in the form of a partnership between Government and Muslim communities is explored; that is, the official denial of the relationship between British foreign policy and extremism.

Foreign policy and radicalization

The relationship between foreign policy and extremism has been (to say the least) marginalized in the Government's post-7/7 counter-terrorism strategy. Hazel Blears (the new Secretary of State for Communities and Local Government under Gordon Brown), when Home Office Minister, was reputed to have walked out of meetings in her post-7/7 'tour' of Muslim community groups if the discussion turned to 'foreign policy' (Home Office Home Affairs Committee 2005). In turn, Tony Blair also rejected the suggestions that there was a relationship between British foreign policy and radicalization when he stated in September 2005 that:

> of course these terrorists will use Iraq as an excuse ... but we must be careful of almost giving in to the sort of perverted and twisted logic with which they argue.
>
> (Blair, in Oliver 2005: 3)

On 4 July 2006 Tony Blair added to his earlier statement when he announced that:

> If we want to defeat extremism we have got to defeat its ideas and we have got to address the completely false sense of grievance against the West.
>
> (Tony Blair, in BBC News 2006a: 2)

Almost a year later, Margaret Beckett, when Foreign Secretary, stated on the BBC News in August 2006 in response to the open letter criticizing the Government's foreign policy[14] that:

> Drawing a link between Government policy and the terror threat would be the gravest possible error ... Let's put the blame where it belongs: with people who wantonly want to take innocent lives.
>
> (Beckett, in Temko 2006: 2)[15]

John Reid hammered home the Government's stand on the issue of the relationship between extremism and foreign policy, or more accurately, the suggestion that British foreign policy should be modified in the light of this relationship when he stated to *BBC News 24* that:

> I think it is a dreadful misjudgment if we believe that the foreign policy of this country should be shaped in part, or in whole, under the threat of terrorist activity ... no Government worth its salt would be supported by the British people if our foreign policy, or any other aspect of policy, was being dictated by terrorists.
>
> (Reid, in *Guardian Unlimited* 2006: 5)

The primary reason that the Blair Government attempted to side-step the issue of the relationship between 'the increased threat from domestic extremists' and the invasion of Afghanistan and Iraq is, according to Brighton, a matter of 'political survival' (2007: 3). Acknowledging the links between these phenomena would amount to the Government admitting that its contribution to the 'war on terror' had resulted in 'terror' being brought closer to home. However, perhaps the gravest possible error for Britain (rather than just being a matter associated with the political survival of the Labour Government under Blair) comes from 'the continued official denial' of the relationship between foreign policy and domestic extremism (Abbas 2007: 7). Kundnani reminds us that the leader of the 7/7 bombers, Mohammad Sidique Khan, explained his actions a response to Governments that 'continuously perpetuate atrocities against my people all over the world'; Khan's warning was 'until you stop the bombing, gassing, imprisonment and torture of my people we will not stop this fight' (Kundnani 2007: 97). By dismissing the relationship between British foreign policy and radicalization, the Government under Blair lost the opportunity to understand and respond to grievances that extremists are all too eager to exploit.

The Government, the Home Affairs Committee and various academics (for example, Parekh, Walzer and Booth and Dunne) are correct; grievances (such as poverty perceived as relative deprivation between Muslims and non-Muslims) alone do not create social movements; they do not necessarily lead to mobilization (Baylouny 2004: 3). However, it would be rather premature to end the discussion there. To do so would be neglectful of the cultural appropriation of highly resonate strains and grievances (McAdam 1994: 38) by 'social movement' entrepreneurs (Crossley 2002: 136) such as Al-Qaeda 'recruiters'. This was the point that the signatories of the open letter to the Government were trying to make. For example, Sadiq Khan MP, one of the signatories of the open letter, attempted to clarify the purpose of the open letter in the following statement: 'we have not said that there is a link between foreign policy and acts of terrorism but rather that there is a link with the sort of materials that are used to radicalize young people' (Khan, in Hencke and Muir 2006: 3).

Rather than dismissing grievances, associated with social exclusion and anger over perceptions of anti-Muslim foreign policy as being unrelated to extremism, social movement entrepreneurs (for example Al-Qaeda recruiters) are, as alluded to above by Khan, more than capable of bridging their extremist 'schemata of interpretation' or frames[16] (Snow et al. 1986: 464) with the aggrieved schemata of interpretation found in unmobilized 'sentiment pools' (or reservoirs of discontent) (McCarthy, in Snow et al. 1986: 467).

Alongside the new terrorism discourse deployed by Governments (see Chapter 2) which is shored up by the security expertise (Huysmans 2006: 8) of 'embedded experts' (Burnett and Whyte 2005: 13), there exists a parallel extremist counter-discursive formation. This alternative discourse on the war on terror 'plays up' rather than 'plays down' Muslim grievances. According to Snow and Benford, one of the things social movements do is frame or assign meaning to and interpret relevant events and conditions in ways that are intended to mobilize potential adherents and constituents (1988: 198). The work of framing, when directly related to the proselytizing outreach work of social movement organizations, involves 'frame bridging' and 'frame alignment' whereby organizations or movements attempt to connect their cognitive orientations to ' ... aggregates of individuals who share common grievances and attributional orientations, but who lack the organizational base for expressing their discontents and for acting in pursuit of their interests' (Snow et al. 1986: 467).

Werbner suggests that Pakistanis living in Britain focus their attention on oppressed Muslim communities beyond the Islamic heartland, that is:

> Pakistanis in Britain have rediscovered their connection to Palestine, Bosnia, Chechnya, Kashmir. In their fund raising efforts they work with major Muslim transnational non-Governmental organizations ... the Muslim diaspora opens up a diasporic space of critical dissent against leaders everywhere: the Arab world, Pakistan, and the West.
>
> (Werbner 2002: 12)

Leweling suggests that Webner's insights on the *ummah*, if read from a social movements perspective, makes a pan-ethnic Muslim mobilization ' ... entirely possible – and perhaps to be expected – among Muslim diaspora communities when the grievance is associated with marginalized Muslim groups outside of the "home" country' (Leweling 2005: 7). Oliver Roy describes this type of solidarity as being possible with globalization, in which 'Islam' is being dissociated from a given culture in order to provide a model that can work beyond given cultures (Roy 2004: 25). From a Government intelligence perspective, British Muslim solidarity with and support of 'brothers and sisters' abroad could be construed as 'proof of Islamic fanaticism' (Fekete 2004: 10). However, if these activities are viewed from a human rights perspective then:

> Coming to the aid of people under occupation and at risk of serious human rights violations, even genocide, could be construed as the same kind of idealism that motivated anti-fascists to join the International Brigades and risk their lives fighting Franco.
>
> (Fekete 2004: 10)

At the same time the *ummatic* frame alignment, described by Werbner as 'diasporic action' (2002: 12), does not have to be extremist in orientation; it could result in Muslims joining non-violent campaigns, for example, the Stop the War Campaign in Britain.[17] It could, however, also lead to an extremely small number of discontented, alienated and therefore susceptible individuals being drawn under the influence of extremist networks. With this in mind, perhaps rather than rejecting the link between foreign policy and extremism, the Government under Tony Blair should have been concerned with the following questions: under what conditions do framing efforts strike a responsive chord or resonate within the targets of mobilization? (Snow and Benford 1988: 198). However, the Government also needed (as suggested in Chapter 2) to take greater care with regard to the differentiation between different responses and types of mobilization that could be initiated from such framing efforts; that is, they needed to understand the difference between violent extremist radicalization and peaceable, non-violent radicalization. At the same time they need to understand that these different types of radicalization are further internally differentiated along continuums of commitment.

The blurring of the distinction between different varieties of radicalization is not only a Government preserve; recent opinion polls have further blurred this distinction. For example, according to the ICM opinion poll published in 2006 (in which 500 Muslims were polled across Britain), 20 per cent of the Muslims polled felt some sympathy with the 'feelings and motives' of the July 2005 bombers, and 1 per cent (representing 16,000 of the 1.6 million Muslims in Britain) felt that the attacks were 'right' (ICM 2006: 4). Despite its far-reaching impact in that this poll has been quoted by political and media pundits alike, the ICM poll has been subjected to criticism and other polls have been conducted to challenge its findings. For example, The 1990 Trust produced a survey in response to the ICM survey. The 1990 Trust set out to survey the views of Muslims on foreign policy and the issues surrounding it (2006: 2). Rather than asking vague questions such as 'irrespective of whether you think the London bombings were justified or not, do you personally have any sympathy with the feelings and motives of those who carried out the attacks?' that were used in the ICM survey. The 1990 Trust asked 'direct' and 'focused' questions. According to the 1990 Trust Survey, only 1.9 per cent of the 1213 Muslim respondents surveyed between 8–27 September 2006 believed that it was justifiable to commit acts of terrorism against civilians in Britain and an 'overwhelming majority – 96% stated emphatically that acts of terrorism against civilians were unjustifiable' (2006: 3).

There have been a number of similar polls focusing on British Muslims between 2005–6, although the July 2005 ICM poll attracted the most attention. Other polls have also been published: the Sky Communication research poll 2005, the NOP poll for Channel 4 in April 2005, the YouGov poll in July 2005, the Populus Poll in February 2006 and the Global Attitudes Study for the Pew Foundation in June 2006 (see Blick et al. 2006 for a review of all these polls).

Despite this, at the Wilton Park Conference in 2006, the findings of the ICM poll were used to describe 'the wider tacit support for terrorism prevalent in up to one fifth of the Muslim community in the UK' (Hart 2006: Para. 5). At the same time John Denham, in his speech to DEMOS in 2007, seems to have been influenced by the findings of the ICM poll that inspired him to talk about the enabling capability of a sympathetic or supportive community with regard to terrorism. According to Denham, it is an uncomfortable truth that:

> few terrorist movements have ever lasted for long without a supportive community. A supportive community does not necessarily condone violence and, certainly, most people in it would not want to become personally involved ... Whether or not they condone violence they see terrorists as sharing their world view, part of the struggle to which they belong.
>
> (Denham 2007: 1)

Denham, in this speech, attempts to draw his audience's attention to how the post-9/11 rush of politicians to reassure the majority of British citizens that the events of 9/11 did not reflect 'real' Islamic values and that only a tiny minority of Muslims in Britain were involved in terrorism were both accurate messages, the danger being that 'if taken too literally, they obscure parts of the real challenge' (2007: 2). He suggests that the real challenge is for the Government and the country to engage with the fact that:

> Beyond the tiny numbers involved in terrorism there are parts of the broader Muslim communities that do repeatedly express some sense that terrorism in Britain can be understandable or even a legitimate response to current concerns.
>
> (Denham 2007: 2)

Taking grievances seriously?

Rather than targeting all Muslims and treating them like suspect communities, an effective 'community-relations' approach to counter-terrorism would tackle the complex grievances of the broader Muslim community and especially the grievances of young Muslims head on. The latter might divert some of the Government's exclusive focus on eradicating undesirable foreign influences, for example, 'hate clerics' and Internet extremists. Rather than being viewed as being beyond the pale, irrational and fundamentalist, 'radicalization' needs to be reclassified in Government, media and academic discourse perhaps as an understandable response to intolerable conditions. At the same time the Government needs to wake up to, rather than dismiss, the grievances that produce feelings of alienation and dislocation as they provide fertile ground for the creation of what Hart describes as the 'tipping point' (2006: Para. 19) at which a small minority fall in with extremist networks. This combination of conditions can lead to a siege mentality in young

Muslims (Hart 2006: Para. 19) that coincides with conflicting emotions: a sense of personal victimhood combined with a sense of global grievance (2006: Para. 19).

It is impossible to build a broader 'community-relations' approach to counter-terrorism that dismisses key components of young Muslims' grievance interpretation schema. According to Parekh:

> We should not put terrorist outside of the pale of rational discourse but engage in a dialogue with them, understand their grievances, see if they are genuine, ask ourselves whether we bear any responsibility for these, mend our ways when we think we do and, when we don't, persuade them why they need to put their own house in order. Although such a dialogue is not easy against the background of spectacular terrorist acts, it is absolutely essential.
>
> (Parekh 2002: 271)

I agree with Parekh, however; I do not think that 'we' should wait until individuals have already made the transition to terrorism. This dialogue should commence immediately in order to attempt to interrupt the frame building and frame alignment work of Al-Qaeda networks.

There was a glimmer of hope, in the Blair Government, in the form of Gordon Brown (as Chancellor of the Exchequer), and some of his closest allies (for example, Ed Balls) who, unlike his colleagues, were willing to talk about the relationship between grievances, material deprivation and extremism. Brown and his allies were obviously less invested in the political survival of 'the Blair' Government and therefore had a wider remit; one that understood the discursive battle between the war on terror and the exploitation of Muslim grievances by 'extremists'. For example, Brown is explicit in his plans to develop a more holistic or 'broader' anti-terrorism approach when he talks about tackling 'the roots of terrorism and not just terrorism' (2006b: 2).

The roots of terrorism, according to Brown, are found in the interdependent relationships between ' ... the extremism that seeks to justify it and the grievances that fuel it, fund it and give it cause' (2006b: 2). Included in the grievances listed by Brown that give extremism ' ... an audience ... ' is Muslim poverty in Britain, he suggests that: 'it is a problem for the whole of society that British Muslims are twice as likely to be jobless, twice as likely to be on low incomes, twice as likely to live in deprived areas' (2006b: 15). Brown's suggested broader counter-terrorism strategy takes in community relations, it understands grievances and root causes, but is importantly national and global in its reach:

> global terrorism must be fought nationally and globally – so we will have to work to root out terrorism and its causes globally and we will

have to do so in circumstances where the instruments of terror operate locally, nationally and globally.

(Brown 2006b: 3)

Both Gordon Brown and Ed Balls have talked about a 'broader' or 'alternative' counter-terrorism strategy. For example, Brown, in his article in *The Sun*, suggested that:

> besides targeting the terrorists themselves, we must win the battle for hearts and minds in their communities. When Britain and America set out to win the Cold War, we realized victory lay both in our military power and in persuading people under soviet control to demand their economic freedom and human rights. It was a battle fought through books and ideas, even music and the arts, and it helped to bring down communism from within.
>
> (Brown 2006b: 2)[18]

It will be interesting to see if Gordon Brown as Prime Minister will make these proposals a reality. Brown, in the weeks prior to him taking office, had already started to promise new tougher measures to combat terrorism. The measures Brown has talked about are: extending the length of time police could hold terror suspects without charge beyond 28 days, calling on judges to be granted greater powers to punish terrorism (by making it an aggravating factor in sentencing) as well as calling for a review of the laws banning the use of phone tap evidence in court (Panja 2007: 1–2). These are a mixed bag of measures that will no doubt prove controversial for civil liberties groups, the opposition parties and the security forces. One thing should be noted, however. Brown is insistent that both the courts and Parliament should be given greater insight over the proposed new measures and that although he was ready to be 'tough in the security measures that are necessary to prevent terrorist incidents in this country', at the same time he still wanted to win 'the battle over hearts and minds' in the Muslim community against extremism (Brown 2007: 1). Brown also insisted that 'at no point will our British traditions of supporting and defending civil liberties be put at risk' (BBC News 2007c: 1).

However, it would appear that Tony Blair had also modified somewhat his opinion of the relationship between Muslim grievances and extremism in his last year in office. Tony Blair and John Reid presented HM Government's *Countering International Terrorism Strategy* to Parliament in July 2006. The contents of this strategy document are rather surprising given their previous statements on foreign policy and Muslim grievances. It was stated in the strategy that:

> Identifying the factors which may lead to radicalization, and some of the arguments used to justify it, are important so that we can focus our responses in order to reduce the risk of terrorism. Of course, setting out these factors does not in any way imply that we accept their validity or that resorting to terrorist violence could ever be justified.
>
> (HM Government 2006: 10)

This statement, although cautious and still suspicious of Muslim grievance, was a major step for the Blair Government. It could potentially signal the beginning of a new Government responsiveness to the frame-working activities of Al-Qaeda recruiters whose 'version of history and recent events is highly negative and partial in its interpretation' (HM Government 2006: 10). As well as recognizing the Government's role in countering extremists recruitment strategies at the level of foreign policy (2006: 10), the Government's strategy also recognized the relationship between radicalization and tackling disadvantage on the domestic front (2006: 11). Personal alienation or community disadvantage arising from socio-economic factors such as discrimination, social exclusion and lack of opportunity were emphasized as potential factors in the process of radicalization (2006: 10). At the same time the role that the Government's community cohesion and integration strategy (see Chapter 4) could play in reducing radicalization was also discussed in this strategy, for example:

> The first area of action to counter radicalization lies in addressing structural problems in the UK and elsewhere that may contribute to radicalization. In the UK, this forms part of the broader equality agenda and we are working with communities and the public and private sectors to address these wider issues. Many Government programmes that are not specifically directed at tackling radicalism nevertheless help to build cohesion in communities across the country.
>
> (HM Government 2006: 11)

This was a major step forward with regard to the Blair Government recognizing the need to counter (rather than dismiss) the radicalizing effect of extremist interpretations of current and past foreign policy interactions between Islam and the West, as well as admitting to the role disadvantage and social exclusion could play in contributing to the alienation and potential radicalization of young Muslims. The worry remains, however, that those individuals who presented this strategy have stubbornly continued to dismiss the relationship between foreign policy and extremism (which was cautiously recognized in this strategy document) in the weeks running up to the presentation of the Government's strategy to Parliament. This strategy in its attempts at grievance appreciation has more of the hallmarks of Gordon Brown's broader counter-terrorism approach than the Blair Government's 'tough' stance on 'evil' extremists (see Chapter 2).

However, despite this progress, the Government's broader 'community-based' counter-terrorism strategy post-7/7 has been somewhat limited. The major obstacle to bring Muslim communities on board against extremism is the Government's refusal to have an open and honest debate on foreign policy. These limitations are explored in the next section.

Preventing Extremism Post-7/7

As noted in the previous chapter, the Bombings in London on 7 July 2005 and the attempted bombings on 21 July 2005 have had a significant impact on Britain's counter-terrorism policies. According to Shami Chakrabarti (Director of Liberty), many of the post-7/7 counter-terrorism provisions can be described as knee-jerk political responses that will result in people being stripped of basic rights and freedoms in the name of fighting terror (2005: 15). Chakrabarti suggested that in the post-7/7 context (just as the Home Affairs Committee suggested in the post-9/11 context) 'community relations must be part of the solution to terrorism' (2005: 15), that is:

> we need active societal and community involvement. The way to achieve that is not by more laws that will target particular groups but by inspiring people with confidence that they are not the enemy, they are not a suspect community.
>
> (Chakrabarti 2005: 15)

However, there is more to the post-7/7 counter-terrorism strategy than controversial legislation. Although John Denham was initially critical of the Government's lack of response to the Home Affairs Committee's *Terrorism and Community Relations* report prior to 7/7 (Denham, in House of Commons Home Affairs Committee 2005), he noted that there was some evidence of 'broader' community-relations-focused counter-terrorism strategies emerging in Britain after 7/7 with the setting-up of seven 'Preventing Extremism Together' working groups. Each of the seven groups focused on one of the following areas: tackling extremism and radicalization; engaging with young people; regional and local initiatives; engaging with women; Imam training and the role of Mosques; meeting Muslim educational needs; and, security, policing and tackling Islamophobia. The *Preventing Extremism Together* report offered an array of findings and recommendations. The Government has been highly selective with regard to the type of findings or recommendations presented in the working groups' report that they have been willing to support and those that they have attempted to marginalize. For example, the Government is keen to support the following initiatives recommended by the working groups: a country-wide Muslim road-show in conjunction with the setting-up of the Islam on-line website; and setting up a National Advisory Council of Imams and Mosques and a National Forum against Extremism and Islamophobia.[19]

Many of these initiatives are concerned with diverting young Muslims from the paths of extremism and to foster and encourage the development of positive British Muslim identities. At the same time the Government is currently running with some of the ideas generated by the working group on 'Imam training and the role of Mosques'. For example, the Home Office, in their *Ministers from Abroad* (second) consultation report (published in March 2005), focused on initiatives to increase English language competence and for increasing and improving the 'community engagement' of foreign ministers of religion in Britain. The proposals made by the working group had a slightly different emphasis to the Home Office's consultation report. The working group report on Imams and Mosques was more in line with the recommendations made by the Home Office's Faith Communities Unit in relation to integration, representativeness (especially including young people and women, see below) and developing the processes of consultation between faith communities and Government, in that the overwhelming emphasis of the working groups was on 'up-skilling' and capacity building (Home Office's Faith Communities Unit 2004). The working group dismissed the view that Mosques and Imams in Britain have been a breeding ground for extremism. They suggest that these institutions and the individuals closely associated with them have been beacons of moderation and tolerance (Preventing Extremism Together Working Groups 2005: 62). The proposals made by the Working Groups were intended to increase the capacity of the Muslim community to match the capacities of 'established faith communities' in influencing policy (2005: 72). Their proposals, for example, included recommendations for setting up a National Advisory Council for Mosques and Imams, a National Resource Unit responsible for designing curriculum and 'training' for Imams, a professional development programme for Imams, and the dissemination of good practice guidelines for Mosques, Islamic centres and Imams in Britain.

All that being said, the Government has attracted a great deal of criticism from some of with the working group participants. For example, participants criticized the Government's agenda- setting (which was established prior to the Working Groups being set up), the rushed nature of project (disbanded after three months), and the Government's cultural ignorance during the process (for example, working groups were established during *Ramadan* and meetings were scheduled on *Eid*). The main source of criticism was the

Government's selective take-up of only some of the Working Group's recommendations. For example, Dr Siddique, the leader of the Muslim Parliament, suggested that the Muslim road-show and other initiatives were on the periphery of the Muslim community and therefore failed to change entrenched attitudes (Ungoed-Thomas 2006: 3). However, many of the participants involved in the Working Groups, including Sadiq Khan, Labour MP for Tooting, Lord Ahmed and Ibrahim Mogra (Chairman of the Muslim Council of Britain's Mosque and Community Affairs Committee) have openly talked about feeling let down by the Government's inaction with regards to the Working Groups' recommendations. Sadiq Khan in his Fabian Society Lecture in 2006 said of the Working Groups and the Muslim Task Force:

> I worry that the Government might become the Duke of York – marching all these talented British Muslims up the hill of consultation and dialogue only to march them down again as very little appears to have changed.
>
> (Khan 2006: 4)

Ibrahim Mogra's suggestion that Government inactivity with regard to Working Group recommendations had put him and many of the other participants in an impossible position in their communities who are now sceptical about future cooperation:

> When we engage with Government we do so on behalf of our communities and they expect to see the results of our engagement ... because they have not seen any progress they now feel it is pointless to engage with the Government ... it is becoming exceptionally difficult for us in terms of our relationship and accountability to our communities.
>
> (Bennett 2006: 2)

Many Working Group participants, interviewed by DEMOS, also feel as if they have had their fingers burned after the process. Just like Ibrahim Mogra, many other Muslim leaders had to ask their communities to make a leap of faith:

> They took personal risks by actively persuading the skeptics among them to participate in Preventing Extremism Together, and, following the hollowness of the exercise, many feel they wasted their hard-earned legitimacy and have undermined their standing within their communities.
>
> (DEMOS 2006: 28)

Despite the Government promising post-7/7 consultation activities, for example setting up the Muslim task force, and initiating the Preventing Extremism Working Groups, this consultation process has in the end become a paper exercise, a Public Relations strategy that has backfired, if the comments of some of the participants above are representative of how these events are perceived by many in Muslim communities in Britain. However, perhaps the most enduring damage that the Government has inflicted upon its broader counter-terrorism strategy with regard to the Working Groups' recommendations is their refusal to engage with the Working Groups' comments on foreign policy. In their report the Working Groups stated that:

> British foreign Policy – especially in the Middle East – cannot be left unconsidered as a factor in the motivations of criminal radical extremists. We believe it is a key contributory factor.
>
> (Home Office 2005a)

The Blair Government chose to marginalize statements such as this. Rather than broaden its counter-terrorism strategy to include a national debate on the possible relationship between British foreign policy and the radicalization of young British Muslims, it has chosen to narrow the parameters of permitted debate. Rather than attempting to foster 'open and honest' debate on 'difficult issues' with the members of Muslim communities in Britain, the Government is clearly attempting to close down debates, especially in relation to Foreign Policy. According to DEMOS, the Blair Government's stubborn and often absurd and damaging reluctance to engage with the many reasonable grievances of the Muslim communities in Britain represents their fear 'that any kind of acknowledgement could suggest that the terrorists have just cause or that the Government is somehow complicit. This has made honest conversations difficult, as too many vital subjects remain out of bounds' (DEMOS 2006: 14).

Damage limitation and getting even tougher on extremism

In the end, the Government's 'community-based' counter-terrorism strategy consists of damage limitation exercises in the form of attempting to counter the negative impact on relationships between police and local communities after counter-terrorism operations have taken place (for example, the Forest Gate police raid).[20] Kundnani reminds us of the impact of some of the police counter-terrorism operations in recent years:

Armed raids across the country, sometimes involving hundreds of officers, have led to children being held at gunpoint, a woman suffering a heart attack and a young man being shot in the chest. The shoot-to-kill operation that led to the killing of Jean Charles de Menezes at Stockwell underground station in July 2005 reveals how brazenly the police resort to lethal violence. Dawn raids on households, involving the rounding-up of family and friends of terrorist suspects, have become familiar . . .

(Kundnani 2007: 170)

It seems the 'broader' or 'community-relations' counter-terrorism strategy that actually exists in Britain is one dedicated to improving 'the way in which counter-terrorist operations are conducted' (HM Government 2006: 21). This amounts to a strategy that will provide local communities subjected to a counter-terrorism operation (for example, a police raid, see Kundnani above) with as much information as possible (without compromising the integrity of ongoing investigations and intelligence) in a transparent and open manner. This is to be achieved through police engaging with local communities through local partnerships and through 'national' mechanisms such as the Muslim Safety Forum (HM Government 2006: 21). The problem is this very limited community-relations strategy is only available in London. The Muslim Safety Forum consists of 'Muslim community' representatives, Metropolitan Police and Association of Chief Police Officers. Representatives from other police forces (other than the Metropolitan Police Service) attend by request or invitation. This group holds monthly meetings in New Scotland Yard, which are described as 'national meetings, albeit mainly London-based' (HM Government 2006: 22).

As well as the mainly London-based damage limitation work of the police, the Blair Government launched a campaign to encourage Muslim communities to work alongside them to root out terrorism. The message that the former Prime Minister was attempting to get across was that 'the Government alone cannot root out extremism' (Blair, in Wintour 2006: 1). At the same time, the former Home Secretary, John Reid, called for a partnership approach to ensure 'our' common security in a speech to DEMOS in August 2006:

Our security forces and the apparatus of the state provide a very necessary condition of defeating terrorism but can never be sufficient to do so on their own . . . our common security will only be assured by a common effort from all sections of society.

(McLaren 2006: 1)

Ruth Kelly placed the responsibility for rooting out extremism with Muslim leaders. A spokesperson for Kelly told journalists from *The Guardian* that Muslim leaders 'have just not done enough and that extremist literature is still circulating ... it is important to get across that if another attack does occur Muslims will be among those who will suffer' (Hencke and Muir 2006: 2). As well as attempting to appeal to a future shared victimhood, Ruth Kelly, in a speech on 11 October 2006, threw down the gauntlet to Muslim leaders and Muslim organizations saying that 'it is not enough to merely sit on the sidelines or play lip service to fighting extremism', while indicating that she was in the process of fundamentally rebalancing the Government's 'relationship with Muslim communities' (2006a: 5). Part of this rebalancing strategy pertains to Ruth Kelly's intention to force Muslim organizations to take the lead on tackling extremism under the threat of financial penalties:

> In future, I am clear that our strategy of funding and engagement must shift significantly towards those organizations that are taking a proactive leadership role in tackling extremism and defending our shared values.
>
> (Kelly 2006a: 6)

Kelly made particular note of the 'wider network of Muslim organizations' that she had been forging relationships with, especially those representing young people and women.[21] Kelly is intent on bypassing the 'usual suspects' in Muslim community-Government consultation if 'they do not play ball'. This is not a bad strategy if one considers what Yahya Birt has to say: 'it is obvious to all that our older generation of leaders is out of touch with febrile and confused sentiment apparent among many younger Muslims after 7/7 ... community leaders rarely know how to direct these sentiments in constructive directions' (2006b: 14). At the same time Kelly's proposed shift in Government engagement and funding to wider networks of Muslim organizations is in line with the recommendations in the Home Office's Faith Communities Unit report *Working Together: Co-operation between Government and Faith Communities* (2004). One of the central recommendations of this report was that faith organizations, especially those that were consulted by Government on various issues (including terrorism), should include within their organization's representative structures 'hard to reach groups'; in the case of Muslim organizations, women[22] and young people. Awan suggests that part of the problem is the existence of tribal or clan-based power structures in such organizations that are epitomized by South Asian *biraderi*, and commensurable systems in other cultures, which can have the ostensive effect of divesting youth from any real tangible control over their own lives' (2007: 215).[23] Kelly's attitude seems to be if these organizations do not transform themselves quickly and sufficiently enough to include women and young people, she will simply select those organizations that do represent women and young people as *the* organizations suitable for Government consultation on terrorism.

Kundnani is rather dismissive of these types of arrangements. He suggests that the much derided (as being socially divisive) model of managing diversity associated with the 1980s' multiculturalist policies that created a new class of 'ethnic representatives' who were encouraged into town halls as the surrogate voice of their own ethnically defined communities is being transposed in recent times onto faith community representatives (Kundnani 2006: 2). Kundnani suggests that this is a colonial arrangement, which in the 1980s resulted in pressing ethnic groups into competition against each other for grants and recognition (2006: 2). There is clearly a risk of promoting division and competition between 'factions', in intra-faith group organizations, with regard to Kelly's 'divide and conquer' rebalancing strategy. At the same time, although Kelly's threats to disengage with established 'Muslim organizations' in order to re-engage with organizations that better represent women and young people seems 'practical', this action could have political implications and further exacerbate 'the clash of generations' (Hussain and Bagguley forthcoming) among Muslim communities.

However, it is not only Muslim leaders and Muslim communities that have been charged with the responsibility of tackling extremism. John Reid, in an infamous speech on 20 September 2006 (in which he was heckled by Abu Izzadeen), called on Muslim families to do more to root out extremism in their own households. Reid urged parents to keep a close eye on their children:

> There is no nice way of saying this but there are fanatics who are looking to groom and brainwash children, including your children ... look for the telltale signs now and talk to them before their hatred grows and you risk losing them forever ... in protecting our families we are protecting our community.
>
> (Reid, in Holden 2006: 1)

Statements such as these, as well as some of the high-profile counter-terrorism raids on Muslim communities since 7/7, have resulted in Muslims in Britain losing what little trust they had in the Government and police. For example, Azad Ali, Chair of the Muslim Safety Forum (the organization the Government hold up as an exemplar of its partnership approach to terrorism, see above), talked of 'a strongly held belief amongst grassroots Muslim communities that the Government and law enforcement agencies operate on the basis that Muslims are terrorists and or harbor them' (Azad 2006: 4).

In many ways this chapter can be described as an exploration of the tension that exists between the Blair Government's recognition and marginalization of the relationship between 'Muslim' grievances and radicalization. This discursive battle was being fought by Blair and his close allies right up to the last few months of the Blair Government being in office. For example, despite the cautious recognition of the relationship between 'Muslim' grievances and radicalization in the Government's Strategy on International Terrorism, Lord Falconer (the former Lord Chancellor) declared in his speech to Royal United Services Institute (RUSI) on 14 February 2007 that the view that British domestic and foreign policies are a ' . . . coordinated effort to subjugate Muslims' as being 'utter, utter nonsense. But nonsense that has regrettably been allowed to take root. And it is a myth which we must take every opportunity to repudiate' (2007: 5). Lord Falconer's solution is that 'we must demonstrate its falseness, and we must ensure that voices within the Muslim communities also attest to its wrong-ness' (2007: 4). In this speech Lord Falconer's treatment of Muslim perceptions on the impact of anti-terror laws and feelings about British foreign policy are once again (as in Blair, Beckett and Reid's speeches above) dismissed; moreover, Lord Falconer insists that Muslim communities themselves must join himself and the Government in demonstrating the falseness of these grievances, thus demonstrating one of the 'features' of Islamophobia listed by Abbas (see Chapter 2), that is 'Muslim criticism of western cultures and societies are rejected out of hand' (Abbas 2005: 12). At the same time this speech once again (see Chapter 2) establishes the extremely narrow parameters of permitted debate on the relationship between 'Muslim' grievances, including foreign policy, and the war on terror.

Conclusion

The Blair Government can be accused of paying lip-service to many of the recommendations and developments associated with this broader counter-terrorism strategy including greater consultation with Muslim communities, and, for example, creating the working groups in the immediate post-7/7 context to inform Government policy. However, like the Home Affairs Committee, the Blair Government, especially in 'the rule-changing' mode associated with the Terrorism Act 2006, is still too fixated on eradicating 'undesirable influences' to be concerned enough with opening up the debate on terrorism to include exploring the relationship between foreign policy and extremism. This strategy is most explicit in their marginalization of the statement in the Working Parties' *Preventing Extremism Together* report that there is indeed a relationship between British foreign policy and extremism. This relationship has been cautiously recognized as a source of radicalization by the Blair Government in its *Countering International Terrorism strategy* in 2006. However, this recognition of the relationship between British foreign policy (and its manipulation in the promotional material distributed by extremist networks) has not had a major impact on the Government's counter-terrorism strategy to date.

According to DEMOS, by refusing to fully engage with this issue, the Government is fast losing the trust of the Muslim community, and is heightening their sense of voicelessness (2006: 63). The only way out of the impasse between the Government conceding the moral high ground in the 'war on terror' and the Muslim communities' retreat from pointless consultation is for the Government to take more risks to ' . . . create spaces within which these discussions can be had' (DEMOS 2006: 63) in order to multiply the legitimate outlets available for especially young Muslims to register protest and dissent (Preventing Extremism Together 2005: 13).

The development of a broader counter-terrorism strategy in Britain will be extremely limited if the Government do not fully consider the relationship between 'Muslim disadvantage' in the domestic context (discrimination, deprivation, social exclusion and Islamophobia) and the perception of British foreign policy in the international context as being 'anti-Muslim' by many Muslims in Britain. Without developing an understanding of the 'respective weight' of each of these potential sources of grievance and how they might relate to one another (Preventing Extremism Together Working Groups 2005: 71) the Government is in danger of developing policy without a clear evidence base (Blick et al. 2006: 24). Any broader, effective community-relations approach to counter-terrorism must take all this on board and be cognizant of and attempt to counteract the 'war on terror' discursive formation in which the distinctions between radicalization and extremism are often collapsed and as a result the continuum among 'radicalizations' and 'extremisms' are effaced. As noted in Chapter 2, failure to do this could lead to dissent being driven underground and debate being stifled by the chilling effect of pernicious legislation justified by a politics of fear. We can only hope that Gordon Brown, and his new Home Secretary, Jacqui Smith, strike a better balance between anti-terrorism legislation and a community-relations approach to counter-terrorism than their predecessors have.

4 Cohesion, citizenship and integration (beyond multiculturalism?)

> We need to consider whether the scale upon which sameness and difference are calculated might be altered productively so that the strangeness of strangers goes out of focus and other dimensions of basic sameness can be acknowledged and made significant.
>
> (Gilroy 2004: 3)

This chapter marks a shift away from security and the impact of anti-terrorism legislation to focus instead on the new integration discourses that have emerged in Britain since 2001. The emphasis of this chapter (and the next two chapters) is on the diverse strategies that have emerged since the disturbances in Oldham, Burnley and Bradford since 2001, which have attempted to improve community cohesion and increase integration in both new immigrant and settled migrant communities in Britain. This examination is achieved through exploring a number of interrelated strategies, consultation exercises and policies produced by or for the Home Office (and the Communities and Local Government Department). In many ways this chapter is a direct sequel to Chapters 2 and 3 of my previous book *Intolerant Britain? Hate, Citizenship and Difference* in which I critically examined the relationship between community cohesion strategies and managed integration strategies for new migrants in the Nationality, Immigration and Asylum Act 2002 (including English language classes and citizenship classes). It is suggested below that the Cantle report in combination with David Blunkett's speeches on the theme of introducing an active, inclusive sense of British citizenship in response to the disturbances in Oldham, Burnley and Bradford in 2001 have cast a very long shadow across a number of areas of public policy, for example, immigration (see below and McGhee 2005a), counter-terrorism (see Chapter 3) and even the necessity of setting up the new Commission for Equality and Human Rights (see Chapter 5).

This chapter begins by focusing on David Blunkett's pronouncements on the weakness of British citizenship and the Cantle discourses on community cohesion. The latter provides the discursive context for examining some of the strategies on community cohesion, 'race' equality and integration, including consultation strategies that have emerged from the Home Office since 2004, for example, the *Strength in Diversity* consultation strategy in 2004, the *Improving Opportunities, Strengthening Society* strategy 2005, and the reports produced by the Commission on Integration and Community Cohesion (CICC) in 2007. Before that, it is important to remind ourselves of what Cantle and Blunkett had to say about community cohesion and British citizenship in the aftermath of the social disorder in 2001. As noted in the previous chapter, Ted Cantle was commissioned to set up the *Community Cohesion Review* in order to examine the factors that led to the eruption of violent clashes between Pakistani-Muslim, neighbouring white communities, members of far-right organizations and police in the spring and summer of 2001 in Oldham, Burnley and Bradford; and to suggest how these problems could be ameliorated. Citizenship, or more accurately the establishment of a 'greater sense of citizenship', based on principles common to all groups was central to the recommendations made by the Community Cohesion Review in relation to Oldham, Burnley and Bradford. However, in their report they extended this recommendation to include the whole of Britain:

> We believe that there is an urgent need to promote community cohesion, based upon a greater knowledge of, contact between, and respect for, the various cultures that now make Great Britain such a rich and diverse nation. It is also essential to establish a greater sense of citizenship, based on (a few) common principles which are shared and observed by all sections of the community. This concept of citizenship would also place a higher value on cultural differences.
>
> (Home Office 2001: 10)

In his response to these recommendations, the former Home Secretary David Blunkett wholeheartedly agreed that the 'weak sense of British citizenship' was a key factor to be considered by the nation. The problem, according to Blunkett, was that:

> The UK has had a relatively weak sense of what political citizenship should entail. Our values of individual freedom, the protection of liberty and respect for difference, have not been accompanied by a strong, shared understanding of the civic realm. This has to change.
>
> (Blunkett 2001a: 2)

The solution to this imbalance between respect for freedom, liberty and difference and the development of shared understanding in the 'civic realm', according to the former Home Secretary, was through developing:

> a stronger understanding of what our collective citizenship means,
> and how we can build that shared commitment into our social and
> political institutions.
>
> (Blunkett 2001a: 2)

As indicated above, these observations and recommendations can be described as laying the groundwork for many of the Government's interrelated
strategies in recent years, for example, Community Cohesion, Managed
Migration, *Strength in Diversity*, *Improving Opportunities*, and the work of the
CICC. All of the latter are intent on replacing the emphasis on the respect of
diversity, as an end-point of political tolerance and political unity in a multicultural, multi-racial and multi-faith context, with a new 'integration'
project that insists on forging a new level of meta-allegiance through establishing shared values.

David Blunkett's conception of citizenship through establishing shared
values has much in common with Etzioni's thesis in *The New Golden Rule* of
the inter-community mosaic of diverse communities and groups held by the
'frame and glue' (Etzioni 1997: 193) of basic agreement. According to Young,
in Etzioni's image of the mosaic, 'the cultures are held separate, their traditions valued and preserved, their separate entities are held together by the
contractual glue of mutual respect and a rather basic collection of common
values' (Young 1999a: 163). The new integration discourse, as suggested by
Blunkett, proposed the development of a stronger understanding of what
'our' collective citizenship means and that the building of 'our' shared
commitments was not about 'cultural conformity' (Blunkett 2001b: 2); rather
it was to involve maintaining 'our' diversity while simultaneously reorienting
'our' allegiances in the movement towards 'a common place'. It should be
noted that what is being called for is not the one-way process of 'integration'
(Parekh 2000a: x); rather, according to Blunkett, this is a matter of encouraging flexible or complex meta-loyalties above and beyond competing micro-
loyalties, that is:

> There is no contradiction between retaining a distinct cultural
> identity and identifying with Britain. But our democracy must
> uphold fundamental rights and obligations to which all citizens and
> public authorities adhere. Citizenship means finding a common
> place for diverse cultures and beliefs, consistent with the core values
> we uphold.
>
> (Blunkett 2001b: 2)

It is suggested below that Blunkett's discourse on 'integration with diversity'
combined with a reactivation of British citizenship as the means of achieving
'unity in diversity' have taken on a hegemonic place in the *Strength in Diversity*

and *Strengthening Opportunities* strategies, and in the associated speeches of the chairs of Commissions, for example, the Commission for Racial Equality (CRE) and the new CICC between 2006 and 2007. In these strategies and these speeches there is evidence of a sustained attempt, following Blunkett, to distinguish the new 'integration' strategy from assimilation and multiculturalism through combining the concept of integration with the concept of active citizenship. It is also suggested that what started out as a debate on 'multiculturalism' led by Blunkett after the social disorder in Oldham, Burnley and Bradford in 2001 has become, post-7/7, an open hostility to the concept of multiculturalism in the speeches of the Communities Minister Ruth Kelly and the head of the CICC Darra Singh in 2006 and 2007. However, all is not what it seems. In many ways this retreat from and open hostility to multiculturalism is, on examination, an exercise in avoiding using the term 'multiculturalism' rather than moving away from the principles of multiculturalism altogether. Therefore, in this chapter I also take the opportunity to explore what can be described as 'the rather confused retreat from multiculturalism' in Britain in recent years (Bagguley and Hussain forthcoming). Here it is suggested that two discourses underpin the centre left's alleged retreat from 'multiculturalism'. The first of these pertains to a 'national level' discourse that suggests that 'multiculturalism' has promoted division rather than unity in British society. Second, there is a discourse at the 'local level' that 'multiculturalism' has contributed to communal tensions through myths of preferential treatment of some groups at the expense of other groups.

The powerful place that these discourses presently command in British society are explored in the final section of the chapter in relation to debates over 'the veil' and the resurfaced calls for English language proficiency testing. In these debates, the focus on young Muslim men, so evident in the *Strength in Diversity* and *Strengthening Opportunities* strategies (and in counter-terrorism strategies, see Chapter 3) has given way to a focus on the cultural barriers to the full participation of Muslim women that brings the debates generated by Jack Straw (on the veil) and the chair of the new CICC, Darra Singh (on the English language proficiency of foreign spouses) back full circle, to Cantle's 'contact hypothesis'.

The chapter is divided into five parts. Part one examines the evolving discourse of integration from figures such as David Blunkett and Trevor Phillips. Here I explore how the discourses of active citizenship have been co-opted in an attempt to differentiate integration from assimilation and multiculturalism.

In part two, the focus is on the relationship between the *Strength in Diversity* and *Strengthening Opportunities* strategies and the Cantle and Blunkett discourses, especially in the eclipse of 'cultural strategies' by 'race equality strategies' in Home Office strategies produced from 2004.

In the final parts of the chapter, the focus is on the integration strategy that is emerging from the CICC and the Communities and Local Government Department. The major point of contrast here is the emphasis on the local and the particular rather than the national and the universal nature of the previous strategies. The CICC's central concerns are exposed as that of attempting to overcome the legacy of 'divisive' multiculturalism associated with local perceptions of preferential treatment. These final parts of the chapter also examine the increasingly hostile tone of debates on the place of Muslims in contemporary British society in what Blackledge (2006a, 2006b) refers to as the combination of the liberal and illiberal in common-sense discourses that have come to focus on cultural practices associated with Muslim women.

In many ways, the last two parts of this chapter can be described as an examination of what Brubaker (1995) describes as the shifts in the boundaries of legitimate discourse in liberal democracies where previously acceptable modes of discourse (for example, multiculturalism) may become stigmatized and excluded; but, on the other hand, previously illegitimate and effectively marginalized themes may gain a foothold in public debate (for example, suggestions that 'the veil' and the lack of English language skills in foreign spouses are sources of, or barriers to integration).

Integration with diversity

The *Strength in Diversity* consultation strategy was launched in May of 2004.[1] In his speech launching the consultation strategy, the then Home Secretary David Blunkett said:

> Integration in Britain does not mean assimilation into a common culture so that original identities are lost. Our approach is pragmatic, based on common sense, allowing people to express their identity within a common framework of rights and responsibilities.
>
> (Blunkett 2004: 6)

Blunkett's attempt to distinguish between assimilation and integration in the *Strength in Diversity* consultation strategy opened the way for the development of a new model of integration. According to Harrison, interest in integration and community relations is an old concern that was evident especially in some earlier phases of 'race relations' work in Britain (2005a: 5). According to Brighton, one of the earliest attempts to introduce integration as a foundational concept within multiculturalism was presented in the then Home Secretary Roy Jenkins's speech to the national Committee for Commonwealth Immigrants in 1966:

Integration is perhaps a loose word. I do not regard it as meaning the loss, by immigrants, of their own characteristics and culture. I do not think that we need in this country a 'melting pot', which will turn everybody out in a common mould, as one of a series of carbon copies of someone's misplaced version of the stereotyped Englishman. I define integration, therefore, not as a flattening process of assimilation but as equal opportunity, accompanied by cultural diversity, in an atmosphere of mutual tolerance.

(in, Brighton 2007: 5)

The concept of integration is now certainly back in vogue. In fact, according to Harrison, on the publication of the *Community Cohesion Review* in 2001 and documents that have followed it, 'integration' and community relations 'have been given something of a makeover' (2005a: 5). Perhaps the most striking aspect of post-Cantle discourses on integration and community cohesion is just how ubiquitous they have become across the political spectrum. For example, in recent years the CRE has also been intent on re-evaluating the policy of 'multiculturalism' (CRE 2006a: 1) through reinstating formerly tabooed terms such as 'integration' (CRE 2006a: 5). According to the CRE, the development of multiculturalism in Britain was an understandable reaction to black and ethnic minority (BEM) disillusionment with policies of the 1950s and 1960s:

when the aim, said to be 'integration', was really assimilation – the absorption of minority migrant communities into the majority community with no noticeable effect on the culture and the way of life of the majority, while expecting that the culture and the way of life minorities brought with them would disappear.

(CRE 2006a: 5)

Trevor Phillips (as chair of the CRE) has been one of the most vocal opponents of multiculturalism in recent years. Perhaps the most surprising thing regarding the latter is just how similar Phillips's thinking on community cohesion and multiculturalism is to the much criticized Cantle–Blunkett discourses. For example, in his controversial speech entitled: '*After 7/7: sleepwalking into segregation*' in September 2005, Phillips declared:

In recent years we've focused far too much on the 'multi' and not enough on common culture. We've emphasized what divides us over what unites us. We have allowed tolerance of diversity to harden into the effective isolation of communities, in which some people think special separate values ought to apply.

(Phillips 2005: 8)

Phillips's diatribe is against a number of multiculturalisms: primordial multiculturalism (Tempelman 1999: 18) that over-privileges identity and culture, as well as universalist multiculturalism that attends to 'special separate values' of minorities (Werbner 2005: 21). Phillips suggests that 'old fashioned types' who think of integration as just another word for assimilation, who adhere to an 'anything goes' multiculturalism, are in danger of throwing out the integrationist baby with the assimilationist bathwater (2005: 8). Integration, according to Phillips, following Blunkett, is about recognizing diversity while rejecting assimilation. Integration is a two-way street in which the settled communities accept that the new people will bring change with them, and newcomers will realize that they too have to change if we are to move closer to an integrated society (Phillips 2005: 10).[2]

Whereas in Phillips's model of integration we find three essential features: equality, participation and interaction (2005: 10–11); At the heart of David Blunkett's model of integration found in the *Strength in Diversity* Consultation strategy is the promotion of ' ... a wider concept of active citizenship' (Blunkett 2004: 7). Blunkett outlined his integrative concept of 'active citizenship' as opposed to assimilation and multiculturalism in a paper published on the Foreign Policy Centre website:

> An active concept of citizenship can articulate shared ground between diverse communities. It offers a shared identity based on membership of a political community, rather than forced assimilation into a monoculture, or an unbridled multiculturalism which privileges difference over community cohesion.
>
> (Blunkett 2002: 6)

The former Home Secretary is correct when he says that he is not advocating a model of 'forced assimilation'. Rather, what is on offer is an invitation to a variety of 'civic assimilation' masquerading as a two-way ('host' and 'migrant') integration strategy. The latter is described by Joppke as a centrist policy of civic integration with respect to immigrants (2004: 243). Parekh describes this strategy as one means of reconciling the demands of unity and diversity in multicultural societies (2000b: 199). This is to be achieved through forging commonality in the public realm, through creating a shared political culture, 'which includes its public or political values, ideals, practices, institutions, mode of political discourse, and self-understanding' (2000b: 200). In this model the public realm represents uniformity. 'Difference' is pushed into the private realm[3] (Parekh 2000b: 200). The intention of this new integration strategy is to ensure that ethnic and religious allegiances, and inter-ethnic conflicts over values are eclipsed by 'the shared identity of citizenship' (Kivisto 2005a:14).

The project of 'integration with diversity' which was first introduced in the *Secure Borders, Safe Haven* White Paper (Home Office 2002: 9) is a model of civic assimilation based upon the idea of forging allegiance to core principles shared by all, through the effective engagement of responsible 'active citizens' located in 'active communities'. Concomitantly, integration with diversity is a major component of the Government's project of 'civil renewal' at the heart of the Home Office's *Strength in Diversity* strategy. That is:

> Civil renewal is at the heart of the Government's vision of life in our 21st century communities. It aims to reconnect citizens with the public realm by empowering them to influence the development of solutions to problems affecting them. It is vital that barriers to participation – from lack of confidence and capacity to express one's views to prejudice which lead to exclusion – are tackled so that the aspiration for wider engagement can be translated into reality.
>
> (Home Office 2004b: 19)

It is important to reflect on what is driving this project of civil renewal especially those strategies dedicated to making the engagement between diverse groups (and between these groups and Government) more effective. According to Giddens (2000) the State and Government do not represent the public domain when they become detached from their roots in civic association. 'Civil society' rather than the State, according to Giddens, supplies the grounding of citizenship and is hence crucial to sustaining an open public sphere (2000: 65). Blunkett's statements above with regard to active citizenship and active communities reflect his adherence to Third Way principles associated with participatory models of democracy which, when combined with his model of integration, takes the form of a republican model of 'popular participation' through dialogue. Dialogue in this model is the path to greater understanding and greater participation and hence the means to the end of the republican ideal of an actively engaged citizenry.[4] Following on from the *Community Cohesion Review*, the *Strength in Diversity* consultation strategy signals the Government's desire to 'manage' the alleged sources of 'non-integration' and hence non-participation through the vehicles of shared citizenship, increasing participation and dialogue. That is:

> To build a successful integrated society we need to promote an inclusive concept of citizenship, which goes further than the strictly legal definition of nationality and articulates the rights and responsibilities we share. Building this wider notion of active citizenship through participation, volunteering and civic action, underpinned by a sense of shared values, is one of the main ways in which we can strengthen the relationships and connections between communities.
>
> (Home Office 2004b: 6)

'Dialogue' is essential to this participatory, active model of citizenship. This is 'a culture of citizenship' in which citizenship is a cipher for 'culture' in that citizenship has been further reduced to the ability to speak the same language. According to Alexander et al., this relationship can be described as 'the culturing of language' (2007: 3),[5] which is an example of the political crafting of the medium of exchange between heterogeneous groups (Goldberg 1994: 25). Dialogic exchange, so central to Charles Taylor's work on multiculturalism that is premised on the interactional nature of identities, becomes transposed here onto the dialogical character (Taylor 1994: 32) of active citizenship. The focus in the *Strength in Diversity* strategy is less on the deliberative quality of identities forged (and modified) in interaction with others (Gutman 1994: 7) than on a rather more 'practical' intervention in which basic skills (English language proficiency) is rendered essential in order to ensure the successful take-up civic responsibilities.

Thus, the ability to speak English forms the bedrock of the dialogic, participatory and active citizenship being advocated in the new integration discourse. The provision of English language training for new and established migrants is described in the consultation strategy as a means of providing 'practical support' that will 'overcome the barriers to integration' that could face those newly arrived in Britain (Home Office 2004b: 18). The relationship between English language skills and the idea of a culture of active citizenship in the new integration discourse was written into law in the Nationality, Immigration and Asylum Act 2002 (see McGhee 2005a)[6] and has resurfaced as being central to the findings of the CICC's interim statement and final report published in 2007. In the latter, which is further examined below, English language proficiency is linked with enhancing participation in civic culture in new and established migrant groups; however, the CICC also associates English language proficiency with the 'practical' issues associated with employment and social exclusion, especially the employment and social exclusion of Asian women who come to Britain through arranged marriages.

Rebalancing 'the economic' and 'the cultural explanations'

The aim of the *Strength in Diversity* consultation strategy, according to Fiona MacTaggart (former Parliamentary Under-Secretary for Race Equality) is to engage as many people as possible in the debate over how to build community cohesion and reduce race inequalities in Britain in order to develop a Government-wide Community Cohesion and Race Equality Strategy (MacTaggart 2004: 1–2). Whereas the emphasis on young people in the *Community Cohesion Review* was on promoting citizenship education in schools, school twinning and other 'contact increasing' interventions between young people from different ethnic groups; the *Strength in Diversity* consultation strategy takes things much further through making explicit connections between political and religious extremism, young people (especially young people from ethnic and religious minority communities) and the wider issues of racism, structural inequalities and discrimination. This is the beginning of the recognition by the Home Office that 'inequality makes recognition of common interests more difficult because people are actually becoming less alike in economic terms' (Gilroy 2004: 132). This in itself is a significant departure from 'the cultural' ('contact hypothesis') emphasis of community cohesion discourses over the material contexts of segregation and inter-community antagonism (found in the *Community Cohesion Review*, see McGhee 2003, 2005a).

Figures that emerge from the Ethnic Minorities and Labour Market Strategy Unit's report (2003) suggest that black and minority ethnic communities have a higher proportion of young people under 25, and that black and minority people are projected to account for over half of the growth in Britain's working-age population over the next decade (Home Office 2004b: 4). These figures (as well as some of the indicators that are listed below) were used by the Government in the *Strength in Diversity* consultation strategy to justify their focus on attempting to reduce widespread race inequalities.[7] In the consultation strategy, it was suggested that the inequalities and limited opportunities facing ethnic minority communities presents a complex picture and are not simply a question of 'White advantage and minority ethnic disadvantage' as: 'People of all races and religions share experiences of deprivation and disadvantage'(Home Office 2004b: 13). However, the consultation strategy pamphlet stated that 'we know that they affect particular groups more profoundly' (Home Office 2004b: 13). It was suggested that, despite the Government's 'huge investments' in regeneration programmes in disadvantaged areas in recent years, the scale of disadvantage experienced in BEM communities appears to have changed little (Home Office 2004b: 13). Black, Pakistani and Bangladeshi communities were singled out as being particularly disadvantaged and relatively untouched by public policy strategies. The pamphlet suggested that these communities 'experience disadvantage in different ways' to other minority groups (Home Office 2004b: 13). For example, quoting from the New Commitment to Neighbourhood Renewal, National Action Plan study (2001) into ethnic minorities and the labour market, it was suggested that Chinese and Indian people perform on average better than their white peers, while black people, Pakistanis and Bangladeshis perform significantly worse (Home Office 2004b: 13–14).

These findings, especially the attention that Pakistani communities in Oldham, Burnley and Bradford have received in recent years, comprise an alternative discourse of 'segregation' that privileges material factors. For example, the wards affected in the disturbances that stretched from Oldham to Bradford are among the 20 per cent most deprived in the country and parts of Oldham and Burnley rank in the most deprived 1 per cent. All these wards have average incomes that are among the lowest in the country and many also have low educational attainment standards in schools (Denham 2002: 8). The other demographic factor that is particularly relevant is that the participants in the disturbances that took place in 2001 were overwhelmingly male, with those arrested predominantly between 17–26 years old. In Bradford the latter demographic is significant as, unlike the wider demographic picture that emerges from Britain, Bradford has a very young population, with over 50 per cent of its ethnic minority communities aged under 18 (Allen 2003: 17).

One of the problems in Bradford is that a significant number of young ethnic minority people are entering the labour market at precisely the moment that there are significantly fewer jobs available (Allen 2003: 17). The result is that second-generation ethnic and religious minority young people in Bradford are experiencing persistent unemployment. Six wards in Bradford have long-term (over one year) unemployment rates of over 25 per cent, with high rates of youth unemployment, in many parts; for example, in the Little Horton ward it is over 20 per cent (Allen 2003: 17). These figures give an alternative picture of the context of the disturbances in 2001 that were further exacerbated by the added factors of far-right agitation and a history of oppressive policing in places like Bradford (McGhee 2005a: 61–3).

A number of commentators, including academics (see Chapter 3), have suggested that the Cantle–Blunkett fixation on weak citizenship and poor integration has been at the expense of understanding the role that social exclusion, racism and oppressive policing have played in these episodes of social disorder. The *Strength in Diversity* consultation strategy can be described as a well-rounded approach to building community cohesion in that it combines the search for overarching commonalities with an appreciation of the impact of material and economic inequalities (Wetherell 2007: 5). The *Strength in Diversity* consultation strategy not only strikes a better balance between 'the cultural' and 'the material' (this is also found in the *Improving Opportunities, Strengthening Society* strategy, see below), it also examines the relationship between these factors and the threat of political extremism in some of Britain's disadvantaged multi-ethnic areas. It was noted in the *Strength in Diversity* consultation strategy that:

> Structural inequalities and the legacy of discrimination have resulted in whole groups that are effectively left behind, with young people failing to share in the opportunities that should be available to all, which in turn fuels their disengagement from mainstream society and creates pathways to extremism.
>
> (Home Office 2004b: 5)

Two significant developments are present in the statement above. The first is that the context of segregation and the material aspects of discrimination and inequality are now also being prioritized, which is significant given just how influential the *Community Cohesion Review* team's 'cultural-deficit' hypothesis on the lack of community cohesion has become in many different areas of public policy. The second significant development is that the Home Office openly admits to the relationship between inequalities and extremism, a relationship disputed by the Home Affairs Committee and many academics (see Chapter 3).

The *Improving Opportunity* strategy was launched on 19 January 2005 by the former Home Secretary, Charles Clarke. The full title of the strategy is: *Improving Opportunity, Strengthening Society: The Government's Strategy to Increase Race Equality and Community Cohesion.* This strategy heralds the Government's intention of stepping up its investment in helping to build cohesive communities through strengthening the social fabric of Britain and developing a sense of common citizenship in Britain (Home Office 2005a: 21). The aim of the strategy was to create a Britain in which:

- Young people from different communities grow up with a sense of common belonging;
- New immigrants rapidly integrate;
- People have opportunities to gain an understanding of the range of cultures that contribute to our strength as a country;
- People from all backgrounds participate in civic society;
- Racism is unacceptable; and
- Extremists who promote hatred are marginalized.

(Home Office 2005a: 21)

The *Improving Opportunities* strategy demonstrates a greater level of awareness of the perception that certain groups are given preferential treatment and allocated more resources than other groups than in previous strategies and reviews. The Home Office attempted to circumvent accusations of pre-ferential treatment in the *Improving Opportunities* strategy by suggesting that reducing race inequalities and improving the life chances of BEM communities would 'make for a better society' (2005a: 11). In this strategy it was suggested that a cohesive society based on equal opportunities is not just important for BEM communities, it is also important for those from 'majority communities' too (Home Office 2005a: 11). Charles Clarke attempted to alleviate 'majority' concerns in the foreword of the *Improving Opportunity* strategy by stating that:

> This strategy is not about putting all people from minority ethnic communities in one category and those from the majority in another ... Rather it is about getting much better at identifying and

responding to the specific needs of different communities, in education, health, employment, housing, security.

(Clarke, in Home Office 2005a: Foreword)

The former Home Secretary was attempting to distance this new strategy and
model of integration from negative associations with 'one-sided approaches'
that focus on improving the opportunities of ethnic and religious minority
groups to the seeming exclusion of other disadvantaged groups such as disadvantaged white communities. Clarke attempted to navigate a course that
was designed to avoid accusations from the liberal left that the strategy was
'pandering to racists' because it included a consideration of the disadvantaged
white 'community' reaction to policies dedicated to alleviating race
inequality. At the same time Clarke attempted to avoid the far-right accusation that such policies pandered to minority groups to the exclusion (and
detriment) of disadvantaged white communities. The Home Office attempted
to present a balanced strategy that 'pandered' to all disadvantaged groups at
the front-line of integration through combining statements such as: 'at the
heart of this strategy therefore is an overarching objective to reduce race
inequalities' (2005a: 3) with reassuring statements that this strategy is dedicated to promoting ' ... equal life chances for all, within the context of an
inclusive British society that helps people come together to thrive economically, socially and culturally' (2005a: 13).

The *Improving Opportunities* strategy shares some similarities with the
recommendations made in the *Government's Countering International Terrorism*
strategy (HM 2006) that was examined in Chapter 3. The *Improving Opportunities* strategy attempts to combine social justice, community cohesion and
'counter-extremism' components within its wider model of integration.
However, the means of marginalizing extremism in the *Improving Opportunity*
strategy is very much in line with the Home Affairs Committee's Cantle-
inspired approach (see Chapter 3), that is strengthening local leadership. It
was stated in the strategy document that:

Combating extremists is not, however, simply a matter of legislation.
Effective local political and community leadership is also crucial.
Hesitant leadership or actions that play into the hands of racist
organizations can allow extremists to gain a hold within communities and spread hate.

(Home Office 2005a: 51)

In the *Improving Opportunity* strategy much of the emphasis on improving
local leadership focuses on improving the quality of local Government leadership in the fight against racism and extremism (Home Office 2005a: 91).
This fight against racism and extremism consists of the following dimensions:

- Support local partners to hold discussions with communities on difficult issues such as extremism and asylum.
- Support local authorities to communicate improvements in local public services where these have been factors in disengagement and dissatisfaction within communities and have led to tensions.
- Support local authorities in establishing media and communications strategies that speedily respond to myths, involve communities in change in their neighbourhoods and include a role for elected leaders, faith groups and voluntary and community sectors in acting as spokespersons.

(Home Office 2005a: 51)

The role of faith leaders was also described in the *Improving Opportunity* strategy document, in similar language to that used by the Home Affairs Committee, for example, faith leaders were being held up in the *Improving Opportunities* strategy as making a 'significant contribution to fostering good community relations' (Home Office 2005a: 51). The overwhelming emphasis of the strategy for 'marginalizing extremism' is on strengthening the capacity of both Local Government and faith leaders 'to deal with the challenges facing their communities including, countering divisive and extremist influences, and providing role models for young people' (Home Office 2005a: 52). Very little is said about the role that young people, especially those which the Government repeatedly tells us are most susceptible to extremist influences, are to play in this strategy against extremism. The *Improving Opportunity* strategy assumes (as did the Home Affairs Committee) that it is enough to (1) ensure that faith leaders demonstrate acceptable levels of spoken English and (2) to build the capacity of faith leaders so that they can adequately support their community and contribute towards community cohesion (Home Office 2005a: 52).

The re-gendering of 'the Muslim problem'

In many ways all the strategies that have been examined above with regard to the new integration strategy are part of the Government's broader project of attempting to prepare for an unpredictable and perhaps disordered future. At the same time, all these strategies add up to a particular risk consciousness, which is observable through explicitly proactive strategies that focus on preventing the social problems associated with inequality, polarization and potential extremism from taking hold in the future. Young ethnic and religious minority people, especially young Muslim men, are at the epicentre of this consciousness. After the Cabinet reshuffle and the splitting-up of many of the Home Office's responsibilities (including Ruth Kelly becoming Secretary for the new Communities and Local Government Department), there has been a change of emphasis with regard to 'integration'. Rather than being content to focus on dialogue, participation, reducing inequalities and improving opportunities, the Government has mirrored their uncompromising anti-terrorism laws with a new uncompromising approach to integration. In this climate (as observed in Chapter 3) Kelly has announced the need for a fundamental rebalancing of the relationships with Muslims in Britain. John Reid has called on Muslim parents to examine their children for signs of extremism and Jack Straw has opened up the floodgates with comments on 'the veil' (see below). According to Ehsan Masood, the Government's punitive new tone makes it impossible to avoid the impression that their wish is to promote the idea that Britain has a 'Muslim problem' (2006: 2). Recent events have signalled a partial retreat from focusing on young Muslim men as *the* alleged 'Muslim problem' to focus on the cultural practices associated with Muslim women, especially the wearing of 'the veil' (the *niqab* or face covering)[8] and arranged marriages between British 'Asians' and foreign spouses with poor command of the English language. In both these examples, we can observe the survival of the Cantle 'contact hypothesis' in debates that emerged in 2006 and 2007.

The 'veil debate' was initiated by Jack Straw when he sent his usual column to the *Lancashire Evening Telegraph* on Wednesday, 4 October 2006. Rather than being located in its customary place in the inner pages of the *Telegraph,* the editor placed Straw's column on the front page (Wainright 2006: 1). It was this column that resulted in Straw being propelled into the centre of what Blackledge has called the concoction of illiberal and liberal discourses with regard to the cultural practices associated with Muslim women in contemporary Britain (2006b: 157). According to Straw, who is the MP for Blackburn (a town with a Muslim community running at 25 per cent of the population), it was during his constituency surgeries that it occurred to him that the veil 'was a visible statement of separation and difference' (BBC News 2006c: 1). Straw reported that he has begun to urge the Muslim women in his constituency to think about the implications for wearing the veil for community relations (BBC News 2006c: 1). Speaking on BBC Radio 4's *Today* programme, Straw defended his opinion through upholding his commitment to 'equal rights', while contextualizing his controversial comments regarding the symbolic power of the veil within Cantle-esque discourses of segregation:

> I come to this out of a profound commitment to equal rights for Muslim communities and an equal concern about adverse developments about parallel communities'
>
> (BBC News 2006c: 1)

Arzu Merali (Head of Research for the Islamic Human Rights Commission) took Jack Straw to task over these remarks, mirroring Straw's Cantle-esque defence of his actions with her own Cantle-esque condemnation of them, arguing: 'these remarks are arrogant and dangerous, particularly at a time when we need to be exploding myths about different religions and moving forwards harmoniously rather than harking back to past stereotypes' (Merali 2006: 2). Merali hammered her point home by countering the 'well-meaning' community-relations intentions behind Straw's comments on the veil with the following: 'far from breaking down barriers, these remarks only serve to build walls between communities' (Merali 2006: 1).

The veil saga continued in October 2006 when the Yorkshire School Authority suspended the Muslim teaching assistant, Aisha Azmi, for refusing to remove her veil in class (Parker 2006: 1). Parker, writing in the *Arab News,* reported that Tony Blair entered the fray by supporting the Authority's decision stating that 'the veil' represents 'a mark of separation' from the rest of society (Parker 2006: 1). The shifting emphasis of integration takes the form of rebalancing the relationship between Government and Muslim communities as suggested by Ruth Kelly (above, and in Chapter 3) is evident in the former Prime Minister's press conference statement on the veil issue. According to Tony Blair, 'the veil' is just one issue in a broader debate about:

> the relationship between our society and how the Muslim community integrates with our society. There's a second issue which is about Islam itself, and how Islam comes to terms with and is comfortable with the modern world ... we need to confront the issue about how we integrate people properly into our society.
>
> (Blair, in Parker 2006: 1)

The repeated use of 'our society' in this statement works to reinforce Ehsan Masood's suspicions above with regard to the construction of Britain's 'Muslim problem' as a problem of non-integration. By shifting attention away from the deficiencies of leaders, and concerns about young men, 'the Muslim problem' has been re-gendered to focus on women. This is a confrontation with cultural practices that allegedly conflict with basic values – such as those that deny the right to participate as equal citizens (Home Office 2002: 30). Thus, illiberal discourses are being co-opted into progressive discourses promoting equality. For example, Adrian Blackledge suggests that 'liberal discourses' that emphasize equality, democracy and increasing political participation, have been used to sanitize related political statements with regard to the English language proficiency of foreign Muslim brides brought to Britain under arranged marriages. Blackledge also exposes what belies the focus on Asian women's cultural practices, including the ability of foreign brides to speak English (and some Muslim women's practice of wearing the *niqab*). According to Blackledge, these discourses refuse to say what they really mean, which is:

> Asian women should be required to learn English as soon as possible, because their failure to do so brings about community segregation and a lack of social cohesion which threatens society.
>
> (Blackledge 2006b: 143)

In his speech to launch the CICC's interim statement in February 2007, Darra Singh followed on from his comments on the inability of newcomers and settled communities to speak English as the most significant barrier to integration in Britain[9] by explicitly stating what Blackledge suggests has only been said between the lines in various chains of discourse since the social unrest of 2001. Singh's rhetorical question is:

> what happens when brides and grooms who do not speak English arrive in families for whom English is already a second language? ... They become parents to children for whom English is not necessarily a primary language. And the language barrier is potentially resurrected for the next generation.
>
> (Singh 2007: 3)

Singh suggested that waiting to provide language lessons for women after they were entitled to them (that is, after being resident in Britain for three years) was not good enough 'as they will have learned to survive without English' (2007: 4). Rather Singh suggested that ' ... we could be braver, and expect spouses to have learned English before they arrive here, which would signal the emphasis we place on its importance' (Singh 2007: 4).[10] These remarks would not be out of place in the Government's latest five-year 'managed migration' strategy,[11] in that this strategy is highly restrictive and overtly 'third-world' phobic.[12] What Singh is proposing is that the Government's response to immigration, including migration through arranged marriages, which number around 40,000 a year (Singh 2007: 3) should avoid the mistakes of the past by being more selective about 'who' we allow into the country. This is directly related to the subtext of the *Controlling our Borders* White Paper that Britain has been 'importing' 'social problems' in the form of migrant communities who have not integrated properly into British society, who are dependent upon State welfare, and who do not seem to serve the country's interests. How did the Government intend increasing public confidence in the asylum and immigration system in this White Paper? This was to be achieved through strictly micro-managing the system through establishing a set of criteria for immigration on a point-based system. Blair states, in the foreword to the *Controlling Borders* White Paper that:

We will replace out-dated and confusing rules with a clear and modern points system so we only allow into Britain the people and the skills our economy needs. Those who want to settle permanently in the UK will have to show they bring long-term benefits to our country.

(Home Office 2005b: Foreword)

In line with the above, Darra Singh's suggestions for breaking the cycle of 'Asian' social and cultural exclusion through forcing would-be 'arranged marriage' migrants to prove that they can speak English to an appropriate standard is tantamount to asking them to demonstrate that they have the skills to bring long-term benefits (rather than the lack of skills that might add to long-term social problems) to counter 'settled migrant' social exclusion and alleged non-integration in Britain. The emphasis in both the *Controlling Our Borders* White Paper and in Darra Singh's comments amounts to the same thing: discrimination on the grounds of 'economic utility' (Billig et al. 2006: 30). These strategies will only allow assimilable immigrants into Britain regardless of whether these migrants are attracted through the labour market or the marriage market.

The CICC's reflexive multiculturalism

When the speeches made by Ruth Kelly and Darra Singh at its launch in August 2006 are examined, the CICC could be described as the 'Commission for the Amelioration of Local Communal Tensions'. This new Commission shifts the Home Office's post-2001 national level strategies dedicated to 'one size fits all' integration models to a new model of integration that attempts to get to grips with British 'diversity' patterns across regions with an emphasis on the particularity of different 'problems' and the solutions they require in many different communities. This new remit, and new way of viewing diversity in Britain, is evident in Kelly's pronouncements that 'we are experiencing diversity no longer as one country but as a set of local communities. Each experiencing changes in a different way, with some being more affected that others' (2006a: 2). Singh also suggests that Britain needs 'a new model of integration that can keep up with the pace of change in our communities. And one that can be flexible enough to accommodate differences in local experience' (Singh 2006: 1). Singh's vision for a new model of integration is one where local ideas have national potential (2006: 2). Rather than national level debates, the CICC's vision is dedicated to helping local authorities deal with local tensions in the competition for scarce resources. Darra Singh confirms this:

> My experience has shown that the way to tackle the tensions caused by diversity is at a local level. The job of local authorities is to balance diverse community interests – to know when to say no, and to hammer out a way forward that manages competing demands and conflicting priorities.
>
> (Singh 2006: 2)

An overtly critical reading of the Kelly and Singh speeches that launched the new integration model promised by the Commission could describe it as a 'hot-spot'-focused 'fire-fighting' strategy. It will be suggested here that the overwhelming focus found in the Commission on Integration and Community Cohesion's (CICC's) interim statement and in their final report is on reducing the tensions surrounding perceptions of preferential treatment in local communities. According to the MORI poll the CICC had commissioned for its final report perceptions of preferential treatment are widespread, that is:

> Our MORI poll found that more than half of the people (56%) feel that some groups in Britain get unfair priority when it comes to public services like housing, health services and schools. Fewer than one in seven (16%) actively disagreed with the statement. This finding highlights that people are sensitive about perceived free-loading by other groups, and about others getting a better deal than them when it comes to certain public services.
>
> (CICC 2007b: 33)

The CICC's analysis of the data from the MORI poll revealed that it was 'settled communities'[13] who were most worried about the fair allocation of public services. In particular many of the respondents from settled communities believed that 'immigrants and minorities were getting special treatment' (CICC 2007b: 33). Now multiculturalism has been attacked on many fronts in recent years in Britain as noted above. Ruth Kelly added her voice to the centre-left critique of multiculturalism at the event launching the CICC. It was at this event that Kelly announced that 'we have moved from a period of uniform consensus on the value of multiculturalism, to one where we can encourage that debate by questioning whether it is encouraging separateness' (Kelly 2006a: 2). As will be revealed below, the term 'multiculturalism' has become shorthand for preferential treatment. The particular aspect of the legacy of multiculturalism that the CICC are trying to distance themselves from is the divisive potential associated with implementing differential resource allocations to underprivileged and marginalized groups (Anthias and Yuval-Davis 1992: 180), especially asylum seekers, refugees and new migrants (CICC 2007b: 33). The problematization of 'divisive' resource allocation that has the potential for generating accusations and perceptions of favouritism in local areas has been around for some time.[14] However, what is interesting about the above is that this critique of multiculturalism, in the end, can be described less as a complete rejection of multiculturalism and more a tactic by the CICC in which they attempt to distance their new model for building community cohesion and increasing integration from the legacy of 'multi-culturalism'. That is, the CICC's 'post-multiculturalism' strategy amounts to literally avoiding using the term, updating their language use, and adopting 'new' terms, that is:

> our view is that we need to update our language to meet the current climate. We therefore intend to avoid using the term 'multi-culturalism' in our report because of its 'catch all' and confusing quality. Our focus is on what practical policies we need to make our complex society work – where race, faith and culture are important, but not the only, elements of that complexity.
>
> (CICC 2007a: 13)

In the end, what is emerging, especially in the CICC's attempts to distance itself from the term 'multiculturalism', can be described as a 'practical' retreat from multiculturalism (Joppke 2004: 237) associated with the advent of a reflexive version of multiculturalism[15] that is cognizant of (1) the simplistic reductionism associated with perceptions of identity, community and culture under multiculturalism and (2) the side-effects (for example, perceived favouritism, preferential treatment and the unequal access to resources) associated with the competition for scarce resources under multiculturalism.

According to Singh, the term 'multiculturalism' 'belongs in 1967 not in 2007' (2007: 1). The term he prefers is 'shared futures' that he describes as capturing what integration and cohesion really means to people.[16] In the interim statement it was suggested that the strategies of integration and cohesion could be brought together to create a vision of a 'shared future' that would paint 'a picture around which all community members can unify' (CICC 2007a: 14).

The replacement of the term 'multiculturalism' with the term 'shared futures' is an attempt to place a collective future consciousness over an established, albeit 'outdated' discourse. Practices such as these have been described by Beck as examples of re-traditionalizations in which traditions become traditions of the future rather than traditions of the past (Beck 2002b: 27). Darra Singh captures the process of re-traditionalization in the sound bite he introduced in the Foreword to the final report. According to Singh, the overall goal of the CICC is to promote a particular image of Britain, one which has 'a past built on difference, a future which is shared' (Singh, in CICC 2007b: Foreword). The use of the term 'shared futures' by Singh captures the essence of the CICC's superficial ambitions with regard to the reflexive re-traditionalization associated with their intention of avoiding certain see-mingly unpopular terms such as 'multiculturalism'. However, there is more to this than the simple replacement of one term for another. The CICC's shared futures discourse is also a discourse of 'mutual interdependence' (2007b: 46) that involves everyone 'moving forward together' as a result of different groups relinquishing their attachments to the past through moving away 'from narrow identities towards a vision of the future shared by different groups' (2007b: 46).

The CICC's combination of the shared futures discourse with a post-structuralist perspective on identities is not just an academic exercise. Mul-tiple identities and multiple identifications are particularly significant for the CICC's shared futures discourse for 'practical' reasons, that is: (1) for the purposes of facilitating the discovery of commonality between diverse indi-viduals. For example, the CICC suggest that 'fluid identities can also act to bring people together as they discover, for example, experiences common to women or sporting interests, which cut across other potential single group conflicts' (CICC 2007b: 34–5). Thus, multiple identifications in people will facilitate the process of people identifying with each other and working towards a shared future together. At the same time; (2) the CICC suggest that research in Northern Ireland 'has found that people with more complex and multiple sources of identity are more positive about other groups, more integrated and less prejudiced' (2007b: 35). Thus, multiple identifications in people could perform the positive social role of reducing conflict between groups; (3) and perhaps lessen tensions surrounding the competition for scarce resources between groups when difference is no longer used as a 'bar-gaining chip' to gain small advantages over other groups (CICC 2007b: 98). Despite the benefits of promoting multiple, fluid and complex identities lis-ted above, it is suggested that the primary reason that the CICC are so keen on introducing the benefits of multiple identifications in these terms is in order to promote and legitimize a 'regime change' in both Government and non-Government funding.

Visible social justice

According to the CICC, all Local Authorities should be more proactive in the 'preventative action' that they take 'to stop the spread of myths that arise from competition for resources' (2007b: 104). The CICC's major recommen-dation is for Local Authorities to maintain a 'communication plan' based on a revised version of existing Local Authority Publicity Codes (2007b: 101). This communication plan will be designed explicitly to prevent myths of pre-ferential treatment being introduced following specific initiatives involving the allocation of resources to particular groups, through ensuring 'that all communities are kept abreast of changes and the reasons for them' (CICC 2007b: 101).[17] As well as recommending proactive action to counter the spread of myths of preferential treatment, the CICC also recommend that the sources of local tensions around perceptions of preferential treatment could also be managed through embedding the principle of 'visible social justice', which they describe as 'a commitment to equal and fair treatment, combined with a transparency and fairness to all communities' (2007b: 97). Alongside the principle of visible social justice, in the final report, the CICC also introduced perhaps its most controversial recommendations with regard to resource allocation, that is, their 'single group funding' recommendation. The single group funding recommendation reveals the Commission's apprecia-tion of social capital theory, especially the hazards associated with encoura-ging bonding rather than bridging social capital implied in the Cantle report of 2001 (McGhee 2003, 2005a).

Putnam et al. suggest that social capital refers to social networks, norms of reciprocity, mutual assistance and trustworthiness (2003: 2). They explain the distinction between 'bonding' and 'bridging' social capital thus: 'some networks link people who are similar in crucial respects and tend to be inward-looking – bonding social capital. Others encompass different types of people and tend to be outward-looking – bridging social capital' (Putnam et al. 2003: 2). The problem is that bridging social capital is harder to create than bonding social capital; and bridging social capital, according to Putnam et al. ' ... is the kind of social capital that is most essential for healthy public life in an increasingly diverse society ... ' (2003: 3). I have suggested that the recommendations with regard to transforming bonding to bridging social capital found in the Cantle report can be described as encouraging local people to alter their ways of thinking about, doing and being communities (McGhee 2005a: 54). When viewed this way Cantle's recommendations can be described as a problematization of habitus (McGhee 2005a: 54).[18]

For example, the CICC's suggestion that single group funding has the potential 'to increase insularity and a sense of separation where the project funded is only or mainly for the group in question' (2007b: 161) is a state-ment informed by social capital theory. The CICC suggest that continuing single group funding is irresponsible as it could lead to 'a sense in which a "comfort zone" could be developed if communities were not encouraged to be outward-facing, and therefore only mixed with others in their group' (2007b: 161). The CICC's solution to the alleged disadvantages of single group funding is that public sector funding for bodies representing particular communities should come with a requirement to demonstrate that their actions support integration and cohesion (CICC 2007b: 161). What becomes clear in Annex D of the final report is that the CICC's opposition to single group funding is linked to their reflexive project of reducing inter-community tensions around perceptions of preferential treatment and the divisive competition for resources through promoting the idea of visible social justice. That is:

> we are clear that whatever the type of area, all funding should be transparent and open to scrutiny – and that funding decisions should be communicated clearly and to all communities. This is particularly important given the evidence we have seen of the damaging myths perpetuated around preferential treatment.
>
> (CICC 2007b: 162)

In many ways the CICC's anti-single group funding policy advances the recommendations on funding found in the Cantle review in that the CICC's recommendations can be described as a funding policy designed to 'manipulate and re-channel existing identity practices in what are seen as more positive directions' (Wetherell 2007: 13) with the intention of re-educating diverse communities 'unarticulated forms of habitus' (2007: 13). This re-channelling and re-education process is to be achieved through breaking what have been viewed since the publication of the Cantle report as bad (insular, bonded, defensive) 'social capital habits' in order to promote outward-looking, collaborative bridging activities and initiatives in local communities.

Therefore, in combination the CICC's single group funding recommendations and its principle of visible social justice are primarily reflexive in that they are dedicated to 'making social justice visible to all groups in the community' (2007b: 98). The CICC state that they have developed this principle in order to reflect 'what we have heard about the importance of transparency in local areas where the allocation of resources is being questioned' (2007b: 98). At the same time the principle is dedicated to 'tackling inequality in all groups', for example, 'the under performance of White working class boys at school just as much as the disproportionate disadvantage faced by Muslim groups' (CICC 2007b: 98). Settled communities are once again the target of this principle. The social exclusion and felt injustice of disadvantaged white communities was particularly emphasized by Singh in his Foreword to the interim report, that is:

> Our consultation has highlighted a question about re-balancing our perspective. We may need to challenge what can be interpreted by some as an obsession with a narrow focus on minorities and think more 'broadband. 39% of the population live in the 86 most deprived areas – that is 19.1 Million people. Although 65% of people from ethnic minority groups live in these areas, the majority – over 16 million – are White. It is time that we created a clear and explicit

strategy to connect with longer term established communities as well as dealing with the most vulnerable of the new and emerging groups?

(Singh, in CICC 2007a: 3)

In many ways, Singh's question above reflects the contemporary concern with regard to a social phenomenon that has been unfolding since the 1960s in Britain, which Roger Hewitt has called the white backlash (2005: 4). According to Hewitt, the white backlash is a response to perceptions of preferential treatment under 'multiculturalism' by the 'white-have-nots' who see themselves as the losers in the everyday struggles for small advantage by the 'black-have-nots' through the development of minority representation in local areas (2005: 2). Singh's recognition of the relative neglect of white disadvantage in 'race equality' and 'integration' strategies amounts to the acknowledgement of what Honneth describes as atypical socially caused suffering (2003: 118) associated with the neglected immiseration of social groups who are rarely included in civil rights movements, new social movements and identity politics. The CICC it seems will attempt to confront the other side of integration strategies focusing on the amorphous and ethnically diverse 'disadvantaged host communities', including long-established BEM and white communities (McGhee 2006).

This is as much a project dedicated to overcoming the perceptions of misrecognition within institutional procedures (2003: 132) as it is of redistribution in that the purpose seems to be one of recognizing the fact that recognition has been withheld (Honneth 2003: 135) that has resulted in certain groups developing feelings of indignation (Irwin 2005: 156). Singh acknowledges this problem when he said: ' . . . our efforts to respect difference are inadvertently leaving some communities out in the cold' (2007: 1). In many ways, Singh and the CICC are not as concerned with navigating a course designed to avoid accusations from the liberal left of 'pandering to racists' by considering the disadvantaged white reaction to policies dedicated to alleviating 'race inequality', while at the same time attempting to avoid the far-right accusation that such policies pander to minority groups to the exclusion (and detriment) of disadvantaged white communities. In fact, in the final report the CICC state that they have developed the principle of visible social justice 'in the context of a greater understanding of how settled communities may feel that positive action for minorities has unbalanced the way services are being provided' (2007b: 98). From this we can assume that what Hewitt refers to as the white backlash associated with the feelings that disadvantaged white communities who perceive themselves to be the losers in the competition for scarce resources under multiculturalism might become a central concern in integration and community cohesion strategies in the future.

Conclusion

This chapter can be described as being a critical engagement with what Hellyer refers to as the new multiculturalism-integration agenda unfolding in contemporary Britain (2007: 252). It has traced the long shadow of Cantle and Blunkett across the 'policy landscape' that incorporates immigration, community cohesion and integration strategies and combinations of the latter with 'race equality strategies'. Numerous shifts in emphasis have been noted as each 'wave' of strategies and consultation strategies have been introduced. For example, the shift from 'cultural' explanations to incorporate considerations of social exclusion (between Cantle and *Strength in Diversity*) to the reversal of the Cantle cultural and material equation in the *Strengthening Opportunities* strategy that emphasized 'the economic' over other related factors. At the same time we have followed the shift in focus from the victim-blaming tone of Cantle (which implied that Muslims were *the* social problem with regard to the lack of community cohesion) to the increasing recognition that community cohesion is not only a BEM or Muslim issue. From the *Strengthening Opportunities* strategy onwards concerns over preferential treatment have increasingly come to the forefront of debate. This has culminated in the CICC's acknowledgement of white disadvantaged communities as being left out in the cold and neglected in cohesion and integration strategies. Another shift found at the boundaries of these debates is the re-gendering of 'the Muslim problem' away from an exclusive focus on 'weak' community leaders, and radicalized 'angry young men', to also focus on the cultural practices associated with Muslim women especially the wearing of the *niqab* and their ability to speak English.

As well as mapping out the shifts and turns in these unfolding strategies, this chapter has also examined Bagguley and Hussain's accurate description of the confused retreat from multiculturalism in British public policy, in which multiculturalism has become a pejorative term associated with 'social bads' such as perceived favouritism, preferential treatment and the competition for scarce resources. What is emerging in the new integration discourses introduced by Kelly and Singh is a rejection of multiculturalism, which is simultaneous with the emergence of what has been described above as reflexive multiculturalism.

Some of the themes developed above re-emerge in the next chapter, which focuses on the proposal for the establishment of a new Commission on Equality and Human Rights (CEHR). The CEHR is dedicated to bringing the Human Rights Act of 1998 into the centre of British life. However, there is rather more to it than that. The CEHR also promise to defuse what the CICC has identified as the common denominator between communities at the forefront of 'integration', that is, the divisive competition for scarce resources.

The CEHR can be described as a parallel 'integration with diversity' strategy in which the dignity of difference is to be upheld through the creation of a culture of respect for human rights that once again promotes a meta-allegiance to an ideal of British national citizenship through attempting to displace what are presented as micro-allegiances.

5 Culture change – the Commission for Equality and Human Rights – future proofing the nation

> The Human Rights Act is unlikely to achieve its potential, either to protect rights or to foster a human rights culture, if there is no statutory body to drive progress forward. Just as the Government in the 1970s saw the need to establish the CRE and the Equal Opportunities Commission (EOC) in order to enforce the anti-discrimination legislation – and just as the Disability Rights Commission has now been set up to do the same in relation to disability – so there must be an effective body to promote and enforce human rights.
>
> (Parekh 2000a: 101)

This chapter focuses on what can be described as a parallel integration strategy to the new integration strategies explored in the previous chapter. This parallel strategy attempts to promote human rights as *the* shared values that are to unite a diverse Britain. Just as the new integration discourses signal a shift away from the inter-community competitiveness associated with 'multiculturalism', this chapter is an examination of how human rights are being promoted as a replacement discourse for multiculturalism through the combination of human rights discourse with post-structuralist discourses that promote intersectional approaches to discrimination, inequality and identity. This was to be achieved through setting up a single commission that would focus on both equality and human rights.

The British Government announced its intention to establish a single Commission of Equality and Human Rights (CEHR)[1] with the publication of the *Fairness for All* White Paper[2] on 12 May 2004. This development in Britain will follow similar developments in the Netherlands, Ireland, Northern Ireland, New Zealand, Australia, Canada and the USA where single statutory structures supporting equality and anti-discrimination rights and, in some instances, human rights too, have been created (Women and Equality Unit 2002: 13). The Equality Bill (which established the CEHR) was introduced to the House of Commons on 2 March 2005. It was given Royal Assent on 16 February 2006, allowing for the establishment of the new CEHR from October

2007. In the *Fairness for All* White Paper it was suggested that the new Commission would be the basis for a healthy democracy, economic prosperity and the effective delivery of public services. In the explanatory notes published by the Government to coincide with the introduction of the Equality Bill, the main duties of the new Commission were listed thus:

> The CEHR will take on the work of the existing Equality Commissions: the Equal Opportunities Commission (EOC), the Commission for Racial Equality (CRE), and the Disability Rights Commission (DRC) and will additionally assume responsibility for promoting equality and combating unlawful discrimination in three new strands, namely sexual orientation, religion or belief, and age. The CEHR will also have responsibility for the promotion of human rights.
>
> (House of Commons 2005: 2)

It was suggested in the *Fairness for All* White Paper that it was necessary to replace the existing Equality Commissions with the new 'single' Commission because 'the extent of the future challenges we anticipate mean that fresh thinking and new approaches will be needed' (*Fairness for All* 2004: 12).This statement is significant as it suggests that 'social change' and the future challenges that will arise as a result of social change will outstrip the existing equality institutions' ability to deal with them. But what are these anticipated 'new challenges of the twenty-first century'? Or perhaps a more appropriate question is how are the new challenges of the twenty-first century presented in the White Paper and to what ends?

In this chapter particular emphasis is placed on the following: (1) the project of instituting a culture in which human rights are respected in Britain; and (2) the promotion of multiple and intersecting identities associated with the appreciation of multidimensional inequalities in order to undermine 'single identity' politics and group-based competition for resources. It is suggested that these two interrelated projects are significant components of the Labour Government's unfolding strategy of attempting to build a cohesive Britain 'at ease' with its diversity, which is in turn related to strategies to increase the social and political participation of marginalized social groups and reduce the discrimination and inequalities throughout the nation.

There is nothing uniquely British about these projects. These projects are part of the European-wide re-examination of social rights alongside the simultaneous questioning of the viability of some of the key institutions that are supposed to promote social cohesion (Joly 2004: 2). According to Joly, ethnicity is at the top of the policy agenda in Europe (and increasingly across the world), especially when attention turns to citizenship rights and debates concerning social integration and or inclusion of minority communities

(2004: 2). Much of this debate focuses on the domination and discrimination to be found throughout the folds of society; in employment, in the schools, in the law, in the media. It is economic, political and ideological (Joly 2004: 3). This chapter focuses on recent British policies and initiatives within these European-wide (and sometimes worldwide) debates. As such, the *Fairness for All* White Paper builds on established themes in many other areas of British public policy examined in the previous chapter, for example, in Community Cohesion strategies, Asylum and Immigration policy, the *Strength in Diversity* consultation strategy and the *Improving Opportunity, Strengthening Society* strategy, and in the creation of the new Commission on Integration and Community Cohesion (CICC). It should be noted that there are many similarities between the evolving integration and community cohesion strategies examined in the previous chapter and the documents promoting the CEHR in that they are both explicitly critical of 'multiculturalism' and they both seek to redefine identities and shared values in Britain.

This chapter argues that the *Fairness for All* White Paper is saturated with a similar risk consciousness found in the community cohesion and integration strategies examined in the previous chapter. This risk consciousness is evident in the Labour Government's presentation of specific 'social problems' in recent years in relation to, for example, the inadequate 'integration' of established migrant communities; the lack of community cohesion in many areas in contemporary Britain and the alleged 'weakness' of British citizenship often associated with ethnic and religious migrant groups. This risk consciousness in turn maps onto the two central political strategies that dominate the areas of public policy listed above (also to be found in the *Fairness for All* White Paper), that is, the necessity of defusing the alleged source of disharmony or social antagonism between groups (especially in community cohesion and 'race equality' strategies) and the project of unifying diverse social groups under a common identity as British citizens.

The contribution of the documents promoting the CEHR to these interdependent strategies comes from its promotion of a culture change in relation to how social groups, especially 'minority' groups (described in the White Paper as 'protected groups'), are defined as objects of public policy that in turn is supposed to transform how these social groups will act socially and politically in the future. This is to be achieved through promoting a culture in which the respect for human rights becomes the universal (albeit differentiated) unifying force in society.

There are, however, a number of problems associated with attempting to initiate this transformative 'proper' human rights culture in Britain. One problem is that the pursuit of shared values associated with the Blair Government's integration strategy does not explicitly include the respect for human rights as a component of 'British' shared values (see Chapter 6). At the same time, in this chapter (and in the next), the contradictory nature of the

Government's promotion of human rights is explored with regard to counter-terrorism. The Government has actively promoted human rights in Britain through implementing the Human Rights Act and supporting the establishment of the CEHR. However, at the same time, the post-9/11 and the post-7/7 counter-terrorism measures that they have introduced have allowed for the infringement and suspension of human rights.

The chapter is divided into four parts. Part one examines the justification behind the proposals for setting up the new Commission. This part of the chapter focuses on the risk consciousness found in the White Paper (and in other recent areas of public policy, mentioned above) associated with the project of helping Britain to become more 'at ease' with its increasing social diversity and the 'urgent' project of building community cohesion. In part two the focus is on the designation of the 'protected groups' that are to be the focus of the new Commission within the context of expanding 'discrimination legislation', and the deployment of 'multiple identities' as a means of undermining 'single identity' politics through a systematic de-emphasis of fixed social categories in favour of an intersectional approach to social identities and discrimination. Part three examines the mutual restructuring of social identities and the polity associated with the promotion of a common place of citizenship forged through the respect for human rights. Part four examines the White Paper through the lens of radical democratic theory and exposes yet another layer to the attack on 'multiculturalism' in contemporary Britain. At the same time it shows how the Government's treatment of human rights in the context of 'the war on terror' is the most significant obstacle to the realization of the human rights 'culture change' promised in the White Paper.

The CEHR offer an institutionalization of a radical democratic framework to overcome discrimination and advance equality and human rights in British society through taking on the responsibility for the 'three pillars': of equality, human rights and good relations between and within communities. The radical democratic aspects of the CEHR are analysed through exploring parallels with the theories of Nancy Fraser, Ernesto Laclau and Chantal Mouffe.

Managing the risks of 'future challenges'

The promotion of good relations and community cohesion did not feature prominently enough, according to the CRE, in the *Equality and Diversity: Making it Happen* Green Paper of 2002 that preceded the *Fairness for All* White Paper, that is:

> A related potential function for any future equality organization, not considered in the Government's consultation document, but

relevant to their vision for society – and ours – is that of promoting social and community cohesion ... further consideration needs to be given to what the role of any statutory body in this area should be.

(Commission for Racial Equality 2003: 8)

In the White Paper, the CRE's suggestion that the new Commission should be involved in promoting community cohesion was taken up in earnest. The promotion of good relations between groups will be achieved, according to the White Paper, by 'Creating a society that is cohesive and at ease with itself, that is able to respect and celebrate difference while at the same time recognizing and challenging discrimination or unfair treatment' (*Fairness for All* 2004: 21). It is not just any community relations that are the source of concern here. In *Fairness for All* the relations between different ethnic and religious communities were singled out, that is, 'The CEHR will promote good relations among different communities, particularly those of different races, religions or beliefs, CEHR activities in this area will also include good relations between these communities and wider society' (2004: 35). These proposals in the White Paper have been formalized in section 10 of the Equality Act 2006 that sets out the CEHR's duties in relation to promoting good relations between members of different groups, within different groups, and between members of different groups and wider society (House of Commons 2006: Para. 33).

Just as in the *Community Cohesion Review* (Home Office 2001) the suggestion for improving relations between ethnic and religious minority communities and 'wider society' in the White Paper was through 'providing support to local projects that promote dialogue and understanding between different communities and groups' (*Fairness for All* 2004: 35). At the same time, the CEHR was promoted in the White Paper as *the* agency to promote 'good relations' in the event of future social disorder:

> The extended good relations function will give the CEHR the voice it needs to play a leading and influential role in national and Great Britain-wide debates. This role will provide the CEHR with the capacity to assist in the process of mediating conflicts between communities, such as the public order disturbances in Bradford, Burnley and Oldham in 2001. It will give the CEHR the focus to comment on, react to, or bring insight and experience to, emerging or pressing policy issues on race equality, faith communities and other equality and human rights fields.[3]
>
> (*Fairness for All* 2004: 6.4)

The Government's promotion of the CEHR's particular good relations or community cohesion function was first suggested in the Joint Committee on

Human Rights March 2003 report. The Committee suggested that 'alternative dispute resolution function' already used by the DRC on disability discrimination cases could be used more widely in the single equality body in order to address inter-communal strife in an even-handed manner (Joint Committee on Human Rights 2003: Para. 141–4). In the White Paper it was suggested that the rationale for moving away from single issue 'equality institutions' that only focus on race, religion, gender or disability was that they were unable to offer an even-handed mediation function in the event of social disorder and tensions between communities. The CEHR's role in promoting good relations between and within different communities, according to the Government in their response to the White Paper, 'will have important benefits in delivering the culture change it seeks', that is, 'putting equality and human rights values at the heart of British society' (Government Response to Consultation 2004: 10).

In part one of the chapter the emphasis was on the context out of which the new Commission has emerged with regard to the risk of future disorder along the lines of Oldham, Burnley and Bradford in 2001. Social disorders such as these were to be avoided through providing an even-handed response to the events in question and by facilitating dialogue between antagonized groups. In part two the focus is on the further justifications for the new Commission based on its role in supporting public authorities through the introduction of new discrimination legislation. At the same time the White Paper also suggests a change of emphasis in response to the 'deepening understanding of the nature of discrimination that affects communities in contemporary Britain. The result of this is that social groups, and the discrimination they experience, are to be understood as intersectional entities (rather than discrete policy objects). The objective of this change in approach is to undermine what has been identified as one of the primary obstacles to social cohesion in Britain (as subsequently identified by the CICC, see Chapter 4), that is, the conceptualization of minority groups (for example, *the* Pakistani community, *the* African Caribbean community, *the* Gay Community) as discrete 'protected groups' in public policies that must compete with each other for services.

'Proper objects'? multidimensional discrimination and protected groups

This part of the chapter explores another justification for replacing the existing equality Commissions with the new Commission, that is, the supportive role that the new Commission is to play in relation to Britain's expanding discrimination legislation. In the White Paper the core functions of the proposed CEHR are listed as the following:

- Encouraging awareness and good practice on equality and diversity;
- Promoting awareness and understanding of human rights;
- Promoting equality of opportunity between people in the different groups protected by discrimination law;
- Promoting good relations among different communities and these communities and wider society.

(Fairness for All 2004: 29)

The different social groups that make up society are defined through a dividing practice that differentiates between 'wider society' and 'different communities'. In the White Paper 'different communities' refers to 'communities of protected groups' *(Fairness for All* 2004: 29). However, in the explanatory notes accompanying the Equality Act 2006, it was suggested that 'groups may or may not consider themselves to be 'communities'. They stipulated that the Commission's work with groups can apply to communities as well as groups (House of Commons 2006: Para. 34). In the White Paper 'protected groups' are differentiated from 'wider society' through their inclusion (or not) under discrimination legislation, that is:

> We use the phrase 'protected groups' to mean the following groups of people to the extent that they are – or soon will be – protected by discrimination legislation in respect of less favourable treatment based on particular characteristics or personal circumstances: men and women; people of different racial groups; people who have or have had a disability; people of different sexual orientations; people of different ages; and people who intend to undergo, are undergoing, or have undergone gender reassignment.
>
> *(Fairness for All* 2004: 17)

Thus, the focus of the CEHR's attention will be on those groups already protected by discrimination legislation associated with race, gender and disability; however, the Commission will also regulate and support the implementation of 'the new anti-discrimination strands: religion, belief, sexual orientation, and age' *(Fairness for All* 2004: 25). Part of the remit of the new Commission will be to provide 'effective support' with regard to the new regulations associated with these new discrimination strands (2004: 25). This regulatory role will benefit, relative to the existing equality Commissions, from the CEHR being equipped with 'modern powers and duties to apply across all of the 'equality strands' *(Fairness for All* 2004: 28). What this means is that the new Commission is not only necessary to respond to the social risks associated with the increasing diversity of twenty-first-century Britain (see part one above); but that the new Commission is also necessary to support and regulate the unfolding anti-discrimination context in contemporary Britain.

A common feature of these justifications for the establishment of the CEHR (and for the replacement of existing equality Commissions) is the particular way 'protected groups' are defined in the White Paper. The White Paper suggests that 'a single agency' with a 'cross-cutting approach' for tackling the barriers and inequalities affecting several groups 'will be better equipped to address the reality of the many dimensions of an individual's identity, and therefore tackle discrimination on multiple grounds' (*Fairness for All* 2004: 17). This approach to identity was first proposed in the Green Paper: *Equality and Diversity: Making it Happen* (2002):

> people are increasingly looking for equal treatment that respects the many facets of their identities. Everyone's identity has multiple aspects, drawing for example on their gender, age, ethnicity and religious affiliations among other characteristics ... Some identities, and combinations of identities, have been associated with disadvantage and discrimination in the past – for example, being an ethnic minority woman can be a double source of disadvantage. Equality policies must respond to this – another reason for a broad-based approach.
>
> (Women and Equality Unit 2002: 9)

In the Green Paper this perspective on identities was attributed to Parekh. According to Parekh, 'Many communities overlap; all affect and are affected by others. More and more people have multiple identities – they are Welsh Europeans, Pakistani Yorkshire women, Glaswegian Muslims, English Jews and Black British. Most enjoy this complexity but also experience conflicting loyalties' (Parekh 2000a: 10). Parekh has been in turn influenced by Mac an Ghail and Hall who have both referred to the cross-cutting and unpredictable ways identities are experienced (Bottero 2005: 100). For example, Mac an Ghail suggest that 'in social relations, people occupy certain positions simultaneously in that a working-class identity is at the same time a sexual identity and an ethnic identity' (1999: 47). As early as 1991 Stuart Hall urged us to recognize that all of us are composed of multiple social identities, not one, that is, we are complexly constructed through different categories, of different antagonisms, and these may have the effect of locating us socially in multiple positions of marginality and subordination (1991: 57).

On the publication of the White Paper the emphasis had shifted from multiplicity to intersectionality (Crenshaw 1994; Collins 1998). The concept of intersectionality is often used to understand the interconnections between the traditional background categories of gender, ethnicity, race, age, sexuality and class (Anthias 1998; Staunœs 2003). Intersectionality in feminist scholarship is associated with an anti-hierarchical appreciation of the multiple dimensions of discrimination that impact on especially women's identities, for example, the gendered aspects of racial and ethnic discrimination, the racialized aspects of gender discrimination, and the sexualized aspects of gender and racial discrimination (Darling 2002: 3). Intersectional theories of identity and discrimination have in turn had an impact on the feminist movement.

According to Fraser, the exclusive focus of the feminist movement on gender was ultimately disrupted by feminists accepting that they shared political space with a proliferation of new social movements from the 1980s onwards (1997: 179). Increasingly, throughout the 1980s, this sharing of political space became less of a parallel, side-to-side coexistence than a recognition that 'all the various movements cut across one another' (Fraser 1997: 179). At the same time the adequate treatment of class-based inequalities was achieved through seeking to conceptualize the articulation and intersection of class and status-related aspects of inequality (Irwin 2005: 155). The intersectional perspective on identity and discrimination was evident in the following passage from the White Paper:

> An important element of the way the CEHR works will be its capacity to better reflect the reality of people's identities. Individual identities usually have several dimensions, for example, their race and sexual orientation, or gender or age, or faith and whether they are disabled. The CEHR, in its policies and approach, will provide more effective support generally, and particularly in cases of multiple discrimination, by providing information, advice and guidance across the full range of discrimination law.
>
> (*Fairness for All* 2004: 60)

Thus, the necessity of both responding to the multiple elements of discrimination (and concomitantly to the multiplicity of protected group identities) and in responding to the potential complexity of intersecting new and established strands of discrimination legislation becomes, in the White Paper, the mutually reinforcing justifications for the establishment of the new 'single' equality Commission.

The presentation of the members of protected groups as intersectional sites of discrimination and as having multiple intersectional identities has significant implications for the future of 'minority' or 'protected' group identities in Britain. Just as with the CICC's promotion of multiple identities (see Chapter 4) the re-conceptualization of 'protected group' identities in the White Paper offers a post-structuralist understanding of identity (Weedon 1987; Fraser 1992) transposed into public policy. At the same time this White Paper is the potential site for the re-articulation of how these social groups are to be conceptualized in the future. Rather than 'communities of identity' associated with conflicts over the competing and mutually exclusive 'rights' and 'values' associated with different communities (Rose 1999b: 135), what is being proposed is a recalibration of the objects of social justice in the form of 'communities of disadvantage' identifiable in relation to the discrimination(s) they experience. The re-articulation of these groups in society as protected groups who suffer multiple forms of discrimination and who are the sites of competing and multiple identities is connected to the wider project (which is examined below) of improving community cohesion and increasing integration through promoting a culture in which human rights are respected with the intention of strengthening or revitalizing British citizenship.

In the CEHR's anti-discrimination culture there is no such thing as just 'ethnic' minorities, or just 'religious' minorities; rather, an expansive and coalitional sense (Butler 1994: 11) of 'minorities' is articulated here in order to undermine what is increasingly perceived as the source of social divisions in contemporary Britain: that is, discrete or 'single' 'communities of identity' in competition with each other under 'multiculturalism'. At the launch of the White Paper on Wednesday, 12 May 2004, Patricia Hewitt, the then Secretary of State for Trade and Industry and Cabinet Minister for Women, stated:

> In a world where individual identities are becoming increasingly important, we need to see people as a whole – not put them into boxes marked race, religion, gender, sexual orientation, disability ... it is not right. And we've all said so. But we've all said so from our individual lobbies and organizations. And the result is that responsibility for challenging discrimination has been sectionalized. ... That is why I agree with those who say we have reached the limits of multiculturalism.
>
> (Hewitt 2004: 4)

Social categories such as 'racial', 'ethnic' and 'religious' identities; and 'racial', 'ethnic' and 'religious' groups are to be rendered indiscrete, in this White Paper, through their location within a discourse of multiple and intersecting aspects of discrimination. At the same time these social categories are dehierarchicalized and devalued; their significance lies in their intersection with the discrimination common to multiple social categories[4] that is seen as an evolution stage beyond the primordial categories associated with multiculturalism.

This strategy kills two birds with one stone: (1) services and resources will be allocated in response to 'needs' that cut across groups; and, (2) the often highly antagonized competition for scarce resources and services between culturally distant but spatially proximate groups (see Chapter 4) could potentially be defused through this allocation of resources to constituents of individuals (across groups) that share multidimensional forms of discrimination, rather than to single social groups. This is yet another aspect of the proposed CEHR's pledge to promote good relations between different groups through a strategy that disrupts how social groups have been viewed by policy-makers, but perhaps even more importantly the CEHR has the potential to promote different ways for the members of social groups (for example, the members of polarized social groups) to view themselves and other groups on the ground, especially in relation to the competition for resources and services.

In the next section, the role the new Commission will play with regard to the promotion of a culture in which human rights 'are to be taken seriously' is the focus of attention.

Promoting a human rights culture

The previous chapter observed the efforts of the Home Office and the CICC to convince multicultural Britain of the need to find shared values to unite around (this theme is further explored in Chapter 6 when we examine the new Britishness discourse). In the *Fairness for All* White Paper, human rights are celebrated as the potential 'common place' of British citizenship, as an 'all purpose' solution for the 'future challenges' facing Britain whether they be: (1) disunity and segregation between social groups; (2) to conflict resolution; (3) and ultimately to build community cohesion. In other words, human rights are viewed as the 'social glue' (the ties that bind) that will make Britain more 'at ease' with its diversity:

> Greater diversity in our society poses a significant challenge to how we shape and promote the shared values that underpin citizenship. While respecting and celebrating our differences, citizenship will need to promote wider ownership of these common values and a shared sense of belonging. Human rights, establishing basic values for all of us, will play an increasingly important role in this, providing a language we can all share. This language is one that means something to, and is useful for, all people no matter what social group they belong to.
>
> (*Fairness for All* 2004: 15)

Part of the brief of the proposed new Commission, according to the White Paper, is to facilitate the change of culture that was promised (but not yet realized) by the Human Rights Act (1998).[5] This is to be achieved by embedding 'a true culture of respect for human rights throughout society' through implementing the Human Rights Act and making full use of the opportunities it affords (*Fairness for All* 2004: 30).

The impact of the Human Rights Act on public services in Britain has been inconsistent and limited. According to the Audit Commission's report *Human Rights: Improving Public Service Delivery* published in 2003, 58 per cent of public bodies surveyed had no clear corporate approach to human rights (2003: 21).[6] Part of the role of the new Commission will be to directly challenge this limited and inconsistent implementation of the Human Rights Act through ensuring 'an increasing awareness and understanding of human rights within the public sector' that will 'support the Government's wider work to enhance the way in which public services are delivered so that they can meet the needs of all users' (2004: 15–16). As well as pledging to create a human rights culture at the point of service delivery within the public sector, the White Paper suggests that the new Commission should promote a culture of 'respect for human rights' throughout British society (*Fairness for All* 2004: 15). The White Paper specified particular episodes when human rights can be used to promote good relations between people, with particular reference to conflict resolution and the necessity of building community cohesion in local areas, for example, 'the CEHR's human rights remit will play a significant role, providing tools and concepts to help find solutions in areas where rights may conflict' (*Fairness for All* 2004: 55). Therefore, the CEHR will perform the duties of a 'United Nations-like' organization for Britain providing a deployable service in order to resolve potentially conflicting rights, to prevent social disorder initiated through, for example, the mishandling of a critical incident[7] through employing the human rights principles of proportionality and reasonableness (*Fairness for All* 2004: 21). For example:

> The CEHR will also be able to help address situations where there are challenges to social integration, and conflicts between different sets of rights. Human rights principles can offer a way to balance rights and encourage communication between diverse individuals and communities. The CEHR will promote awareness of this approach and a better understanding of what a culture that respects human rights really means.
>
> (*Fairness for All* 2004: 30)

The White Paper argues that the promotion of a culture that respects human rights will benefit everyone, not just 'protected groups' (*Fairness for All* 2004: 15).[8] The new Commission is to be 'an engine of transformation' (Joint Committee on Human Rights 2003: 11) that will introduce a culture of human rights based on institutional and ethical dimensions (2003: 5). The institutional dimension refers to the creation of a culture in public life in which the effective protection of rights is seen as central to the design and delivery of policy, legislation and public services (Joint Committee on Human Rights 2003: 5). The ethical dimension is associated with the understanding that individual men and women have of their equal dignity and worth as the bearers of rights. However:

> A culture of human rights is not one which is concerned only with rights, to the neglect of duties and responsibilities, but rather one that balances rights and responsibilities by fostering a basic respect for human rights and dignity, and creating a climate in which such respect becomes an integral part of our dealings with the public authorities of the state and each other.
>
> (Joint Committee on Human Rights 2003: 5)

Thus, the new Commission is to institute a culture change in which human rights are to become a new way of being in relationships (Kennedy 2005: 301); a thread that should run through all our human interactions, as colleagues, as parents, as lovers, as spouses, as neighbours, or as strangers (2005: 302). From this perspective, human rights become less about the negative human potentialities associated with harm, in which human rights stipulates what should not be done; rather human rights becomes a language for speaking about what ought to be striven for (Gearty 2006: 5). Gearty refers to this as the 'upbeat' dimension of human rights that celebrates difference and diversity, that upholds the right that each of us has to view our humanity, to make the best of our capacities (2006: 6). Gearty's vision of proper human rights culture is one where human rights are embedded in society as a set of realizable political goals that are to be achieved through a sustained programme of political action (2006: 61).

The sustained programme of political action for achieving the culture change necessary for the embedding of human rights as the new common ground of British citizenship involves yet another step away from the respect for diversity fostered under multicultural policies. That is, just as the social categories of race, ethnicity, religion, gender and sexuality, and so on are to be displaced in favour of a response to the multiple dimensions of discrimination (see above); the championing of human rights in the White Paper suggests another negation and displacement, especially in relation to disputes between groups. Here the demands and complaints of different groups will be displaced in order to make room for the emergence of a perspective that will view 'events' in terms of competing and conflicting human rights. What this means is, for example, the social categories of race, ethnicity and religion as well as the social reality of ethnic, racial and religious minority 'communities' and their relationship with 'wider society' will be displaced in favour of viewing each 'group' as a bearer of rights that may or may not have been violated. It is the respect for human rights, and the balance of rights that is paramount here, not the demands of the communities involved. This is to be achieved through introducing 'a common political identity of persons who might be engaged in many different purposive enterprises and with differing conceptions of the good' but who are in turn 'bound by their common identification with a given interpretation of a set of ethico-political values' (Mouffe 1992: 378), namely, human rights.

The promise of the human rights culture, as depicted above, has much in common with David Blunkett's civic assimilationist model for revitalizing British citizenship (see Chapter 4). Moreover, the main limitations of the civic assimilationist approach, that is the promotion of uniformity in the public realm at the expense of relegating 'diversity' to the private realm of 'the family and civil society' (Parekh 2000b: 200) could be potentially ameliorated through forging a common identification with human rights, in which a range of both public and private rights and responsibilities are enshrined. For Parekh the civic assimilationist model attempts to separate the public and the private realms too neatly. The civic assimilationist model also ignores the fact that the 'public realm' in the form of the political culture of advanced western democracies is a product of history and the culture it institutionalizes enjoys State patronage, power and access to resources, and therefore 'sets the tone of the rest of society' thus disadvantages newcomers (Parekh 2000b: 204).

This 'setting of the tone of the rest of society' is associated with the significant differences of power, resources, access to publicity, and so on among different classes, groups, or interests the result being, according to Iris Marion Young, that 'decision making procedures that are impartial in the sense of allowing equal formal opportunity to all to press their interests will usually yield outcomes in the interests of the more powerful' (1990: 114). According to Parekh, 'the logic of multiculturalism qualifies and informs the logic of human rights, just as the logic of human rights qualifies the logic of multiculturalism'(2000a: 91) when one considers that human rights provide the 'ground rules' in law for protecting minimum standards and for negotiating conflicts of interest, they also provide an ethical code on how individuals should minimally treat their fellow citizens, for example, 'respecting their privacy, their freedom of religion or belief, or their right to a fair hearing. They are therefore central to achieving an equal sense of belonging' (Parekh 2000a: 91). Thus, a human rights culture could be the means of rescuing 'the spirit of multiculturalism' from the dustbin of British public policy. The principles of common humanity, minimum guarantees of protection and a framework for handling conflicts of interest enshrined in the European Convention of Human Rights and Fundamental Freedoms alongside the re-articulation of discrimination as intersectional discrimination found in the *Fairness for All* White Paper is one potential way of refashioning citizenship in contemporary Britain to fit with the shared futures discourse that emerged in the CICC.

A human rights culture beyond multiculturalism?

According to Nancy Fraser, the pluralist multiculturalism project tends to:

> Substantialize identities, treating them as given positivities instead of as constructed relations. It tends, consequently, to balkanize culture, setting groups apart from one another, ignoring the ways they cut across one another ... losing sight of the fact that differences intersect, it regresses to a simple additive model of difference.
>
> (Fraser 1997: 185)

In response to these tendencies in pluralist multiculturalism, Honig calls for a resignification of defensive unitary identities as 'coalitional arrangements' in order to disable certain conceptions of agency (for example, the inter-community competition for resources) and enable other conceptions of agency that 'animates more coalitional varieties of social democratic organization and affiliation' (Honig 1996: 270–1).

Chapter 4 examined the retreat from multiculturalism in British public policy (Joppke 2004: 237) since the disturbances in Oldham, Burnley and Bradford in 2001. Since the July 2005 bombings in London this retreat from multiculturalism has accelerated. It is in this context that a balance is being sought between encouraging loyalty and commitment to particular cultures, traditions and identities but with one overriding requirement, that is, these loyalties and commitments are conducive to the fostering of broader civic and political allegiances (this is further developed in Chapter 6). This is an attempt to introduce on the ground what Yuval-Davis described as a 'transversal' or dialogic political identities, which is a process involving 'rooting' and 'shifting' in which participants remain 'rooted' in their cultures, traditions and values (as long as they are cooled down, deradicalized, moderate) and as long as they demonstrate their willingness to have their views shifted and challenged through dialogue with those who have different cultures, traditions, identities and values (1994: 193).

It is suggested that there is common ground between the promotion of a culture that respects human rights (complete with the decentring of intersectional subjectivities) in the proposals for the new Commission with what Benhabib describes as Nancy Fraser's 'thought experiments' in radical democracy. Like the CEHR, radical democratic theory, for example in the work of Laclau and Mouffe (1985),[9] has been held up as a rubric for mediating various struggles over multiple intersecting identities. In many ways radical democratic theory is dedicated to correcting the balkanizing tendencies of identity politics and to promote broader political alliances (Fraser 1997: 181).

Laclau and Mouffe were the first to propose the reconceptualization of citizenship by suggesting that citizens should be unencumbered by compartmentalizing categories and the constraints of discrete group membership (Trend 1996a: 15). Within Laclau and Mouffe's formulation, according to Trend, each individual is conceived as belonging to numerous overlapping groups and multiple intersecting identities (1996a: 15). The problem, however, according to Fraser, was that such advances in cultural theory with regards to identity (especially post-structuralism) were until fairly recently underdeveloped in democratic theory (1997: 181).[10] It was Nancy Fraser who took up the challenge of attempting to connect a cultural politics of identity and difference (what she calls a politics of recognition) to a social politics of justice and equality (what she calls a politics of redistribution) by developing a 'credible model' of radical democracy adequate to our time (1997: 186–7). This was to be achieved through re-coupling 'cultural politics' with 'social politics', that is, the politics of difference with the politics of equality (Fraser, in Fraser and Honneth 2003: 8). Fraser describes the task of such a political fusion in the following passage:

> The task is to foster democratic engagement across current divides in order to build a broad-based programmatic orientation that integrates the best of the politics of redistribution with the best of the politics of recognition.
>
> (Fraser, in Fraser and Honneth 2003: 27)

There are a number of broad similarities between Fraser's 'task' and the CEHR's stated 'core functions' (see part two above). Both demonstrate what Fraser describes as 'perspectival dualism' (2003: 63), which can appreciate multiple domains (for example, 'the economic' and 'the cultural') and the intersections between them. What this perspectival dualism ensures is that it is not only the intersectionality of discrimination that can be appreciated by the proposed new Commission as it impacts upon overlapping constituents of individuals from different social groups but that the CEHR will also be able to identify and map the impact of policy between domains too. That is, the CEHR will be able to identify the 'cultural dimensions' of, for example, 'economic' (and other) policies' in order to map the complex patterns of interpenetration between domains and the equally complex patterns of subordination created by them (Fraser, in Fraser and Honneth 2003: 63, 217).

At the same time the 'bottom-up' or 'grass-roots' task of the political strategy advocated by Fraser for the coalitionization of new social movements is rather closely related to the 'top-down' task of the CEHR devised in the White Paper.

The drafters of the White Paper and post-structuralist-influenced radical democratic theorists (such as Fraser, Mouffe and Laclau) are trying to achieve the same thing, that is, social transformation through the de-emphasis of fixed categories that reify, essentialize and homogenize identities. However, the driving force of these two 'approaches to identity' is different. Fraser, Mouffe and Laclau's theories focus on oppositional social interventions in the form of political action for social transformation that avoids the pitfalls of single identity categories (Martínez 2003: 92). This is a politics dedicated to the powerless, the minorities, with the intention of generating different kinds of political mobilization among these constituents. In the White Paper, on the other hand, post-structuralist approaches to identity are being deployed to undermine single identity politics in order to promote greater equality, social order and integration.

Surprisingly, the aspects of the White Paper that I have focused on in this chapter, that is, the radical mutual restructuring of political subjectivities and the polity promised by the CEHR, has not featured in the responses from the statutory Equality Commissions (EOC, DRC, CRE).[11] The emphasis of the responses to the White Paper was on 'practical concerns'; in fact, Trevor Phillips, when chair of the CRE, adopted a mocking tone in relation to the wider remit of the CEHR:

> Fundamentally, what *Fairness for All* is proposing is less a single champion enforcing strong legislation, and more a hopeful chorus of voices, which *Fairness for All* speculates can be made to sing in tune. This may be a worthy aim for a body whose job is just about spreading goodwill. It may even be a way of allowing those who suffer from inequality to make common cause, in reminding the privileged that we are still far from an equal society. But there has to be more to cooperation than a common declaration of victimhood, and these tasks are but a small part of the mandate of a serious, statutory equality regulator.
>
> (Trevor Phillips, CRE 2004: 5)

Phillips suggested that it was:

> Simplistic to suggest that all forms of discriminatory treatment are similar, and misleading to suggest that they will all be susceptible to similar remedies. This does not make one kind of inequality more important than another – but it does make the task of explaining why both need to be addressed by the same body extremely challenging. Yet, this White Paper does not even ask this question.
>
> (CRE 2004: 4)

Trevor Phillips has, subsequent to these statements, accepted the Government's invitation to be the first chair of the CEHR. Birt suggests that this move was rather surprising given Phillips's previous campaign to preserve the CRE, and his description of the CEHR as a 'train wreck waiting to happen' (2006c: 3). At the same time there has been a substantial backlash against Trevor Phillips in the run up to the Government's announcement of the CEHR Chair. For example, in polls conducted by the BLINK (Black Information Link) on who should be the first Chair of the CEHR, the Director of Liberty, Shami Chakrabarti received 43 per cent of the vote; the former head of the CRE, Lord Herman Ouseley, received 36 per cent and ex-trade union leader Sir Bill Morris received 17 per cent. Trevor Phillips trailed far behind receiving only 4 per cent of the votes (BLINK 2006: 1). According to BLINK, Phillips's relatively lower score in this poll reflects 'the widespread view within Black communities that Mr. Phillips has damaged the drive for greater race equality since taking over the CRE in 2003' (BLINK 2006: 1).

I would suggest that the image of a new Britain achieved through the introduction of a 'proper human rights culture' that is to be found on the pages of the White Paper needs to be fully grasped by organizations such as the CRE and the people of Britain. There is more to the CEHR than a 'common declaration of victimhood' and 'spreading goodwill'. Phillips described the White Paper as a 'theoretical blueprint' (CRE 2004: 5), I agree that in many ways the White Paper contains a sophisticated theoretical (and theoretically informed) blueprint for the transformation of British society (which does appear to be light on detail). However, I do not think that the White Paper should be dismissed so quickly. The value of the White Paper lies in the way that certain 'social problems', mostly associated with ethnic and religious minority groups, are constructed. Of equal value are the solutions proffered for overcoming these 'social problems'. The White Paper provides a portal through which we can view how British society might be transformed in the early twenty-first century. All that being said, there is at least one major obstacle to fulfilling the ambitious project of creating a culture that respects human rights. That is, the Government's inconsistent record with regard to human rights (see Chapters 1 and 2) that is further developed in the next chapter.

Human rights cannot be promoted as the foundation upon which 'our' core values are to be established in one breath, when in the next breath the Government is perceived as attacking human rights. If human rights are to become the core values to be shared by all in Britain, then all individuals must be protected by them.

The Government's hostility to human rights is damaging the chances of enacting a culture in which human rights are respected. Rather than providing 'a language we can all share', the Government is sending out mixed messages. The British people cannot be asked to sign up to a culture change founded on respect for human rights when the Government itself shows little respect for them.

Conclusion

In this chapter I have attempted to demonstrate that some of the key proposals found in the *Fairness for All* White Paper are a direct response to the future challenges associated with the promotion of good relations among different communities, particularly those of different races, religions or beliefs and the promotion of good relations between these communities and 'the wider society'. At the same time, the proposals in the White Paper offer a fascinating confection of political-philosophical and sociological inferences and exchanges on, for example, the nature of identity, the politics of difference, the limits of multiculturalism, which are in turn developed into a broad-based 'blueprint' (in the form of the new Commission) of a 'radical' new framework in response to the 'anticipated future challenges' emerging in contemporary Britain.

From a 'community cohesion and integration' perspective the two most significant suggestions that emerged in the White Paper for ensuring good relations between different groups were (1) that, in line with the CICC's suggestions (see Chapter 4) fixed social identities should be de-emphasized as they become the sites of polarization and non-integration between groups; and (2) that competing demands for resources and services should be defused by introducing a human rights approach. In turn these two processes are associated with the much more ambitious project of restructuring how social identities and discrimination are understood and how social and political demands are made (by minority groups and the members of 'wider society') in a potential Britain of the near future redefined by a human rights culture that is to be 'taken seriously' by all.

This project of promoting a culture of human rights in this context could prove to be a very radical strategy indeed. Furthermore, the new Commission can be described as a civic assimilationist radical democratic project in that the outcomes of its strategy is to make our belonging to different communities of values, language and culture compatible with our common belonging to a political community whose rules we have to accept (Mouffe 1995: 34). According to Trend, the expanded view of the multiple 'intersectional' subjects of radical democracy is in turn connected to a much broader definition of 'the political' in which new 'sites' in the form of 'new political spaces' beyond the conventional jurisdiction of State institutions in the more dynamic domain of cultural representations and social practices will emerge (Trend 1996a: 15). With regard to the CEHR this could, for example, encompass the expansion of alternative conflict resolution mechanisms that would perform the task of balancing competing rights claims.

The new Commission with its 'good relations function', its intersectional perspective on discrimination and its project of promoting a culture in which human rights are respected is only part of the wider strategy of initiating a radical mutual restructuring of political subjectivities and the polity (Isin and Wood 1999: 12). However, the CEHR and the new culture of human rights that was promised to Britain with the enactment of the Human Rights Act in 1998 have been marginalized by seemingly more pressing debates on 'Britishness' and 'shared British values' that are on the whole neglectful of human rights (see Chapter 6). The CEHR has only had a fleeting mention in recent strategies and statements (for example, in the *Improving Opportunities* strategy in 2005 and in the Interim Statement of the CICC). The most significant obstacle to the culture change promised by the new Commission is the Government's own disrespect for human rights in its response to global terrorism. For a 'true' culture of human rights to emerge in Britain the Government needs to stand firm on human rights. It needs to resist the temptation to rewrite the underlying principles of law during 'trying times'; here I agree with Helena Kennedy who argues that 'Rights are not expendable entities to be dumped when exigencies require' (2005: 302).

6   Shared values, Britishness and human rights

> Six years on, the ground has shifted subtly. But decidedly, in political
> and policy terms away from this pluralist vision of Britain as a
> multicultural mosaic, and in favour of a reinvigorated and assim-
> ilative national project ...
>
> (Alexander 2007: 115)

In this passage Alexander is referring to the vision of Britain as a 'community
of communities' presented by Parekh in the Runnymede Trust commissioned
report *The Future of Multi-ethnic Britain* published in 2001. I agree with her.
Britain's relationship with multiculturalism has taken an assimilationist turn
in recent years. Rather than disappearing altogether I have suggested in
Chapter 4 that the demands of integration have resulted in multiculturalism
surviving in a reflexive version of its once pluralist form. Multiculturalism
seems to have been eclipsed by various strategies containing varying combinations of assimilation and integration all of which focus on identifying 'the
norms of acceptability' and the responsibilities of citizenship in contemporary Britain (Alexander 2007: 116).

In the light of the latter, in this chapter 'integration' will be contextualized once again (see Blunkett, Chapter 4) within the discourse of the
nation and nationhood. In particular this chapter examines the post-7/7
discourses on 'Britishness' introduced by Gordon Brown and Tony Blair. Like
the community cohesion, civic assimilationalism, and the discourses promoting 'a proper human rights culture' explored in Chapters 4 and 5, 'the
new Britishness' discourse is a component of the new integration discourse
associated with the project of searching for core, shared values for all in
multicultural Britain. The focus of this chapter is on how Brown and Blair
present the new Britishness as being distinct from older, 'ethnic models' of
Britishness. What is emerging in the new discourses is a particular conception
of patriotism and nationalism that emphasizes civic engagement over ethnic
and biological attributes. Gordon Brown's speeches on the 'new Britishness',
as detailed below, falls back on the civic assimilationist reliance on dominant
cultural institutions and histories as providing the foundations upon which
British shared values have been and should be forged. Tony Blair's speeches
on the new Britishness, in contrast, takes on a rather more authoritarian tone,

especially his insistence that the right to call oneself British comes down to the ability to live by 'British values'.

In many ways this chapter begins the work of concluding this book in that the two parts of the chapter re-engage with the major themes examined in previous chapters, that is, integration, security and human rights. The chapter is divided into two parts. Part one contextualizes the new Britishness discourse in the new integration strategies examined in Chapters 4 and 5. In particular, part one examines how the civic assimilationist project that emerged in response to the social disorder in Oldham, Burnley and Bradford in 2001 is being further developed with regard to the new Britishness discourses in the post-7/7 context. In this part the parallel process of updating values to match changing circumstances and the construction of new outsiders, that is, those who do not share 'our' values are examined. Some of the issues discussed in relation to counter-terrorism and the impact on Muslim communities (see Chapters 1–3) are also explored. This part of the chapter examines the slide from a communitarian contractual discourse of 'rights with responsibilities' to a more authoritarian new Britishness discourse targeting specific communities.

Part two examines the relationship between the shared values emphasized in the new Britishness discourses with the establishment of a 'proper human rights culture' in contemporary Britain. In this part themes developed in Chapters 1–3 with regard to human rights, counter-terrorism and Muslim communities are connected to the themes developed in Chapters 4 and 5 in relation to the challenges of finding common ground in a multicultural context. These themes are examined in the context of the reflexive turn in human rights discourse in post-7/7 Britain that is being translated into calls to (re)balance human rights to champion the rights of 'the law-abiding majority' over the rights of 'the criminal' or 'extremist' minority.

This chapter, therefore, forms part of the conclusion in that it attempts to draw together a number of themes included in earlier chapters with regard to multiculturalism, integration and citizenship in the context of, for example, 'the war on terror'. At the same time the chapter is provocative in its attempts to comment on the future developments in public policy, legislation and 'our' relationship to human rights.

Towards a patriotism of shared purpose

Chapter 4 explored some of David Blunkett's speeches on the necessity of promoting a new British citizenship, based on values shared by all in contemporary Britain. Blunkett was not alone in this project. A year before in 2000, Tony Blair stated in his speech entitled 'Britishness and the Government's agenda of constitutional reform' that 'a new Britain is emerging with a revitalized conception of citizenship' (2000: 3). In this new Britain, according to Blair, 'a new modern form of patriotism is needed' (2000: 5). This new British patriotism was to be made possible through 'rediscovering our strength and values' and 'uniting those values to a common purpose' (Blair 2000: 5). Leggett describes this process as the New Labour strategy of periodically 'updating values' to meet 'changed circumstances' (2005: 52). This strategy is common to numerous New Labour 'vision' speeches since they took office (Leggett 2005: 35). However, there is more to this process than just updating values. In many ways these 'vision speeches' are strategic in that they can be described as a project of wrestling patriotism away from the centre right and far right in order to redeploy a new type of patriotism that will coincide with a particular vision of 'Britishness'. Many key New Labour figures have deployed the distinction between what Ignatieff describes as 'ethnic nationalism' and 'civic nationalism' in their presentation of a particular image of Britain.

According to Billig et al., civic nationalism, in contrast to traditional 'ethnic nationalism' depicts the nation as based on shared values, not shared ethnicity (2006: 4). Michael Ignatieff made the distinction between civic and ethnic nationalism. For Ignatieff ethnic nationalism 'defines the nation in terms of ethnic origins and birth' (Ignatieff 1996: 219). On the other hand, civic nationalism 'defines the nation not in terms of ethnicity but in terms of willingness to adhere to its civic values' (Ignatieff 1996: 219). In this particular speech, Blair attempts to promote the civic nationalist idea by saying that 'blood alone does not define our national identity'; rather, for Blair 'our identity lies in our shared values' (Blair 2000: 4). My reason for selecting this particular speech is because some of its themes, especially the shift to an overt civic nationalism discourse, in the face of changing circumstances (in this case associated with the planned devolution of Scotland) forms a precursor to later speeches, made in response to other changing circumstances in post-7/7 Britain made by both Gordon Brown and Tony Blair. For example, Gordon Brown in his 'The future of Britishness' speech delivered at the Fabian Britishness Conference in January 2006[1] was keen to make the distinction between ethnic nationalism and his vision of patriotic civic nationalism that he described as a 'sense of common patriotic purpose' (2006c: 3), that is:

> This British patriotism is, in my view, founded not on ethnicity nor race, not just on institutions we share and respect, but on enduring ideals which shape our view of ourselves and our communities – values which in turn influence the way our institutions evolve.
>
> (Brown 2006c: 4)

In this speech Brown manages to distinguish the 'old' discourse of patriotism associated with right-wing jingoism to promote, in its place, a new variety of patriotism that coincides with civic nationalism in that it stresses 'the importance of political loyalty to a democratic polity and citizens' through a commitment to the common principles underpinning liberal democratic cultures (Kostakopoulou 2006: 75). Whereas Tony Blair in his speech above states the importance of standing up for our 'core British values' (which he lists as: fair play, creativity, tolerance and an outward-looking approach to the world) and having the strength to realize them in the modern world (2000: 1), Gordon Brown is rather more specific when it comes to what he considers to be 'our enduring British values':

> In addition to our qualities of creativity, inventiveness, enterprise and our internationalism, our central beliefs are a commitment to – liberty for all, responsibility by all and fairness to all.
> (Brown 2006c: 3)

In these speeches Blair and Brown envisage the nation as 'a community of equal, rights-bearing citizens, united in patriotic attachment to a shared set of political practices and values' (Ignatieff 1993: 6). The civic nationalistic flavour of Blair and Brown's vision statements are explicit. For example, for Blair, establishing values and standing up for these values are essential if Britain is to survive 'the huge changes we are living through' (2000: 1). At the same time, for Brown, shared purpose as a country is found through being 'more explicit about what we stand for' and as a result 'we will meet and master challenges best' (2006c: 4). According to Brown, it is the heated 'debates about immigration, asylum and multiculturalism in particular' that 'challenge us to be more explicit about Britishness' (2006c: 2). At the same time, it is the events of 7 July 2005 that 'lead us to ask how successful we have been in balancing the need for diversity with the obvious requirements of integration in our society' (Brown 2006c: 2). It is in looking to the future, to Britain's ability to meet and master the challenges of the global economy, but also the international, demographic, constitutional and social and security challenges ahead, according to Brown, 'that requires us to rediscover and build from our history and apply in our time the shared values that bind us together and give us common purpose' (2006c: 3). However, it is here where the future-orientated discourse of moving to 'our' shared future (see Chapter 4) becomes infused with the backward-looking rediscovery, in Brown's speech, of 'our' values that are expressed through 'our' history and 'our' institutions:

> British people should be able to gain great strength from celebrating British identity which is bigger than the sum of its parts and a union that is strong because of the values we share and because of the way these values are expressed through our history and our institutions.
> (Brown 2006c: 2)

Brown, like Blair, assumes that the shift from 'ethnic' nationalism to 'civic' nationalism in which 'national identity is defined by the values we share in common' (Brown 2006c: 2) is enough to sanitize British identity of cultural bias, or accusations of assimilationism. Brown's project can be described as a re-articulation of Britishness in which:

> the presence of others who do not share the dominant culture's memories and morals poses a challenge to the democratic legisla-turers to rearticulate the meaning of democratic universalism ... through which they refashion the meaning of their own peoplehood.
>
> (Benhabib 2006a: 69)

However, this refashioning is rather superficial for Britain, as Brown points out, has never been ethnically pure in that 'we have always been a country of different nations' (2006c: 2). Brown's constitutional settlement is less about the re-articulation of Britishness from a racially coded 'white' Britishness (Parekh 2000a: 38) and more about demanding the universal respect for British institutions that reflect 'our values'. Thus, shared values do not in fact involve a two-way process of 'sharing' (for example, 'host' and 'newcomer') values. The 'shared values' associated with the new Britishness discourse are traditional 'British values'.[2] The patriotism that the new Britishness dis-courses are promoting is fast becoming compulsory in the aftermath of the events of July 2005 in which the contractual discourses (for example, of rights with responsibilities) has begun to slide into authoritarian discourses (Fair-clough 2000: 43).

For example, in her speech to Muslim Organizations in 2006, Ruth Kelly outlined her vision of a universal British citizenship in which non-negotiable rules will be shared and followed by all:

> I want to see a clear understanding that although fundamental rights must be equal for everyone, with rights come responsibilities. Even within a framework of mutual tolerance, I believe that there are non-negotiable rules, understood by all groups, both new and established. We must be clear and unafraid to say that we expect these will be shared and followed by all who live here.
>
> (Kelly 2006b: 4)

What is emerging especially in Kelly's speeches (above), and in Blair's 'Our Nation's Future' Lecture in December 2006 (see below), is a clear demarcation of what Kearns and Muir describe as 'the essential minimum' duties of poli-tical citizenship in Britain (2006b: 2). That is, according to Blair:

> Obedience to the rule of law, to democratic decision-making about
> who governs us, to freedom from violence and discrimination are
> not optional for British citizens. They are what being British is about.
> Being British carries rights. It also carries duties. And those duties
> take clear precedence over any cultural or religious practice.
>
> (Blair 2006b: 3)

The 7/7 bombers, according to Blair, were 'integrated' at one level in that they
were integrated in terms of lifestyle and work (2006b: 2), but they were not
integrated fully:

> Integration is not about culture or lifestyle. It is about values. It is
> about integrating at the point of shared, common unifying British
> values. It isn't about what defines us as people, but as citizens, the
> rights and duties that go with being a member of our society.
>
> (Blair 2006b: 2)

The partial integration of the 7/7 bombers and their willingness 'to harm us'
(Blair 2006b: 2) has resulted in Blair re-articulating the desirability of establishing 'shared values' in speeches made by Blunkett (see Chapter 4) and
Brown (see above) into an essential duty, which he describes as 'the duty to
integrate' (2006b: 3) for all Britons. This is clearly a major shift that perhaps
signals the emergence of post-multiculturalism in Britain. Alexander seems to
think that this is the case. She describes the discourses of integration and
nationhood as marking a dramatic shift away from the public lip-service paid
to the ideals of multiculturalism and celebrating cultural diversity towards
'one which simultaneously marks out minority communities and cultures as
an obstacle (or threat) to a viable modern national identity and demands
their submission and dissolution within it' (2007: 116). An example of Blair's
authoritarian mentality (Dean 2007: 109) and anti-multiculturalism can be
found in the following passage in which he promotes a civic assimilationist
model (including pushing differences, including faith, into the private realm,
see Chapters 4 and 5) with the demand for uncompromising duty to integrate
at the point of shared values associated with civic nationalism:

> Christians, Jews, Muslims, Hindus, Sikhs and other faiths have a
> perfect right to their own identity and religion, to practice their faith
> and to conform to their culture. This is what multicultural, multi-
> faith Britain is all about ... But when it comes to our essential values
> – belief in democracy, the rule of law, tolerance, equal treatment for
> all, respect for this country and its shared heritage – then that is
> where we come together, it is what we hold in common; it is what
> gives us the right to call ourselves British. At that point no distinctive

culture or religion supersedes our duty to be part of an integrated
United Kingdom.

(Blair 2006b: 2)

Berkeley argues that the ideals associated with pluralist multiculturalism
found in, for example, Parekh's depiction of Britain as a 'community of
communities' has been eclipsed in political discourse, such as Blair's above,
by the depiction of Britain as a 'community of citizens' (2006: 2) in which it is
the rights and responsibilities that link an individual to the State that are
always paramount rather than membership of a 'community of identity'
(Alexander 2007: 122). This could signify, as suggested in Chapter 3, that the
Blair Government's 'anti-multiculturalism' has resulted in simultaneous
movement away from its 'government through community' approach (Rose
1999b: 136) in that the relationship between Government and particular
communities, namely Muslim communities, seems to be one based on
mutual suspicion.

According to Billig et al., what is fascinating about the new Britishness
discourse based on shared values (including tolerance) is that it creates new
outsiders (2006: 25). These new discourses clearly demarcate the line between
tolerance and intolerance through stating who is 'un-British' and therefore
intolerable; that is, those who are suspected of not sharing our values. Blair's
comments are more far-reaching than just designating the intolerable, the
extremist enemies of British values. Blair can also be described as attempting
to attack the order of loyalties in specific communities. Blair's 'duty to integrate' could be interpreted as an attack on the privileging of the *ummah* in
Muslim communities. For example, the assumption he is making is that
loyalty to the *ummah* will come at the expense of being loyal to the political
community of the nation.

According to Parekh, British citizens who prioritize their loyalty to the
ummah over their loyalty to Britain can be described as 'Muslim Britons'
(2006b: 3); these are individuals who want to be British in a Muslim way,
rather than Muslim in a British way (2006b: 3). In contrast British Muslims
privilege their British identity; they practice their religion according to British
values and practices (Parekh 2006b: 3). Blair's lecture is yet another component of the creation of limited subject positions for Muslims in contemporary
Britain (see Chapter 2). It is not enough for Blair that Muslims are to be
discouraged from becoming involved in extremist activities by anti-terrorism
legislation. Muslims must now also be 'Muslim' in the correct way; more than
that Muslims must be British in the correct way. This, according to Blair, is a
duty expected of them. Seddon has problems with the Islamophobic
assumptions present in the 'Muslim loyalty discourses'. In particular, Seddon
considers the question 'are they British Muslim or Muslims in Britain?' (2004:
141) to be discriminatory as the same questions of allegiance and identity are

not transposed onto, for example, non-Muslim anti-war campaigners (2004: 141). Seddon et al. counter Blair's 'duty to integrate' discourse by suggesting that by holding contentious and alternative views, for example, on British foreign policy, is evidence that Muslims can synthesize their religious and national identities in a British context:

> When British Muslims disagree with their Government on issues of political, moral and religious values as with the Satanic Verses Affair, the Gulf War or the recent events in the Middle-East, their contentions should not be viewed in terms of their specific loyalties or belonging to Britain. Rather, their alternative views should be interpreted as an expression of their democratic right to oppose Government policies and as an indicator of active integration, that Muslims are aware and concerned with Government policies.
>
> (Seddon et al. 2004: x)

Dilwar Hussain views the 'Muslim loyalty discourses' that present the notion of the *ummah* as something 'sinister and somehow contradictory to being British' rather than what it is; a bond of common faith and belief as being one of the 'main threads' of the 'Inquisitorial climate' that 'could be alienating the very people who need to be won over if there is any hope of preventing another attack on our country' (Hussain 2005: 1).

What is being contested is a variety of compulsory or forced patriotism that demands Muslims, in particular, to prioritize their loyalty to Britain over all other cultural and religious 'duties' and creeds. Brighton suggests that these calls for increased civic integration and 'shared' – centrally dictated – values might meet with more success if they were accompanied by some guarantee of accountability for State projects such as military intervention abroad (2007: 16). Hussain concurs with this view when he suggested that when two million people march on London to protest against the war and this has no influence on policy 'there is a serious democratic deficit' (2005: 2). The solution, according to Hussain, is for Britain to provide a vision for democratic participation that channel 'the legitimate frustrations and anxieties faced by many people in this country' (2005: 2).

I further suggest that it is not the forced patriotism in Tony Blair's speech above that is the most controversial aspect of the new Britishness discourse. Rather, I think it is the relationship between 'the said' and 'the not said' in speeches such as these that is the most controversial aspect of the new Britishness discourse, that is, the complete absence of any mention of human rights, the Human Rights Act or the new Commission on Equality and Human Rights in speeches that are attempting to determine shared values, common purpose and the essential duties and responsibilities of British patriots. In the next part of the chapter the relationship between a civic nationalist patriotism and a human rights culture are examined.

The Human Rights (re)balancing Act

During his address to the Civil Service College Seminar in December 1999, the then Home Secretary, Jack Straw, described the Human Rights Act in the following terms: 'the Human Rights Act will, I believe, be seen by future social historians as one of the defining events in British constitutional history' (Straw 1999: 2). In the same year, in his speech entitled 'Building a human rights culture', Straw saw the Human Rights Act as an opportunity for 'strengthening citizenship' (1999: 2) for building a 'rights and responsibilities culture in the UK' (1999: 1). However, Straw also described the Human Rights Act as providing the 'formal shared understanding of what is right and what is wrong' (1999: 5) in a multicultural society. That is:

> The Human Rights Act provides that formal shared understanding. It's an ethical language we can all recognize and sign up to. An ethical language which doesn't belong to any particular group or creed, but to all of us. One that is based on principles of our common humanity ... those are the rights that will form the anchor for our policy making – and a sail for service delivery. They will provide a common set of values to help unite a diverse society.
>
> (Straw 1999: 5)

A human rights culture in Straw's vision is an evolutionary stage beyond both civic assimilation (see Chapters 4 and 5) and civic nationalism in Britain, both of which promise unity in diversity, but in the end they demand the universal respect for British institutions that reflect 'British values'. Straw's vision of a proper human rights culture is based on three key arguments: (1) ethical neutrality (providing an ethical language we can all sign up to); (2) rights with responsibilities (where the balances and limitations on many individual rights reflect the rights of others, the wider community and the State itself and form a statement of responsibilities); and (3) a fairness guarantee for all (through providing an ethical bottom line for public authorities). The argument for ethical neutrality is perhaps the most significant of these 'key arguments' for this chapter. Habermas has suggested that the primary question multiculturalism raises is 'the question of the ethical neutrality of law and politics' (1994: 122). Civic nationalism (and by extension the civic assimilationist flavour of David Blunkett's pronouncements on British citizenship) also raises questions with regard to the ethical neutrality of law and politics:

> According to the civic nationalist creed, what holds a society toge-
> ther is not common roots but law. By subscribing to a set of demo-
> cratic procedures and values, individuals can reconcile their right to
> shape their own lives with their need to belong to a community.
> (Ignatieff 1993: 7)

For Habermas, the problem with this (as pointed out by Parekh above) is that
the interpretation of these democratic procedures and values enshrined in law
'cannot be ethically neutral' as they are situated 'within the historical context
of a legal community' (1994: 134). On the other hand, rights related to
'universal personhood', for example the European Convention on Human
Rights do, according to Straw, provide an ethical language that does not
belong to any particular group.[3] The problem is, as mentioned above, that 'a
proper human rights culture' discourse (see Chapter 5) and 'shared values –
new Britishness' discourses, above have rarely intersected in recent years. For
example, human rights did not feature in Blair or Brown's recent speeches on
the new Britishness in 2006. The reason for this, according to Gearty, is that
anxiety about terrorism has gripped public discourse exactly at the same time
as human rights 'has at last been securing centre-stage' (2006: 106); terrorism
and human rights, according to Gearty, 'are strong rivals for the same public
space' (2006: 106). 'Human rights respecting administrations' such as the
Labour Government, according to Gearty, have since 9/11 launched draconian attacks on 'the basic DNA of human rights – dignity, legality and
democracy' (2006: 107) while also enacting the Human Rights Act 1998 and
are working hard to establish the new Commission of Equality and Human
Rights (2006: 107). As a result contemporary Britain is defined by the tension
between two processes: the creation of a human rights culture and a backlash
against human rights.

  Protection is at the heart of these processes: the protection of the rights of
'vulnerable (sometimes unpopular) minorities' and the protection of rights of
'the law-abiding majority'. With regard to the latter, much effort has been
expended on overcoming 'the damaging myths' surrounding the Human
Rights Act by the Department for Constitutional Affairs and the Joint Commission on Human Rights. For example, the Department for Constitutional
Affairs suggest that with regard to the media's reporting on the Human Rights
Act 'too much attention has been paid to individual rights at the expense of
the interests of the wider community' (Department for Constitutional Affairs
2006: 1). The Department for Constitutional Affairs and the Joint Committee
on Human Rights (2006b) have both called for a re-education of the public as
to the benefits of the Human Rights Act (Department for Constitutional
Affairs 2006: 42). For the Joint Committee on Human Rights, the Human
Rights Act has an important role to play in protecting the rights of 'unpopular
minorities and vulnerable or marginalised groups ... but we also think that

there is a danger that the ways in which the Act benefits ordinary people in their everyday lives ... does not attract the same public attention ... we think the legitimacy of the human rights machinery in the eyes of the public depends on this part of the picture also being known' (Joint Committee on Human Rights 2006b: Para. 75).

The tension between 'special rights' and the rights of 'ordinary people' has resulted in calls to rebalance human rights and to reinterpret the Human Rights Act so as to deprioritize the rights of protected groups (see Chapter 5) and terrorists in order to prioritize public security (Department for Constitutional Affairs 2006: 39). Terrorism is joined here by other tensions associated with, for example, balancing the human rights of those in prison with the human rights of the general public. The right of the general public to be protected from 'dangerous criminals' has come to public attention through the media's reporting of specific cases, for example, the murder of Naomi Bryant by Anthony Rice (who had been released from a life sentence) in 2004. According to the Chief Inspector of Probation, Andrew Bridges's conclusions on the case of Anthony Rice are that, 'the people managing this case started to allow its public perception considerations to be undermined by its human rights considerations' (Lea 2005: 1). The public furore resulting from cases such as this has resulted in the Home Office's pledge to 'build a Criminal Justice System which puts protection of the law-abiding majority at its heart' (Blair, in Department for Constitutional Affairs 2006: Foreword). It is in this context that Tony Blair stated in his speech entitled 'We are the change-makers' in September 2005 that:

> Our primary duty should be to allow law-abiding people to live in safety. It means a complete change of thinking. It doesn't mean abandoning human rights. It means deciding whose come first.
>
> (Blair 2005: 31–2)

Counter-terrorism is clearly central to this tension between individual rights and the rights of the law-abiding majority. According to the Department for Constitutional Affairs, the problem with human rights in contemporary Britain is associated with key decision-takers 'getting the balance wrong by placing undue emphasis upon the entitlement of individuals' (2006: 39) with the result being that judges in British courts, as well as judges sitting in the European Court of Human Rights[4] have being paying insufficient regard to 'the overarching importance of a State's duty to maintain public security under Article 2 of the European Convention on Human Rights' (Department for Constitutional Affairs 2006: 39). The recommendation made by the Department for Constitutional Affairs was that the Government should consider using the Human Rights Act to effect a rebalancing (within Britain's margin of appreciation) in the way Article 2 (the right to life) is applied in relation to other Articles (2006: 39)[5]; this is explored further below.

The calls to strike a new balance between individual rights and public security is just one of a series of reflexive rebalancing process, as noted in the Introduction of this book, observable in contemporary Britain (Zedner 2005: 508). This emphasis on public security in the rebalancing human rights discourse that has emerged since 9/11 and has gathered pace since 7/7 is potentially further reaching than some of the other rebalancing discourses encountered in previous chapters.

Lord Falconer stipulated in his Royal United Services Institute speech in the series *Legislating for terrorism* that in order to defeat terrorism 'policy must come first, the law second' (2007: 2). He elaborates: 'By this I mean that whilst the response must be lawful the policy-makers not the lawyers must determine that response ... ' (Lord Falconer 2007: 2).[6]

Lord Falconer was adamant that the Human Rights Act should not be regarded as a straitjacket that limits 'our ability to defend ourselves'; rather, 'human rights and the Human Rights Act are essential in identifying, defining and protecting the values that we must put to the forefront of the struggle against terrorism' (2007: 2). However, Lord Falconer is advocating a re-prioritization of human rights and specific aspects of the European Convention, namely Article 2, in order to better equip the State in the fight against terrorism, that is:

> the first duty of Government is to protect its citizens. And faced with new and changing threats the Government must develop its response. New steps must be taken in order to meet these changing circumstances and to continue to provide protection to the public. But in doing so, there must be a strategy. A strategy that must be driven by what will provide public protection.
>
> (Lord Falconer 2007: 3)

This prioritization of public protection (driven by the executive) over the rights of the individual (protected by the judiciary) does carry some risks. Lord Falconer, above, is engaging directly with what Ignatieff describes as the question as to what role human rights should play in deciding public policy during terrorist emergencies (2005: viii). Ignatieff reminds us that most human rights conventions, including the European Convention on Human Rights, allow for the derogation or suspension of some rights in times of emergency (2005: ix). Ignatieff suggests that the danger associated with such actions is they can compromise the status of human rights as a set of unchanging benchmarks (2005: ix). In many ways 'the changing circumstances' associated with 'the terrorism threat', which has resulted in the declaration of a national state of emergency, can jeopardize some of the 'core', 'shared values' associated with the new Britishness-civic nationalism discourse: especially if one considers that one of the key 'core British values' is 'obedience to the rule of law' (Blair, in Department for Constitutional Affairs 2006: 3). Ignatieff's two rhetorical questions associated with a 'state of emergency' are helpful here:

> How can the rule of law be maintained if law can be suspended as necessity dictates? How can the effectiveness of human rights as a guarantee of dignity be sustained, if rights are suspended in emergency?
>
> (Ignatieff 2005: 26)

My interest in terrorist legislation and derogation applications is not with regard to the legality of the latter[7] but rather focuses on the impact of abridging, suspending, circumventing and rebalancing human rights on the wider projects of establishing 'shared values', 'integration' and 'winning hearts and minds' that have been explored in various chapters throughout this book. The rebalancing of human rights protections away from the rights of the individual to prioritize public security is an example of what Ignatieff calls the logic of 'the lesser evil' (see Chapter 1). The logic of the lesser evil is associated with the willingness of a State to sacrifice the interests of a minority of its own people (for example, terror suspects) on the condition that this action guarantees an increase in security to the majority (2005: 87). This comes down to (as observed in Chapters 1 and 2) striking a balance between 'our' security and 'their' liberty, of sacrificing the rights of the many over the rights of the few (Dworkin 2003).

By rebalancing human rights in this way, the anomaly of emergency measures could fast become a turning point (Mamdani 2005: 2003) in which human rights, which prior to this point have been associated with the protection of the weak, the vulnerable and the marginalized, that is, the 'people who need human rights protection the most' (Gearty 2006: 5) will become associated with the protection of the rights of 'the law-abiding'. This is no bad thing, on the one hand, but when the process of rebalancing human rights is placed, on the other hand, in the context of the governmental attack on Muslim dissent (through vaguely construed unacceptable behaviour prohibitions associated with equally vague definitions of terrorism) and in the context of the Islamophobic turn in the new Britishness discourse, where the right to call oneself British comes down to whether one shares 'our essential values', this is a worrying development. For Gearty, the supposed lack of conflict between counter-terrorism laws and human rights (see Lord Falconer above) is an ominous development that flows from the redefinition of human rights, the effect of which is to excuse repression as necessary to prevent the destruction of human rights values (2006: 108). As a result of this 'dangerous embrace' between counter-terrorism laws and human rights: 'messing about aggressively with people, suspending the ordinary processes of law, narrowing the civic space so as to exclude alternative points of view all turn out to be okay from a human rights perspective' (Gearty 2006: 108). Gearty's parting shot in his book is to reassert what he sees as the emancipatory ideal of human rights:

> it should always be on the side of the underdog, perpetually trying to force an invisible individual or group of individuals into public view, giving them a language with which to shout for attention, and then having secured it to demand an end to suffering and a better set of life-chances.
>
> (Gearty 2006: 157)

However, the new human rights discourse that is emerging in post-7/7 Britain is a radical reversal of Gearty's description of an Esperanto of the virtuous, and of Jack Straw's 'ethical language which doesn't belong to any particular group or creed, but to all of us' (1999: 5). Instead, human rights have become distorted by the 'good and evil' discourse of the war on terrorism (see Chapter 2), which divides humanity into two basic types: good and bad humans (Gearty 2006: 136). The co-option of human rights into security discourse has resulted, for Gearty, in the single greatest disastrous legacy of the war on terror from a human rights point of view; 'the supersession of the criminal model based on justice and due process by a security model that is based on fear and suspicion' (2006: 137). In the following passage, the Council of Europe's Human Rights Commissioner Alvaro Gil-Robles incorporated a timely reminder in his report on human rights in Britain:

> It is perhaps worth emphasising that human rights are not a pick and mix assortment of luxury entitlements, but the very foundation of democratic societies. As such, their violation affects not just the individual concerned, but society as a whole; we exclude one person from their enjoyment at the risk of excluding all of us.
>
> (Gil-Robles 2005: 5)

It should be no surprise then that Gordon Brown and Tony Blair did not include human rights in their pronouncements on Britishness, patriotism and duty. As Jack Straw pointed out in his speech in 1999, human rights 'provide a common set of values to help unite a diverse society' (1999: 5); they 'provide an evolving ethic which establishes rights and responsibilities for all' (Klug 2000: 139); they are the 'universal values of human and democratic rights that all communities share' (Kundnani 2006: 2). Moreover, the broader human rights framework promised by the CEHR could encourage a more comprehensive and principled approach to tackling the problem of terrorism by the reduction of social exclusion, inequality and discrimination (Blick et al. 2006: 67).[8] Unfortunately, it is human rights that are most under attack in the 'war on terror' and as a result it is little wonder that the Government 'prefers to look elsewhere for common denominators to bind society' (Kundnani 2006: 2). That being said, there is evidence of a convergence of the new Britishness, new security and new human rights discourses under Gordon Brown. Within a few weeks of Gordon Brown taking office, the *Governance of Britain* Green Paper was published by Jack Straw in his role as the new Secretary of State for Justice and Lord Chancellor. The last chapter of this Green Paper entitled 'Britain's future: the citizen and the state' introduced the topic of a British Bill of Rights, or more accurately a British Bill of Rights and Duties. Once again, multiple identities were employed in this Green Paper to separate out the different weights between the different components of 'our' identities in order to promote our meta-allegiance as citizens of the State:

> Each of us possesses multiple identities because we define ourselves in different ways depending on the factors that matter most to us. Factors such as gender, race, ethnicity, age, disability, class and faith are shared with some and different from others. But in addition to these there is a national identity that we can all hold in common: the overarching factor – British citizenship – that brings the nation together.
> (*Governance of Britain* Green Paper 2007: 53)

The final chapter of this Green Paper can be described as an advertisement for the forthcoming debate on British citizenship and 'common British values' that will take the form of a series of discussion documents and materials to inform this national debate (2007: 59). This is to be 'a process of developing a British statement of values' through 'a range of engagement methods' that are intended to promote 'dialogue with the people of Britain and between the people of Britain' in order to facilitate 'a fuller articulation of British values' (2007: 59). The authoritarian tone associated with the acceptance of compulsory, indisputable shared values found in Blair's speech (see above) are fully present in the Green Paper, as is the trumping of multiple allegiances and identities by 'our' identity as British citizens:

> It is important to be clearer about what it means to be British, what it means to be part of British society and, crucially, to be resolute in making the point that what comes with that is a set of values which have not just to be shared but also accepted. There is room to celebrate multiple and different identities, but none of these identities

should take precedence over the core democratic values that define what it means to be British.

(*Governance of Britain* Green Paper 2007: 57)

The initial discussion with regard to the potential Bill of Rights and Duties in the Green Paper is significant in terms of the strategy of rebalancing human rights explored above. According to the Green Paper, a Bill of Rights and Duties will provide explicit recognition that human rights come with responsibilities and must be exercised in a way that respects the human rights of others (2007: 61). It was further stipulated that the Government recognizes:

> the importance which must attach to public safety and ensuring that Government agencies accord appropriate priority to protection of the public when balancing rights. A Bill of Rights and Duties might provide a means of giving greater clarity and legislative force to this commitment.
>
> (*Governance of Britain* Green Paper 2007: 57)

What this statement suggests is that the Government under Gordon Brown will be pushing forward the convergence of anti-terrorism legislation, authoritarian shared values and Britishness discourses with an emergent human rights culture that prioritizes 'public security'. By so doing the new Government under Brown, like their predecessors, have chosen to bind themselves to the people 'through fear rather than hope' through 'the politics of a phoney Britishness rather than a genuine universalism' (Kundnani 2007: 7).

Conclusion

Gearty's predictions are becoming a reality. There is evidence of a securitization of human rights in the *Governance of Britain* Green Paper that is converging with the shifting authoritarian integration discourses around shared values, loyalties and duties in contemporary Britain. In many ways the discursive battle that has been waging across all the chapters contained in this book can be described as a Government-derived battle over identity that is being driven by the Government's recent security, integration, cohesion and citizenship strategies. As noted in previous chapters, the discourse of multiple, complex and intersectional identities appears in numerous places in this book; for example, in the CICC's interim statement and final report, in the Green and White Papers associated with the CEHR and in the *Governance of Britain* Green Paper introduced by Gordon Brown and Jack Straw. These

perspectives on identity have been used as a weapon against the alleged rei-
fication of fixed and discrete identities under 'multiculturalism'. At the same
time these discourses of fragmented identities have been used to promote
particular ways of being 'British first' through attempting to establish a
'master identity' in the form of 'our' British citizenship underwritten by 'our'
acceptance of 'our' shared 'British' values and duties.

This is more than just the desire to transform the social capital habits of
local communities (see Chapter 4). This is an assimilationist project with an
authoritarian edge, legitimized by a convergence of Government-derived
discourses justified through a politics of insecurity (Huysmans 2006). This
politics of insecurity that is legitimized by 'insecurity minimizing' discourses
(see Afterword) such as 'we need to give up a little freedom to protect freedom' is made possible by a politics of fear. If the *Governance of Britain* Green
Paper is any indication, the relationship between rights and duties will continue to shift in favour of duties under Gordon Brown. In many ways New
Labour has been influenced by Etzioni's communitarian reassertion of duty
and responsibility (see Chapter 4). However, it is becoming increasingly
obvious that New Labour have not followed Etzioni's observation that individuals abide by and are committed to a set of core values because they
believe in them rather than being forced to comply with them (Etzioni 1997:
12). Tony Blair's 'duty to integrate' is part of a tradition that has increasingly
placed duty before rights. This tradition was established in Tony Blair's
Labour Party Conference speech in 1997, where he stated that 'a decent
society is not actually based on rights. It is based on duty. Our duty to each
other' (Blair, in Klug 2000: 61). The problem is both the compulsory shared
values and duties discourses and the salutary intentions of the post-9/11 anti-
terrorism laws could be somewhat counterproductive. They could very well
exclude and radicalize the very people that they are intended to include and
control, that is, young Muslims. The convergence of compulsory values, the
rebalancing of duties over rights combined with counterproductive anti-
terrorism legislation that has created 'communities of suspicion' could very
well create, as Biling et al. suggest, new outsiders who are unable to fully and
unquestioningly accept British values as dictated by the State.

Afterword

Has multiculturalism had its day? Have we reached the end of multiculturalism? Well, yes and no. Blunkett's civic assimilationism and Blair and Brown's civic nationalisms' projects are indeed the dominant discourses that shape the new 'common-sense', 'practical' approaches to integration in contemporary Britain. I have suggested that we have entered into a phase of reflexive multiculturalism in which the term 'multiculturalism' has been driven underground, while some of the strategies associated with multiculturalism continue to influence policy and practices at the 'local' level (see Chapter 4). However, I also suggest that in debates on citizenship and Britishness, multiculturalism is under sustained attack (see Chapter 6). The conclusion we can draw from this is that the principles of multiculturalism endure at the 'local level' (however, the term itself has, or is becoming, taboo). In 'national level debates', however, Britain has entered an authoritarian 'anti-multiculturalism' period in which multiple identities, loyalties and allegiances are both being problematized and deployed in order to facilitate 'our' primary identification as British citizens who must accept British values above all else. At the level of these national debates we will see attempts to 'soften' these strategies through employing terms such as 'shared futures' (as invoked by the Commission on Integration and Community Cohesion, see Chapter 4). However, 'we' should be under no illusion that the 'shared values' that allegedly provide the foundation for 'our shared futures' will be dictated by political exigencies in which ensuring public safety will be the first and foremost priority.

In the Preface and Introduction of this book I stated that the emergence of hostility to multiculturalism and the associated new integration discourses could not be examined without considering the impact of terrorism, or more accurately the impact of the response to 'the terror threat' on contemporary British society. The 'war on terror' in general and the specific 'war on extremism' that has unfolded in Britain has resulted (as noted in Chapter 2) in the re-emergence of seemingly archaic terms in public discourse, for example, loyalty, allegiance and treason. The latter are associated with the fear of the inner enemies, fifth columnists and suspect communities that exist within Muslim communities in Britain. These discourses and the range of anti-terrorism laws that have been introduced in response to the terror threat since 2001 have ushered in a new ethics of inhospitability and an even stronger sense of the precariousness and conditional nature of citizenship for certain communities. This has in turn influenced the new integration discourses and has undermined the possibility of a 'proper' human rights culture emerging in British society.

Security is becoming the dominant discourse in contemporary Britain. Securitization is taking the form of institutional reflexivity driven by the desire to minimize insecurity and maximize security. The politics of insecurity and fear explored in the previous chapters must be placed in its institutional context. In many ways this book is an exploration of the institutional reflexivity associated with the unintended consequences, the side-effects, the dangers or the 'bads' (Lash 1994b: 198, 200) associated with super diversity. The reflexive processes of minimizing insecurity and risk have underwritten what Burnett and Whyte refer to as the new terrorism hegemony (see Chapter 2). Insecurity minimization has legitimized the introduction of the post-9/11 and post-7/7 anti-terrorism laws in Britain. At the same time insecurity minimization also structures and justifies the new integration discourses that emerged in response to the episodes of social disorder in Oldham, Burnley and Bradford in 2001. The various chapters of this book have examined the responses to 'insecurity', whether this has taken the form of the desire to eradicate terror suspects from British soil by deportation (see Chapter 1) or the attempts to stifle debate in the name of eradicating extremist ideas (see Chapter 2); or in the risk consciousness evident in a number of areas of public policy, for example, community cohesion, integration, 'race' equality (see Chapter 4) and creating unity for an unpredictable future through promoting a 'proper human rights culture' (see Chapter 5). The latter are as much associated with Government-derived discourses associated with the reduction of communal antagonisms and reducing radicalization as they are simultaneous with the search for elusive unifying 'shared values'.

I agree with many of the commentators (see Chapters 1 and 2) who have suggested that the greater threat to democracy does not come from terrorism but from the West's response to terrorism. I will suggest that it is human rights rather than democracy *per se* that is most under threat from 'the war on terror'. Dworkin is correct when he says that it is not all of 'our' human rights that are under threat since 9/11 but rather the rights of certain members of Muslim communities in the West. It is a fact that anti-terrorism laws and the Islamophobic flavour of media and political discourses since 9/11 have impacted negatively upon Muslim communities in the USA and in Britain and this has in turn amplified their sense of insecurity.

However, I think the greater damage to human rights as a result of 'the war on terror' has been on the possibility of introducing a proper human rights culture whereby 'human and democratic rights' (Kundnani 2007: 9) rather than particularly 'British' values can be promoted as the fundamental shared values to galvanize the nation. That being said there are signs, as indicated in the last chapter, that a new human rights culture is emerging in contemporary Britain. The problem is this is a human rights culture has been co-opted by security. This securitization of human rights will transform human rights discourse and practice. This will be achieved through the process of re-prioritizing human rights to grant the greatest protection to the greatest number. Rather than the terrorist's and criminal's charter, Human Rights could be radically modified in the process of establishing a new British Bill of Rights and Duties (see Chapter 6), which could codify the authoritarian shared values discourse and securitization of human rights in the name of public protection above the protections afforded to individuals. The combination of this reflexive human rights culture (and associated anti-terrorism legislation) with the new assimilationist integration strategies could well result in the emergence of a new Britain founded on a set of non-negotiable 'British' values legitimized by the doctrine of the lesser evil. Rather than an inclusive concept of citizenship (see Chapter 4), what is on offer here is an exclusive concept of citizenship complete with new compulsory membership norms and a new order of inhospitability.

Notes

Introduction

[1]   The process whereby events become 'key' is highly 'selective'; for example, one would think that the disturbances in Lozelles, Birmingham on 22 and 23 October 2005 would have become a key event. It wasn't only the newspapers who have gone extraordinarily quiet (very quickly) with regard to these disturbances. The Government has also been rather quiet on this event. There has certainly not been a Government or quasi-Government review of the events like the ones that followed the disturbances in Oldham, Burnley and Bradford in 2001. The major difference between the events in Lozelles and earlier disturbances in Brixton, and in Bradford, according to Cole, was the sheer scale of the event. The Lozelles disturbances were of a smaller scale in terms of the numbers involved and the damage caused. However, the striking difference that emerged in Lozelles in contrast to the other examples of social unrest was that the Lozelles disturbances were a violent conflict between black and Asian communities (Cole 2005: 1). This was an intra-ethnic 'race riot', rather than a disturbance involving ethnic minority youths and white neighbours and police. The disturbances were ignited by allegations that a young black girl was raped by a group of Asian men (BBC News 2005a: 1).

[2]   These events were described by Joppke as marking the beginning of the Labour Government's move 'beyond multiculturalism' (Joppke 2004: 251).

[3]   There is no such thing as a single monolithic Muslim community in Britain. The 1.6 million Muslims in Britain which constitute 3 per cent of the British population, are remarkably diverse in terms of ethnicity, generation, British-born or new immigrant, birthplace and class (Blick et al. 2006: 18).

[4]   For example, in a speech delivered in 2006, Gordon Brown stated after 7/7 that:

> In effect the Treasury itself had to become a department for security. For as Chancellor I have found myself immersed in measures designed to cut off the sources of terrorist finance. And I have discovered that this will require an international operation using modern methods of forensic accounting as imaginative and path breaking in our times as the achievement of the enigma code breakers at Bletchley Park more than half a century ago. And I have found that it is not just the Treasury that is a department of security. So too is almost every other department.
>
> (Brown 2006a: 1)

At the same time certain Government departments are being reorganized in order to better focus on 'security'. For example, it was announced in March 2007 that the Home Office will be further divided into the Ministry of Justice (focusing on probation, prisons, prevention and reoffending) while the Home Office will exclusively focus on terrorism, security and immigration (Shaw 2007: 1).

5   At least four of these 'investigations' or consultation strategies were introduced in Britain between 2001 and 2007. They are examined in Chapter 4.

6   Parekh makes the useful distinction between multiculturalist and multiculturalism. According to Parekh, the former is a society that includes two or more cultural communities, that is 'multicultural 'refers to the fact of cultural diversity', whereas the term multiculturalism is the normative response to that fact (2000b: 6).

7   The current backlash against 'multiculturalism' is certainly wide ranging, but it is inaccurate to say that the backlash from those on the left of the political divide is sudden considering the anti-racist critiques of, for example, multicultural education practices in the 1980s and early 1990s in Britain (for example, Brandt 1986; Troyna 1987, 1993; Gillborn 1990, 1995; Troyna and Hatcher 1992). Anti-racists accused multicultural education policies of reifying culture and cultural differences while failing to address the central issues of structural racism in the education system (May 1999: 2). But it should be noted that the British brand of 'official multiculturalism' has always been *laissez-faire,* de-centred and only instituted in some branches of Government, especially at Local Government level (Joppke 2004: 249). Joppke reminds us that British Governments in the past (for example, the Conservatives under Thatcher) have repudiated multiculturalism or at best ignored it (2004: 249). Thus, multiculturalism as an ideology influencing public policy has been for a number of decades rather patchy.

8   These strategic texts fall within Kooiman's definition of formal and informal instruments. The examples of strategic texts that Rose includes are: the manifestos of political parties, Government documents such as Green Papers, White Papers and the reports of Commissions of Enquiry, all those texts 'which analyse particular difficulties and propose remedies' (1999: xxii). In this book a number of these strategic texts are analysed including consultation documents, reports, court proceedings, pressure group and think-tank reports across a number of Government, Parliamentary, Judicial, non-government organizations (NGOs) and journalistic interpretations of events and commentary on strategic texts and associated strategies.

Chapter 1

[1] Britain was the only European Union (EU) Member State to opt for derogation from Article 5 after 9/11.

[2] The Terrorism Act 2000 was described by the European Commission in their proposal for a Council Framework Decision (on Combating Terrorism) after 9/11 'as the largest piece of terrorist legislation in the EU Member States' (European Commission 2001: 7).

[3] According to Hillyard, in Northern Ireland internment was accompanied by the 'torture' of a select number of internees (2006: 6). This torture involved what Ewing and Gearty describe as the 'five techniques': wall-standing, hooding, continuous noise, deprivation of food and deprivation of sleep (1990: 211).

[4] According to Gearty, the Prevention of Terrorism Act 1974 allowed the authorities to exclude British citizens from Britain and restrict them to Northern Ireland if the Home Secretary (and not a court) decided that such persons have 'been concerned in the commission, preparation, or instigation of acts of terrorism connected with Northern Ireland' (1991: 144).

[5] The Government, fuelled by the tabloids, has been trying to rid Britain of foreign and dual-national 'inner enemies' such as Abu Hamza (the tabloid-coined 'hook-handed' Muslim 'hate cleric') from British soil. In fact, the Nationality, Immigration and Asylum Act 2002, which strengthened the Home Secretary's powers to revoke citizenship from people with dual nationality (Branigan 2003: 1), has been referred to as the 'Abu Hamza law' by commentators in Britain, in that this legislation was thought to have been specially developed just to rid Britain of this 'extremist' individual (Hayes 20006: 52).

[6] DEMOS, in its *Bringing it Home* report, suggest that Al-Qaeda had been building its base in Britain for 15 years prior to 9/11, and that London was one of the main global hubs, evidenced by the fact that between 1996 and 1998 nearly one-fifth of the calls from Osama Bin Laden's mobile phone were to mobile phones in Britain (DEMOS 2006: 1). According to DEMOS, the Government's policy of 'active appeasement', which enabled Al-Qaeda to put down strong roots in Britain (2006: 1) has been transformed into their current war on extremism in response to the events of 11 September 2001.

[7] The Council of Europe's Human Rights Commissioner is of this opinion:

> The inability to return foreigners suspected of being involved in international terrorism to their countries of origin owing to their risk of torture they face there was one of the reasons behind the introduction of the Anti-terrorism, Crime & Security Act in 2001
>
> (Gil-Robles 2005: Para. 28)

8 Karamjit Singh Chahal (an Indian national and Sikh separatist) who was resident in Britain was suspected by the Home Secretary of being involved in terrorist activities in support of the Sikh separatist cause in India. The Home Secretary wished to deport Chahal; however, Chahal claimed that if he was returned to India he would be tortured by the authorities because of his support of Sikh separatism (House of Commons Constitutional Affairs Committee 2005: Para. 46).

9 According to the Constitutional Affairs Committee, one of the complaints made by Chahal to the European Court of Human Rights was that although judicial review was available to challenge the Home Secretary's decision to deport him, the effective determination of his risk to national security was made by an internal Home Office advisory panel on the basis of sensitive intelligence material that he had no opportunity to challenge for two reasons: (1) the evidence presented regarding the risk to national security was precluded from disclosure by public interest immunity; and (2) he was not entitled to any form of legal representation before the panel (House of Commons Constitutional Affairs Committee 2005: Para. 46).

10 The SIAC Act was further amended in 2005 under the Prevention of Terrorism Act where the use of special advocate procedures will be transferred to the High Court for cases involving control orders (House of Commons Constitutional Affairs Committee 2005: 3).

11 *A, X, Y and Others* v. *Home Secretary* [2004] EWCA Civ 1123 [2005] 1 WLR 414.

12 To date seven foreign nationals have been deported from Britain on the grounds of national security (six to Algeria and one to France). It was reported on *Newsnight* on BBC 2 on 26 February 2007 that the man thought to be Al-Qaeda's spiritual leader in Europe, Abu Qatada, will be deported from Britain to Jordan after the SIAC had accepted the memorandum of understanding from Jordan. However, two Libyan terror suspects (known as DD and AS) have won their 'deportation appeal' in front of the SIAC in April 2007, despite the SIAC ruling that both DD and AS were a threat to national security, as the SIAC ruled that the appellants risked being tortured or executed if returned to Libya. This case was described as the first real test of the diplomatic agreement with Libya that was set up to allow the removal of terror suspects to their country of origin without breaching their human rights (Sturcke 2007: 1).

13 Žižek sites Jonathan Alter's post-9/11 *Newsweek* column 'Time to think about torture' on 5 November 2001 as epitomizing the logic of the lesser evil, in which Alter stated 'we can't legalize torture; it's contrary to American values. But even as we continue to speak out against human rights abuses around the world, we need to keep an open mind about certain measures to fight terrorism' (Žižek 2002: 102). See also Dershowitz's (2004) article 'Should the ticking bomb terrorist be tortured?: A case study in how a democracy should make tragic choices'.

Chapter 2

[1]   The *ummah* is an Islamic internationalism (Yaqoob 2007: 280). Birt defines the *ummatic* as the attachment Muslim feel to their fellow believers (2005: 109) who form the imagined global Muslim nation – the global community of Muslims – (Modood 2006: 46). According to Birt these attachments can vary according to ethnic, sectarian, national and generational proclivities (2005: 109).

[2]   This was further exacerbated by the realization by Muslim communities in Britain that existing blasphemy laws did not protect all religious groups equally (McGhee 2005a).

[3]   There is nothing necessarily new about this. At the Lord Mayor's annual banquet in the Guildhall in November 1988 Mrs Thatcher had the following to say about her Government's legislative response to terrorism connected with Northern Ireland:

> We do sometimes have to sacrifice a little of the freedom we cherish in order to defend ourselves from those whose aim is to destroy that freedom altogether – and that is a decision we should not be afraid to take because in a battle against terrorism we shall never give in. The only victory will be our victory: the victory of democracy and a free society.
>
> (Ewing and Gearty 1990: 209)

[4]   There is some evidence to support this assertion in Britain. In its October 2006 survey The 1990 Trust reported that 81 per cent of the Muslims questioned believed that the war on terror is a war on Islam (2006: 5).

[5]   It should be noted that reflexivity in the face of an alleged unprecedented threat from 'the new terrorism' is not a British Home Secretary's preserve. For example, a similar reflexivity in the face of the new terrorism threat can be found in the European Commission's Council Framework Decision (on Combating Terrorism) presented a few days after 9/11. According to the European Commission 'modern day terrorism' should be contrasted with the 'terrorist acts of the past' in that 'the actual or potential impact of armed attacks is increasingly devastating and lethal' and as a result of 'the profound changes in the nature of terrorist offences ... the inadequacy of traditional forms of judicial and police cooperation in combating it' is highlighted (2001: 3).

[6]   This strategy of eradicating 'Muslim extremist' is not unique to Britain. See Liz Fekete's article 'Speech crime' and deportation cases for a link to a table of cases (across the EU) in which foreign nationals have been deported from EU countries after breaching new citizenship and residence rights measures that constrain freedom of speech (Fekete 2005b).

[7]   Section 56 of the Immigration, Asylum and Nationality Act lowers the

threshold for the removal of British citizenship by replacing one of the existing criteria with a new power to deprive where such action is held by the Home Secretary not to be 'conducive to the public good' (HM Government 2006: Annex A).

8   It is not accurate to say that the 7/7 bombers were working under the radar. The cross-party Intelligence and Security Committee (ISC) found 'intelligence gaps' in the security services' monitoring of the potential terrorist threat to Britain prior to 7/7 (Batty 2006: 1). It has come to light that two of the men (Mohammad Siddique Khan and Shazad Tanweer) involved in the 7/7 bombings had been under surveillance by MI5 for a year before carrying out their attacks. Subsequent to this report the BBC published the transcript of a conversation bugged by MI5 between Omar Khyam, the now jailed ringleader of the fertilizer bomb plot, and Mohammad Sidique Khan, one of the 7/7 bombers. The conversation took place on 21 February 2004 in Khyam's car that MI5 had bugged (BBC News 2007a: 1). The result of all of this is that the survivors and relatives of victims of the 7/7 attacks have begun to step up the pressure for a public inquiry into MI5's handling of the intelligence (BBC News 2007b: 1)

9   The 'dual-national ontological insecurity' that could be unleashed by this legislation should not be underestimated. For example, Bill Morris, General Secretary of the Transport and General Workers' Union, said of the Nationality, Immigration and Asylum Act 2002: 'after nearly 50 years residency in Britain, doing my bit for Queen and country, including national service ... I feel a sense of fear and insecurity as someone with dual citizenship' (Morris, in Branigan 2003: 1).

Chapter 3

1   The Home Affairs Committee is one of a number of departmental Select Committees appointed by the House of Commons to examine expenditure, administration and policy of the Home Office, Attorney General's Office and the Crown Prosecution Service, and so on. John Denham chairs the Committee that consists of 13 mostly Labour and Conservative MPs. Blick et al. describe the Home Affairs Committee as the 'lead' committee on counter-terrorism policy, although other select committees may also investigate aspects of counter-terrorism, for example, Defence, Foreign Affairs, Science and Technology and the Joint Committee on Human Rights (2006: 61). At the same time, the Intelligence and Security Committee, whose members are appointed by the Prime Minister, has the exclusive remit for scrutiny of the work of the intelligence and security agencies (Blick et al. 2006: 32).

2   This suggestion was made before the Cabinet reshuffle in 2006 where some of the responsibilities of the Home Office, for example in relation to community

cohesion, was allocated to the new Communities and Local Government Department.

3   The House of Commons Foreign Affairs Committee was adamant that dialogue on terrorism was essential, regardless that such discussions could sometimes be difficult (2005: 49). The Committee found the attitudes of some (former) Home Office Ministers, especially Hazel Blears, in relation to engaging the members of Muslim communities in a discussion about terrorism, problematic. Blears suggested that:

> In terms of engagement with the community, it is quite difficult to go and have a discussion about terrorism ... I think it needs to be a broader conversation than simply about terror threat because anybody just having a conversation about that is going to find it quite difficult.
>
>   (Blears, in House of Commons Home Affairs Committee 2005: 37)

4   This has resulted in a number of initiatives across Europe, especially in France and the Netherlands. Perhaps the best example in Britain is the pilot programme launched to develop a management and leadership qualification for Imams. This programme has been developed by the Learning Skills Council in conjunction with the Home Office and 'the Muslim Community' (Inside Employment Studies 2005: 3).

5   Figures that emerge from the Ethnic Minorities and Labour Market Strategy Unit's report (2003) suggest that black and minority ethnic communities have a higher proportion of young people under 25 and that black and other ethnic minority people are projected to account for over half of the growth in Britain's working-age population over the next decade (Home Office 2004b: 4). In relation to Muslim groups in Britain 38 per cent of the Bangladeshi community and 35 per cent of the Pakistani community are under 16; the equivalent figure for the majority white group is 19 per cent (House of Commons Home Affairs Committee 2005: 22).

6   There are a number of studies that have suggested that 'a large proportion of British Muslims form an underclass' (Birt 2006a: 1). For example, according to the Commission on British Muslims and Islamophobia (CBMI), Pakistani and Bangladeshi communities have much lower employment rates and higher unemployment rates than national averages (for example, 9.1 per cent of Pakistani men aged between 16–74 are unemployed, and 10.2 per cent of all Bangladeshi men between the ages of 16–74 are unemployed) (CBMI 2004: 30). The CBMI also state that even when Muslim men were in employment their average earnings were 68 per cent of that taken home by non-Muslims (2004: 30). According to the Home Affairs Committee, Muslims are also subject to other disadvantages besides disproportionate rates of unemployment; for example, they are largely concentrated in areas of multiple deprivation, living in 'unfit' dwellings and experience disproportionate rates of

illness and disability and means-tested benefit dependence (House of Commons Home Affairs Committee 2005: 23). It is important to note that this 'racial underclass' (Modood 1992: 261) is not a recent phenomenon that has emerged out of nowhere since the late 1990s. Modood informs us that throughout the Labour Force Surveys of the 1980s Pakistanis and Bangladeshis suffered the highest rates of unemployment, had the lowest number of educational qualifications and the highest profile in manual labour (1992: 261).

7   Walzer is particularly dismissive of the suggestion from liberals and leftists in the aftermath of 9/11 that 'inequalities' were the root cause of international terrorism. According to Walzer this argument is false ' . . . for both domestic and global society, because otherwise terrorism would be far more widely dispersed than it is' (2004: 32).

8   Like the Home Affairs Committee, the 9/11 Commission stated that terrorism is not caused by poverty and that many terrorists come from relatively well-off families (The National Commission on the Terrorist Attacks Upon the United States 2004: 378).

9   This is not to say that the Committee did not adequately review other reports from other Government departments. They offered a wide-ranging and sympathetic review of Community Cohesion panel reports, ODPM reports, regional development agency reports and initiatives, as well as an analysis of Immigration and Asylum policy. They did not, however, as stated above, adequately review key Home Office reports and consultation exercises that are directly related to and further developed the recommendations made in the Cantle report.

10 According to Awan, one glaring commonality emerges when the biographies of those implicated in terrorist acts are examined: 'their political radicalisation, culminating in terrorism, is somehow inextricably linked to, or perhaps even contingent upon, the complex phenomenon of sudden or increasing religiosity' (2007: 208). Such transitional religiosity experiences, according to Awan, do not occur in a social vacuum, rather they are a product of an 'ambient social, cultural and political milieux' (2007: 211).

11 Booth and Dunne concur with the Home Affairs Committee's rejection of poverty as being the cause of radicalization when they dismiss explanations that suggest ' . . . that poverty itself breeds extremism' (2002: 9). Booth and Dunne also point out that Osama Bin Laden and Al-Qaeda do not belong to the poor of the Middle East; however, they suggest that they exploit the material dispossession of others for their own gains, that is, ' . . . they belong to an old tradition in which self-serving elites seize upon and manipulate the grievances of the poor' (2002: 9).

12 For example, it has come to light, after the 7/7 bombings, that one of the men involved, Mohammad Saddique Khan, gave an interview to the *Times Educational Supplement* in relation to his job as a learning mentor, in which he

expressed utter disdain at the lack of regeneration funds needed to raise Beeston, the area in Leeds where he lived, 'from its endemic squalor' (Awan 2007: 213).

[13] According to the 9/11 Commission, the combined gross domestic product of the 22 countries in the Arab League is less than the gross domestic profit (GDP) of Spain. Forty per cent of adult Arabs are illiterate (two-thirds of them women). One-third of all individuals living in the 'broader Middle East' live on less than two dollars a day (The National Commission on the Terrorist Attacks Upon the United States 2004: 376).

[14] This open letter to the Government condemned British foreign policy, especially in Iraq, and suggested a relationship between British foreign policy and extremism. The letter was signed by a number of MPs, three Muslim members of the House of Lords and nearly 40 Muslim community organizations (Temko 2006: 2).

[15] Margaret Beckett's dismissive comment here misrepresents the Foreign Office's efforts to combat radicalization. For example, the Foreign Office set up the Engaging with the Islamic World Group (EIWG) in September 2004 (Brighton 2007: 3). The EIWG has undertaken a range of activities at home and abroad including 'outreach work' designed to explain British foreign policy to domestic audiences as well as bolstering community-led projects to counter the ideological and theological underpinnings of the terrorist narrative (Brighton 2007: 3–4).

[16] The term 'frame' (or 'frame work') is borrowed from Goffman (Snow et al. 1986: 464).

[17] According to Yahya Birt, in the report from the seminar: *Anti-terrorism Laws: The Experience of the Irish and Muslim Communities in the UK* in 2006, a great many Muslims are mobilized through the Stop the War Coalition. Rather than being an exclusively 'Muslim' organization, the Stop the War campaign can be described as a Muslim and non-Muslim coalition. Birt suggests that in Birmingham it was the second generation of young British Muslims who mobilized the community (cutting across ethnic, sectarian and generational divides) through family networks and the mosques. Birt suggests that the involvement of Muslims in anti-war marches disproved the Islamophobic presumption that opposing the war meant sympathizing with terrorism, as many Britons opposed the war on terror as well (2006a: 6). In his summary of the seminar, Mac an Ghail suggested that the participation of Muslims in the anti-war movement was key in that 'Muslim communities have found new ways of engaging politically and making their voices heard' (2006: 8). Hart describes this type of political dissent as an example of 'peaceable radicalism' (2006: Para. 33).

[18] At the same time Balls told BBC Radio 4 that the 'war on terror' needed a 'cultural element'; this passage was quoted in the *Arab News*:

you can't fight against Islamic extremism simply by security ... we have
to win the battle over hearts and minds and persuade people in communities in Britain and around the world that the values of fairness,
stability and opportunity and turning away from extremism is the way to
go.

(Balls, in Parker 2007: 1)

[19] A national forum against extremism has been set up. This forum has been
created out of the membership of 12 Muslim organizations. At the same time
six regional forums are in the process of being set up that will bring together
members of Muslim communities, law enforcement agencies and other public
service agencies.

[20] At 4.00 a.m. on 2 June 2006 250 police officers raided two houses on
Landsdown Road in Forest Gate, East London with a warrant to search the
premises under the authority of the Terrorism Act 2000. This operation was
launched on the back of intelligence received from an unnamed informant
(*Guardian Unlimited* 2006: 1). During the operation two brothers were arrested
– Mohammed Abdulkahar, aged 23 and Abul Koyair, aged 20. The former
received a gunshot wound to his shoulder during the operation. Both
brothers were subsequently released without charge (BBC News 2006b: 1).

[21] Kelly is not alone in this activity. For example, the Muslim Public Affairs
Committee (MPAC) include the empowerment of youth and women in their
five-point action plan '5 things you can do to stop terror' (Muslim Public
Affairs Committee 2006). At the same time Tony Blair held a high-profile
meeting with Muslim women on 10 May 2006 at Downing Street: He said in
the closing remarks during this meeting 'we decided to have this engagement
because we wanted, really arising out of all the events in the past few years, to
have a different type of engagement with people ... until very recently, when
we met with the Muslim community, we would basically meet some very
identifiable and well known Muslims, mainly men ... ' (Blair 2006a: 1).
Moreover, one of the Preventing Extremism Together working groups was
specifically set up to address the issues of the engagement of Muslim women.
However, according to Zareen Roohi Ahmed, despite the commitment and
goodwill of the individuals involved, there has been no tangible outcome that
will change the predicament of Muslim women in Britain or enable them to
help solve the problems of young people becoming radicalized (Ahmed 2006:
5).

[22] The Muslim Council of Britain's study: *Voices from the Minarets* study found
that only 43 per cent of Mosques provide specific services for women; 32 per
cent have general women's facilities and 57 per cent report having separate
prayer facilities for women (Muslim Council of Britain 2006).

[23] It is worth noting that the cumulative marginalization of youth voices by
decision-makers and community leaders has been a staple of many of the

reports that emerged after the social disorder in Oldham, Burnley and Bradford in 2001 including the Cantle report (2001) and the Denham report (2002). According to the Preventing Extremism Together Working Groups' report 'young British Muslims face a double exclusion: from wider society and from conventional leadership roles within their own community' (2005: 13).

Chapter 4

1   This strategy consists of three components: the *Strength in Diversity* consultation strategy pamphlet; the *Strength in Diversity* consultation strategy toolkit; and a special *Strength in Diversity* consultation strategy pamphlet for young people.

2   Phillips insists that 'we' need to develop a 'modern highway code for multi-ethnic Britain' (2005: 9). Just as the highway code contains 'a set of rules of behaviour that allows us all to get along on the road without too many conflicts', Phillips suggests that a highway code for multi-ethnic Britain will 'reconcile respect for our common values and traditions with that of individual liberty' (2005: 8). This amounts to formalizing the 'unspoken rules, which are the equivalent of the Highway Code for our multiethnic society' (Phillips 2005: 9). In many ways Phillips's interpretation of these unspoken rules is an example of the civic assimilationist ambition (see below) of pushing 'the private' out of 'the public realm':

> We respect each others' ways of worshipping. We compromise on dress codes – what we wear at work may not be what we wear at home. And above all we use the English language for everyday intercourse with others – even if there is only one person in the group who does not speak some other language.
>
> (Phillips 2005: 9)

3   In the next chapter the problems associated with distinguishing a clear boundary between 'the public' and 'the private' in models of civic assimilation are examined.

4   Dialogue, in the form of communication and interaction across boundaries, is also 'the highest norm' of civic assimilationism (Tempelman 1999: 24).

5   These authors are following Bhabha's (1993) analysis of Fanon's (1967) observation that 'to acquire language is to do more than acquire the ability to communicate; it is to acquire culture' (Alexander et al. 2007: 3).

6   According to the Crick report, the Nationality, Immigration and Asylum Act 2002 requires that residents of the UK seeking British citizenship to be tested to show 'a sufficient knowledge of English, Welsh or Scottish Gaelic', to have 'a sufficient knowledge about life in the United Kingdom' and to take a

citizenship oath and a pledge at a civic ceremony (Life in the United Kingdom Advisory Group 2003: 3). Development in 2006 suggests that English language and associated tests will be extended to those seeking permanent residence in Britain, for example, migrant workers who have come to Britain from EU accession countries since 2004. According to a Home Office press release in December 2006, the Government has strengthened its commitment to integration by announcing that from 2 April 2007 those seeking to live in Britain permanently will have to pass 'English language' and 'Knowledge of life in the UK' tests before being granted permanent settlement rights. According to this press release, introducing mandatory tests for applicants wishing to settle in Britain will bring them into line with the requirements of those seeking British nationality. 'It will maximize their contribution to the economy by increasing their job prospects, assist their integration into local communities and generate a greater understanding of the rights and responsibilities that come with living in Britain' (Home Office Press Release 2006: 1).

7 For example, ethnic and religious minority groups are disproportionately represented in the most deprived 88 neighbourhoods in England (67 per cent compared to 37 per cent of the white population), the wage gap or 'ethnic penalty' in the labour market, and the gap in the levels of educational attainment on the basis of ethnic origin persists despite the Department for Education and Skills (DfES) evidence that indicates some improvement in educational attainment on the basis of ethnic origin (Home Office 2004b: 13).

8 It should be noted that the recent debates concerning 'the veil' ignited by Jack Straw have emerged in the context of other debates, court proceedings and school suspensions in Britain and abroad associated with the wearing of the *niqab*, the *jilbab* (a gown covering the whole body, arms and legs) and *hijab* (headscarf) by Muslim women. For example, Shabina Begum was sent home from Denbigh High School in Luton for deciding to wear a *jilbab* rather than the permitted *shalwar kameeze* (skirt worn over trousers) in 2002. This case was eventually heard before the Administrative Court in 2004 and the appeal was heard in the Court of Appeal in 2005 (Ward 2006: 119). According to Zine, girls and young women have been excluded from school and universities in France, Turkey and Canada for wearing the *hijab* (2006: 239); the most famous case being the *L'affur du foulard* (the affair of the scarf) in 1989 in which three Muslim girls were denied acces to a public school in France because the wearing of the *hijab* contravened legislation introduced in 1937 in France that prohibits the wearing of conspicuous religious symbols in Government-run schools (2006: 241). The British case of Aisha Azmi, a teaching assistant from Yorkshire, who was suspended from her duties because she wore a *niqab*, is discussed below.

9 According to the MORI poll commissioned by the Commission on Integration and Community Cohesion (CICC), 60 per cent of people polled

identified language as a key issue (CICC interim statement 2007a: 18). It was stated in the interim statement that lack of English language skills found in new arrivals and in 'settled communities' was a source of 'social distance' that is a barrier to integration and cohesion. It also hampers people's efforts to integrate economically and to access the labour market and it prevents them from developing a sense of belonging to bring them together with others (CICC Interim statement 2007a: 18). It was suggested in the report that the provision of translation services by local authorities is part of the problem. In his speech at the launch of the interim statement, Darra Singh (2007) stated that translation services had become a crutch upon which many non-English speakers members of settled communities depended.

10   Blackledge reported that Ann Cryer, the Labour MP for Keithley (a neighbouring district to Bradford), in her speech to the House of Commons on 17 July 2001 (in the weeks following the social unrest in Oldham, Burnley and Bradford) suggested that the main cause of the social disorder was ' ... the lack of a good level of English, which stems directly from the established tradition of bringing wives and husbands from the subcontinent who have often had no education and have no English' (Cryer, in Blackledge 2006b: 147). The significance of Cryer's interventions should not be underestimated. Tony Blair referred to her speech in his 2006 lecture series 'Our Nation's Future' to justify his comments on the necessity of everyone in Britain being able to speak English (2006c).

11   This strategy was proposed in the *Controlling our Borders: Making Migration Work for Britain* White Paper (2005b). In the Foreword to this White Paper, Tony Blair suggested that this five-year strategy for managing migration is about winning back public confidence in Britain's asylum and immigration system and stated that: 'The challenge for the Government is to maintain public confidence in the system by agreeing immigration where it is in the country's interests and preventing it where it is not' (Home Office 2005b: Foreword). This White Paper can be described as directly related to the attack on multiculturalism combined with the introduction of 'managed integration' in the *Secure Borders, Safe Haven* White Paper (2002). The *Secure Borders* White Paper was described by Joppke as connecting planned new immigration strategies with 'reduced multiculturalism' that attempted to assure the general public that the newcomers would not be a threat to 'their sense of belonging and identity' (2004: 252).

12   In the executive summary of the White Paper it was stated that: 'Our starting point is that employers should look first to recruit from the UK and the expanded EU before recruiting migrants from outside the EU' (Home Office 2005b: 2). From this we can deduce that the solution to the alleged social problem of immigration in Britain is to reduce immigration from non-EU countries. Therefore, the social problem of immigration (and hence integration) in Britain in this White Paper seems to be being closely associated with

non-EU migration. At the same time the solution to Britain's immigration (and perhaps 'community-relations' problem) is to encourage more EU (European, white, Christian) migration and discourage non-European (non-white, ethnic and religious minority) migration.

13 By settled communities, the CICC is referring to white communities and settled migrant communities.

14 For example, the Community Cohesion Review suggested that funding bodies should: 'presume against separate funding for distinct communities, and require collaborative working, save for the circumstances where the need for funding is genuinely only evident in one section of the community and can only be provided separately' (Home Office 2001: Para. 6.45). The issue of separate funding is examined further below.

15 The reflexive variety of multiculturalism described above should be distinguished from Ali Rattansi's 'framework of reflexive multiculturalism' (1999: 103). What is being described here is more akin with Beck's work on institutional reflexivity whereby societies attempt to rectify the side-effects of existing practices, policies and laws. This is very much a top-down reflexivity concerned with the maintenance of social order and conflict resolution. Rattansi's framework for a reflexive multiculturalism, on the other hand, bears 'many similarities with critical multiculturalism', as well as being influenced by Giddens's notion of reflexivity that emphasizes 'the reflexivity of agents and subjects' and the significance of 'expert systems' of knowledge (Rattansi 1999: 104) in combination with Derridean deconstruction (1999: 103).

16 Singh has borrowed the term 'shared futures' from the high-profile discussions associated with improving community relations in Northern Ireland (Darby and Knox 2004). The term 'shared' was used in this context rather than an 'integrated' future to avoid connotations of assimilation of one group by the other group (2004: 12). Shared futures discourse prioritizes the creation of a sense of common purpose rather than prioritizing the creation of a common identity (Holloway 2004: 17). The shared futures discourse has much in common with Gordon Brown's new 'Britishness' discourse in which he attempts to de-emphasize ethnic nationalism in favour of a nationalism of 'common purpose' (see Chapter 6).

17 Another major recommendations made by the CICC to stop the spread of myths of preferential treatment in local areas is the setting-up of 'rapid rebuttal units' by the new Commission for Equality and Human Rights (CEHR), the Communities and Local Government Department and the Local Government Association (CICC 2007b: 105).

18 According to Bourdieu, habitus can be defined as a system of dispositions that designate ways of being, habitual states; in particular predispositions, tendencies, propensities and inclinations (1977: 214).

Chapter 5

[1] This was based on the Joint Committee on Human Rights' recommendation that an independent Human Rights Commission should be established in Britain in their report of March 2003.

[2] This White Paper is a consultation document that built on the responses to the Green Paper entitled *Equality and Diversity: Making it Happen* that was produced by the Women and Equality Unit in October 2002, which sought views on the future role and structure of statutory equality institutions.

[3] The Government, in their statement announcing their intention to establish the Commission, issued in October 2003, proposed that one of the functions of the new body would be:

> Promoting community cohesion through providing support to local initiatives to promote dialogue and understanding between different communities and groups, where relevant drawing upon the balance between rights and responsibilities contained in the Human Rights Act.
> (in Joint Committee on Human Rights 2004: Para. 41)

[4] This process has been contested by existing equality institutions. For example the Commission for Racial Equality (CRE), in its response to the Green Paper, urged the Government to recognize the 'real differences in terms of identity, needs and requirements between different groups' (2003: 3). According to the CRE, ethnic minority communities experience discrimination differently to other disadvantaged groups 'such as white women and disabled people' (2003: 4). There are concerns, especially among ethnic minority communities, 'that a broad-based, generic approach to equality may fail to recognize some of the real differences in the experience of, and issues affecting, different strands, especially race' (CRE 2003: 6).

[5] The Human Rights Act was enacted in November 1998 and implemented in October 2000 (Gearty 2005b: 205).

[6] The Audit Commission's findings in this area was that most local authorities reviewed policies in a piecemeal basis; in the health sector the picture was worse with little monitoring of performance in this area; in police authorities there is evidence of a more positive response; however, probation and fire services followed a similar pattern to local authorities (2003: 10).

[7] The Metropolitan Police Service Racial and Violent Crime Task Force define a critical incident as: 'Any incident where the effectiveness of the police response is likely to have a significant impact on the confidence of: the victim, their family and/or community' (Metropolitan Police Force 2002: 4).

[8] In the next chapter the Government's attempts to promote the Human Rights Act to 'the majority' (as opposed to minority or 'protected groups') is explored

in the context of ' ... the damaging myths which have taken root in the popular imagination' (Department for Constitutional Affairs 2006: 1) that human rights are the preserve of the weak, the vulnerable and the marginalized.

9 In *Hegemony and the Socialist Strategy* Laclau and Mouffe's intention was to encourage the common recognition among different groups (for example, women, workers, blacks, gays, ecological, as well as other 'new social movements') that despite their differences they all have a common concern: the extension of democracy (Mouffe 1992: 378–9).

10 The impracticality or 'theoretical' nature of radical democracy has been commented upon by numerous commentators, for example, according to Epstein, 'radical democracy' suggests grass-roots politics, diversity, a playful political practice that is not bound by rigid structures but is continually in the process of transformation (1996: 128). For Trend, despite its common-sense appeal, radical democracy has yet to be implemented on any large scale, he adds: 'the theoretical character of radical democracy has drawn fire from those who fault the program for lack of specificity. These critics accuse radical democracy of offering little more than a set of philosophical ideals, lacking any concrete explanation about its implementation in practical circumstances' (1996b: 3).

11 For example, although the Disability Rights Commission (DRC) welcome much in the Government's White Paper (2004: 3), a number of concerns remained for them, especially the need for dedicated resources to underpin the disability unit and that the broader remit of the single Commission might lead to loss of focus and impact (2004: 8). The Equal Opportunities Commission (EOC) support the principle of the single Commission; however, they also had significant concerns about the aspects of the White Paper relating to resources, enforcing equality legislation and powers (2004: 4).

Chapter 6

1 A number of commentators have suggested that this was a strategic speech for Brown (a Scot) in which he attempted to present himself as a suitable 'Prime Minister for the whole of the UK' (Cleverly 2006: 2).

2 In the Life in the United Kingdom Advisory Group report *The New and the Old*, it was deemed unnecessary to define Britishness too precisely nor to redefine Britishness since to be British: 'Is to respect those over-arching specific institutions, values, beliefs and traditions that bind us all, the different nations and cultures, together in peace and legal order' (2003: 11). This is very much Appiah's view. According to Appiah, the project of arguing out democratically a common culture on which to centre 'our' national life is unnecessary, rather ' ... to live together in a nation, what is required is that

we all share a commitment to the organization of the state – the institutions that provide the overarching order of our common life' (Appiah 1998: 102).

3   This is not necessarily the case given the Eurocentric and gendered nature of human rights discourse.

4   Lord Falconer, the former Lord Chancellor, in his Introduction to the Department for Constitutional Affairs *Review of the Implementation of the Human Rights Act* (2006), stated that two cases in particular (*A and others* v. *the Home Secretary in the House of Lords* and the *Chahal* v. *United Kingdom* case in the European Court of Human Rights in 1996, both examined in Chapter 1) highlight the impact that human rights have had upon British law (Falconer, in Department for Constitutional Affairs 2006: 3). The analysis of the overall effects of the human rights on the activities of security agencies, according to the Department for Constitutional Affairs' review, is that it is the Strasbourg Court (in cases such as Chahal) rather than the Human Rights Act that has had an impact on their ability to deal with 'dangerous terrorist suspects' (2006: 35). John Reid, in his statement to the House of Commons on the three non-derogating control order absconders on 24 May 2007, referred to the Chahal judgment: as 'an outrageously disproportionate judgment' that prevents a State deporting 'a terror suspect if there would be any threat to him if he were sent abroad' (House of Common (Hansard) 24 May 2007: Column 1433). Reid followed the latter with 'we must have regard to that, but we are prohibited from having regard to the threat that will be posed to the other 60 million people in the country if he remains here.' (House of Common (Hansard) 24 May 2007: Column 1433).

5   Blick, Choudhury and Weir, refer to 'human security' as 'the principle human right' (2006: 11). For them, 'the right to life' is the central component of the carefully assembled and interdependent package of civil and political rights and responsibilities contained in the European Convention on Human Rights (ECHR) (2006: 11). Zedner refers to the employment of the 'public interest' or 'national security' by Governments as the 'trump card against which any individual claim to liberty cannot compete' (2005: 513).

6   This statement cuts to the heart of the uneasy relationship between the executive and the judiciary in recent years with regard to anti-terrorism legislation. According to Sivanandan, the executive's arrogation of power since 9/11 undermines the judiciary (2006: 4). In a similar vein, Lord Hoffman in his 'controversial' statement in his ruling in *A and others* v. *Secretary of State for the Home Department* [2004] UKHL 56 on part 4 of the Anti-terrorism, Crime and Security Act 2001 said that: 'The real threat to the life of the nation, in the sense of living in accordance with traditional laws and political values, comes not from terrorism but from laws like these' (Lord Hoffman, in Lord Phillips 2006: 5). This statement was deemed controversial, according to Lord Phillips, because the Government considered it a violation of the rule that Judges should not descend from interpreting the law into politics (2006: 5).

7   For an examination of the legality of the Anti-terrorism, Crime and Security Act 2001 derogation form the ECHR, see Bates (2006).

8   Blick, Choudhury and Weir understand terrorism as having social, economic and cultural roots, both within Britain and internationally, and they present human rights as a potential antidote to the roots of terrorism as human rights encompass the right to 'equality' and freedom from discrimination associated with the full spectrum of economic, social and cultural rights (2006: 67). Weir takes this approach further by suggesting that a greater balance needs to be struck between the civil and political rights enshrined in the ECHR and economic and social rights, in which social exclusion would be defined in terms of the denial of human rights (Weir 2006: ix, xi). According to Weir, the existing patchwork of laws and regulations does not provide the legal, or constitutional protection of socio-economic rights that the Human Rights Act does for civil and political rights (2006: xiii). In many ways Weir's suggestion that British democracy requires both political equality and social inclusion is central to the approach adopted by the Equalities Review in their *Fairness and Freedom* report (2007). The Equalities Review approach to political equality and social inclusion can be described as yet another shift in the emphasis of human rights from the emphasis on civil and political rights to emphasizing social justice and social and economic rights first. Rather than abstract rights, the approach adopted by the Equalities Review is a 'practical' one based on an appreciation of the freedoms and activities that people have reason to value 'derived from international human rights principles' (2007: 6). According to the review, 'achieving equality means narrowing the gaps in people's educational attainment, employment rates and real opportunities open to them' (Equalities Review 2007: 6). At the same time they are explicit who will be the target of their interventions; that is, those groups who experience persistent disadvantage (Equalities Review 2007: 6).

Bibliography

A and others v. *Secretary of State for the Home Department* [2004] UKHL 56.

A and others v. *Secretary of State for the Home Department* [2005] UKHL 71.

Aaronovitch, D. (2004) Stop and search: a defining moment, *The Guardian*, 6 July, p. 5.

Abbas, T. (2005) British South Asian muslims: State and multicultural society, in T. Abbas (ed.) *Muslim Britain: Communities Under Pressure*, pp. 3–17. London: Zed Books.

Abbas, T. (2007) Introduction: Islamic political radicalism in western Europe, in T. Abbas (ed.) *Islamic Political Radicalism: A European Perspective*, pp. 3–14. Edinburgh: Edinburgh University Press.

Agamben, G. (1998) *Homo Sacer: Sovereign Power and Bare Life*. Stanford: Stanford University Press.

Ahmed, Z.R. (2006) Kashmiri, Pakistani muslim women and security in Britain (retrieved from: http://www.bmf.eu.com/zareen.pdf).

Alba, R. and Nee, V. (2005) Rethinking assimilation theory for a new era of immigration, in P. Kivisto (ed.) *Incorporating Diversity: Rethinking Assimilation in a Multicultural Age*, pp. 235–76. Boulder and London: Paradign Publishers.

Alexander, C. (2003) Violence, gender and identity: re-imagining 'the Asian gang'. Unpublished paper presented to the *Youth and Gender: Transnational Identity and Islamophobia Seminar*, European Commission, Brussels, 22–24 May.

Alexander, C. (2007) Cohesive identities: the distance between meaning and understanding, in M. Wetherell, M. Laflèche and R. Berkeley (eds.) *Identity, Ethnic Diversity and Community Cohesion*, pp. 115–26. London: Sage Publications.

Alexander, C., Edwards, R. and Temple, B. (2007) Contesting cultural communities: language, ethnicity and citizenship in Britain, *Journal of Ethnic and Migration Studies*, 33 (5), 783–800.

Alexander, J. (2005) Theorizing the 'modes of incorporation': assimilation, hyphenization, and multiculturalism as varieties of civic participation, in P. Kivisto (ed.) *Incorporating Diversity: Rethinking Assimilation in a Multicultural Age*, pp. 320–36. Boulder and London: Paradigm Publishers.

Alibhai-Brown, Y. (2000) *After Multiculturalism*, The Foreign Policy Centre: London.

Allen, C. (2003) *Fair Justice: The Bradford Disturbances, the Sentencing and the Impact*. London: Forum Against Islamophobia and Racism.

Allen, C. (2005) From race to religion: the new face of discrimination, in T. Abbas (ed.) *Muslim Britain: Communities under Pressure*, pp. 49–65. London: Zed Books.

Amin, A. (2002) Ethnicity and the multicultural city: living with diversity. Draft report for the ESRC Cities Programme and the Department of Transport, Local Government and the regions (DTLR) (retrieved from: http://www.livjim.ac.uk/cities/papers/ash_amin.pdf).

Amnesty International Press Release (2005) UK: new security measures are a serious attack on human rights, 24 August (retrieved from: http://news.amnesty.org/library/index/ENGEUR450332005).

Anthias, F. (1998) Connecting ethnicity, 'race': gender and class in ethnic relations research, in D. Joly (ed.) *Scapegoats and Social Actors: the Exclusion and Integration of Minorities in Western and Eastern Europe*, pp. 173–91. Basingstoke: Palgrave Macmillan.

Anthias, F. and Yuval-Davis, N. (1992) *Racialized Boundaries: Race, Nation, Gender, Colour and Class and the Anti-racist Struggle*. New York and London: Routledge.

Appiah, K.A. (1998) Cosmopolitan patriots, *cultural politics*, 14, 91–114.

Appiah, K.A. (2006) *Cosmopolitanism: Ethics in a World of Strangers*. New York and London: W.W. Norton & Company.

Arendt, H. (1968) *Between Past and Future*. New York: Viking Press.

Arendt, H. [1951] (1979) *The Origins of Totalitarianism*. New York: Harcourt Brace Jovanovich.

Ashby Wilson, R. (2005) Human rights in the 'war on terror', in R. Ashby Wilson (ed.) *Human Rights in the 'War on Terror'*, pp. 1–36. Cambridge: Cambridge University Press.

Audit Commission (2003) *Human Rights: Improving Public Service Delivery* (retrieved from: www.audit-commission.gov.uk).

Awan, A.N. (2007) Transitional religiosity experiences: contextual disjuncture and Islamic political radicalism, in T. Abbas (ed.) *Islamic Political Radicalism: A European Perspective*, pp. 207–30. Edinburgh: Edinburgh University Press.

Azad, A. (2006) Chair of Muslim Safety Forum, *Anti-terrorism Laws: The Experience of the Irish and Muslim Communities in the UK*. Report from the Seminar held on 21 April 2006 (retrieved from: http://www.cre.gov.uk/about/birmingham_seminar.html).

Back, L., Keith, M., Khan, A., Shukra, K. and Solomos, J. (2002) The return of assimilationism: race, multiculturalism and new labour, *Sociological Research Online*, 7 (2), 1–13.

Bagguley, P. and Hussain, Y. (forthcoming) Non-Muslim responses to the 7th July Bombings in London, in D. Zimmerman (ed.) *Terrorism and Diaspora*. Zurich: Centre for Security Studies.

Balibar, E. (2004) *We, the People of Europe? Reflections on Transnational Citizenship*. Princeton and Oxford: Princeton University Press.

Barnett, C. (2004) Deconstructing radical democracy: articulation, representation, and being-with-others, *Political Geography*, 23, 503–28.

Barry, B. (2001) *Culture and Equality: An Egalitarian Critique of Multiculturalism.* Cambridge: Polity Press.

Bates, E. (2006) A 'public emergency threatening the life of the nation'? The United Kingdom's derogation from the European Convention on Human Rights of 18 December 2001 and the 'A' Case, in *The British Year Book of International Law 2005*, pp. 245–35. Oxford: Clarendon Press.

Batty, D. (2006) Two 7/7 bombers were under surveillance, *Guardian Unlimited*, 11 May (retrieved from: http://www.guardian.co.uk/attackonlondon/story/ 0,,1772529,00.html).

Bauböck, R. (1997) Citizenship and national identities in the European Union (retrieved from: http://www.jeanmonnetprogram.org/papers/97/97-04-.html).

Baylouny, A.M. (2004) Emotions, poverty, or politics: misconception about Islamic movements, *Strategic Insights*, III (1), 1–9 (retrieved from: http:// www.ccc.nps.navy.mil/si//2004/jan/baylounyJan04.asp).

BBC, Bradford and West Yorkshire, News (2001) 'Serious disorder' flares in city, Sunday 8 July (retrieved from: http://www.bbc.co.uk/bradford/news/indepth/ bradford_riot080701_seriousdisorder.shtml, 1–4).

BBC News (2001) Oldham hit by fresh violence, Monday 28 May (retrieved from: http://news.bbc.co.uk/1/hi/uk/1355379.stm, pp. 1–4).

BBC News (2004) Q&A: Secret Court Explained, 28 April (retrieved from: http:// newsvote.bbc.c.uk/mpapps/pagetools/print/news.bbc.co.uk/s/hi/uk_news/ 3666235.stm).

BBC News (2005a) Man killed in Birmingham clashes, 23 October (retrieved from: http://news.bbc.co.uk/1/hi/england/west_midlands/4367654.stm).

BBC News (2005b) Lords Reject Torture Evidence, 8 December (retrieved from: http://newsvote.bbc.co.uk/mpapps/pagetools/print/news.bbc.co.uk/2/hi/ uk_news/politics/4509530.stm).

BBC News (2005c) Clarke unveils deportation rules, 24 August (retrieved from: http://www.news.bbc.co.uk/1/hi/uk_politics/4179044.stm).

BBC News (2006a) Muslims 'must root out extremism', BBC News, 4 July (retrieved from: http://newsvote.bbc.co.uk/mpapps/pagetools/print/news.bbc.co.uk/2/ hi/uk_news/politics/5144438.stm).

BBC News (2006b) No charges for Forest Gate victim, 27 October (retrieved from: http://www.newsvote.bbc.co.uk/mpapps/pagetools/print/news.bbc.co.uk/2'/ hi/uk_news/england.pdf').

BBC News (2006c) In quotes: Jack Straw on the veil, 6 October (retrieved from: http://news.bbc.co.uk/1/hi/uk_politics/5413470.stm).

BBC News (2007a) Revealed: bomber transcript, 1 May (retrieved from: http:// newsvote.bbc.co.uk/mpapps/pagetools/print/news.bbc.co.uk/2/hi/uk_news/ 6611803.stm).

BBC News (2007b) Pressure grows for a 7/7 inquiry, 1 May (retrieved from: http:// newsvote.bbc.co.uk/mpapps/pagetools/print/news.bbc.co.uk/2/hi/uk_news/ politics/6610209.stm).

BBC News (2007c) Brown pledge to protect liberties, 3 June (retrieved from: http://newsvote.bbc.co.uk/mpapps/pagetools/print/news.bbc.co.uk/2/hi/uk_news/politics/6716865.stm).

Beck, U. (1992) *Risk Society: Towards a New Modernity*. London: Sage Publications.

Beck, U. (1997) *The Reinvention of Politics: Rethinking Modernity in the Global Social Order*. Cambridge: Polity Press.

Beck, U. (2002a) The terrorist threat: world risk society revisited, *Theory, Culture & Society*, 19 (4), 39–55.

Beck, U. (2002b) The cosmopolitan society and its enemies, *Theory, Culture & Society*, 19 (1–2), 17–44.

Beck, U. (2003) Conversation 1: postmodernity or the second modernity, in U. Beck (ed.) *Conversations with Ulrich Beck*, pp. 11–61. Cambridge: Polity Press.

Beck, U. (2005) Neither order nor peace: a response to Bruno Latour, *Common Knowledge*, 11 (1), 1–7 (retrieved from: http://muse.jhu.edu/jpornals/common_knowledge/v011/11.1beck.html).

Beck, U. (2006) *The Cosmopolitan Vision*. Cambridge: Polity Press.

Beck, U., Bonss, W. and Lau, C. (2003) The theory of reflexive modernization: hypotheses and research programme, *Theory, Culture & Society*, 20 (2), 1–33.

Benhabib, S. (1992) *Situating the Self: Gender, Community and Postmodernism in Contemporary Ethics*. Cambridge: Polity.

Benhabib, S. (2002) *The Claims of Culture: Equality and Diversity in the Global Era*. Princeton and Oxford: Princeton University Press.

Benhabib, S. (2006a) Democratic iterations: the local, the national, and the global, in R. Post (ed.) *Seyla Benhabib: Another Cosmopolitanism*, pp. 45–82. Oxford: Oxford University Press.

Benhabib, S. (2006b) The philosophical foundations of cosmopolitan norms, in R. Post (ed.) *Seyla Benhabib: Another Cosmopolitanism*, pp. 13–44. Oxford: Oxford University Press.

Bennett, R. (2006) Muslim task force 'snubbed', *Times Online*, 20 June (retrieved from: http://www.timesonline.co.uk/article/0,,17129-2233399,00.html).

Berkeley, R. (2006) An interview with the Power Commission, *Runnymede's Quarterly Bulletin*, 346 (March), 2–5.

Berlins, M. (2007) New Law Lord took defiant stand on torture evidence, *The Guardian*, 1 January (retrieved from: http://www.giardian.co.uk/terrorism/story/0,,1980895,00.html).

Berman, P. (2003) *Terror and Liberalism*. New York: W.W. Norton & Company.

Bhabba, H. (1993) *The Location of Culture*. London: Routledge.

Billig, M., Downey, J., Richardson, J., Deacon, D. and Golding, P. (2006) *'Britishness' in the Last Three General Elections: from Ethnic to Civic Nationalism*. Report for the Commission for Racial Equality (retrieved from: http://www.CRE.gov.uk/downloads/britishness_elections.pdf).

Birt, J. (2005) Lobbying and marching: British Muslims and the State, in T. Abbas (ed.) *Muslim Britain: Communities Under Pressure*, pp. 92–106. London and New York: Zed Books.

Birt, Y. (2006a) Islamic foundation, *Anti-terrorism Laws: The Experience of the Irish and Muslim Communities in the UK*. Report from the Seminar held on 21 April (retrieved from: http://www.cre.gov.uk/about/birmingham_seminar.html).

Birt, Y. (2006b) Sir Trevor, the Muslims and the New Equalities Commission, 20 September (retrieved from: http://www.yahyabirt.com/?p=32).

Birt, Y. (2006c) Islamic citizenship in Britain after 7/7: tackling extremism and reserving freedoms, in A.A. Malik (ed.) *The State We Are In: Identity, Terror and the Law of Jihad*, pp. 14–31. Bristol and England: Amal Press.

Blackledge, A. (2006a) The magical frontier between the dominant and the dominated: sociolinguistics and social justice in a multilingual world, *Journal of Multilingual and Multicultural Development*, 27 (1), 22–41.

Blackledge, A. (2006b) The men say 'they don't need it': gender and the extension of language testing for British citizenship, *Studies in Language and Capitalism*, 1, 143–61.

Blair, T. (2000) Britishness and the Government's agenda of constitutional reform, Speech to the Regional Newspaper Executive, 28 March (retrieved from: http://www.guardian.co.uk/britain/article10,2763,184950,00.html).

Blair, T. (2005) We are the change-makers. Speech at the Labour Party Conference, 27 September (retrieved from: http://www.labour.org.uk/index.php?id=news 2005&ux_news%5BID%5D=ac05tb&cHash+d8353c3d74).

Blair, T. (2006a) PM meets with Muslim women, Number 10 Downing Street, 10 May (retrieved from: http://www.number10.gov.uk/output/page 9421.asp).

Blair, T. (2006b) Multicultural Britain to be celebrated. Our Nation's Future Lecture Series, 8 December (retrieved from: www.number10.gov.uk/output/ page10562.asp).

Blair, T. (2006c) The duty to integrate: shared British values, 8 December (retrieved from: http://www.number10.gov.uk/output/page10563.asp).

Blick, A., Choudhury, T. and Weir, S. (2006) *The Rules of the Game: Terrorism Community and Human Rights*. Report by the democratic Unit, Human Rights Centre, University of Essex for the Joseph Rowntree Trust (retrieved from www.jrrt.org).

BLINK Press Release (2006) Black Communities Reject Trevor Phillips for Top Equality Job, 5 July (retrieved from: http://www.blink.org.uk/print asp?key=11972).

Blunkett, D. (2001a) Blunkett calls for honest and open debate on citizenship and community. 10 Downing Street Newsroom (retrieved from: http:// www.number10.gov.uk/news.asp?newsID=3255, 17/12/01).

Blunkett, D. (2001b) Securing order, basic safety, and underpinning our freedoms. Speech to the Labour Party Conference, Brighton 2001 (retrieved from: http:// www.number10.gov.uk).

Blunkett, D. (2002) Integration with diversity: globalization and the renewal of democracy and civil society, Foreign Policy Centre (retrieved from: http://www.fpc.org.uk/articles/182).

Blunkett, D. (2004) New challenges for race equality and community cohesion in the 21st century, Institute of Public Policy Research, 7 July 2004 (retrieved from: http://www.homeoffice.gov.uk/comrace).

Bonnett, A. (2000) *Anti-racism*. London and New York: Routledge.

Booth, K. and Dunne, T. (2002) Worlds in collision, in K. Booth and T. Dunne (eds.) *Worlds in Collision: Terror and the Future of Global Order*, pp. 1–26. Basingstoke: Palgrave Macmillan.

Bottero, W. (2005) *Stratification: Social Division and Inequality*. London and New York: Routledge.

Bottomley, A. (1992) Feminism: paradoxes of the double bind, in I. Grigg-Spall and P. Ireland (eds.) *The Critical Lawyers' Handbook*, pp. 23–31. London: Pluto Press.

Bourdieu, P. (1977) *Outline of a Theory of Practice*. Cambridge: Cambridge University Press.

Bradford District Race Review (2001) *Community Pride Not Prejudice: Making Diversity Work in Bradford*. Bradford: Bradford Vision.

Brandt, D. (1986) *The Realisation of Anti-racist Teaching*. Lewes: Falmer Press.

Branigan , T. (2003) Yemen seeks to extradite Hamza, *The Guardian*, 27 April (retrieved from: http://www.guardian.co.uk/uk_news/story/0,3604,931103,00.html).

Brighton, S. (2007) British Muslims, multiculturalism and UK foreign policy: 'integration' and 'cohesion' in and beyond the State, *International Affairs*, 83 (1), 1–17.

Brody, R. (2005) The road to *Abu Ghraib*: torture and impunity in U.S. detention, in G. Robertson (ed.) *Torture: Does it Make Us Safer? Is it Ever OK? A Human Rights Perspective*, pp. 145–54. New York and London: The New Press.

Brown, C. (2007) Brown talks tough on terrorism with plans to increase 28-day limit, *The Independent*, 4 June (retrieved from: http://news.independent.co.uk/uk/politics/article2611738.ece).

Brown, C. and Woolf, M. (2005) Rights laws to be overhauled as Blair says 'the game has changed', *The Independent*, 6 August, p. 4.

Brown, G. (2006a) Chancellor writes for *The Sun*, *The Sun*, 8 September (retrieved from: http://www.thesun.co.uk/0,,2-2006410725,00.html).

Brown, G. (2006b) Securing our future, at the Royal United Services Institute, 13 February (retrieved from: http://www.hm-treasury.gov.uk/newsroom_and_speeches/speeches/chancellorexchequer/speech_chex_130206.cfm).

Brown, G. (2006c) The future of Britishness. Speech at the Fabian Britishness Conference, 14 January (retrieved from: http://www.fabiansociety.org.uk/press_office/news_latest_all.asp?pressid=520).

Brubaker, R. (1995) Comments on 'modes of immigration politics in liberal democratic states', *International Migration Review*, 29 (4), 903–8.

Buck-Morss, S. (2003) *Thinking Past Terror: Islamism and Critical Theory on the Left*.

London: Verso.

Burnett, J. and Whyte, D. (2005) Embedded expertise and the new terrorism *Journal of Crime, Conflict and the Media*, 1 (4), 1–18.

Burnley Task Force (2001) *Burnley Speaks, Who Listens?* Burnley.

Butler, J. (1994) Against Proper Objects, *Differences*, 6 (2 and 3), 1–26.

Cantle, T. (2001) *Community Cohesion: A Report of the Independent Review Team* Home Office (retrieved from: http://www.homeoffice.gov.uk/comrace).

Chakrabarti, S. (2005) The way to let terrorists win is to shut down free speech (interview by Maire Woolf), *The Independent*, 11 July, p. 15.

Clarke, C. (2005) Speech by Charles Clarke, British Home Secretary, to the European Parliament, 7 September (retrieved from: http://www.eu2005.gov.uk servlet/Front?pagename=OpenMarket/Xcelerate/ShowPage&c=Page&cid= 1107293561746&a=KArticle&aid=1125559979691).

Cleverly, J. (2006) My Britishness article in full, 17 January (retrieved from: http:// jamescleverly.blogspot.com/2006/01/my-britishness-article-in-full.html).

Cohen, S. (2001) *States of Denial: Knowing About Atrocities and Suffering*. Cambridge Polity.

Cole, P. (2005) A race riot in Lozells? So what's going on? *The Independent* 30 October (retrieved from: http://news.independent.co.uk/media/article 323298.ece).

Collins, P.H. (1998) It's all in the family: intersections of gender, race and nation *Hypatia*, 13 (3), 61–82.

Commission for Racial Equality (2003) *Response to Equality and Diversity: Making i Happen* (retrieved from: http://www.cre.gov.uk/Default.aspx.LocID-0hgnew03g RefLocID-0hg00900c008001002.Lang-EN.htm).

Commission for Racial Equality (2004) *Fairness for All: A new Commission fo Equality and Human Rights – a Response* (retrieved from: http://www.cre.go v.uk/downloads/docs/ffa_cre_response_prn.doc).

Commission for Racial Equality (CRE) (2006a) *Immigration, Asylum and Nationality Bill*, House of Lords Committee stage, 9 January (retrieved from: http:// www.cre.gov/default.aspx.locid-0hgnew0ae.htm).

Commission for Racial Equality (2006b) *Equality Bill*, House of Commons final stages, 16 January (retrieved from: http://www.cre.gov.uk/Default.aspx. LocID-0hgnew09v.RefLocID-0hg00900f006.Lang-EN.htm).

Commission on British Muslims and Islamophobia (CBMI) (2004) *Islamophobia Issues, Challenges and Action*. Stoke on Trent: Trentham Books.

Commission on Integration and Community Cohesion (CICC) (2007a) *Our Interim Statement* (retrieved from: www.integrationandcohesion.org).

Commission on Integration and Community Cohesion (CICC) (2007b) *Our Shared Futures* (retrieved from: www.integrationandcohesion.org).

Community Cohesion Panel (2004) *The End of Parallel Lives?* (Retrieved from: http://www.communities.gov.uk/index.asp?id=1505128).

Crenshaw, K.W. (1994) Mapping the margins: intersectionality, identity politics and violence against women of colour, in M.A. Fineman and R. Mykitiuk (eds.) *The Public Nature of Private Violence*, pp. 93–118. New York and London: Routledge.

Crossley, N. (2002) *Making Sense of Social Movements*. Buckingham: Open University Press.

Darby, J. and Knox, C. (2004) 'A shared future'. Consultation paper on Improving Relations in Northern Ireland, final report, 21 January (retrieved from: http://www.asharedfutureni.gov.uk/colin_knox_john_darby.pdf).

Darling, M. (2002) Intersectionality. Plenary Presentation, AWID. 9th International Forum (retrieved from: http://www.awid.org/forum/plenaries/intersectionality/ppt).

Dean, M. (1999) *Governmentality: Power and Rule in Modern Society*. London: Sage Publications.

Dean, M. (2004) Opinion (The Commission for Racial Equality is wrong to oppose a Single Equality Body), *Society Guardian*, 1 September, p. 5.

Dean, M. (2007) *Governing Societies: Political Perspectives on Domestic and International Rule*. Berkshire: Open University Press and McGraw-Hill Education.

DEMOS (2006) *Bringing it Home: Community-based Approaches to Counter-terrorism* (retrieved from: www.demos.co.uk).

Denham, J. (2002) *Building Cohesive Communities*. A report of the Ministerial Group on Public Order. London: HMSO.

Denham, J. (2007) Terrorism. Speech to DEMOS think tank, 15 January (retrieved from: http://www.johndenham.org.uk/blog/2007/01/terrorism-speech-to-demos-to-think-tank.html).

Department for Constitutional Affairs (2006) Review of the implementation of the Human Rights Act (retrieved from: http://www.dca.gov.uk/peoples-rights/human-rights/pdf/full_review.pdf).

Dershowitz, A. (2004) Should the ticking bomb terrorist be tortured? A case study in how a democracy should make tragic choices, in K. Darmer, R. Baird and S. Rosenbaum (eds.) *Civil Liberties vs. National Security in a Post-9/11 World*, pp. 189–215. New York: Prometheus Books.

Disability Rights Commission (DRC) (2004) *Government White Paper 'Fairness For All': a New Commission for Human Rights – response form the Disability Rights Commission* (retrieved from: http://www.drc_gb.org).

Douzinas, C. (2000) *The End of Human Rights: Critical Legal Thought at the Turn of the Century*. Oxford: Hart Publishing.

Doward, J. and Hinsliff, G. (2004) British hostility to muslims 'could trigger riots', *The Observer*, 30 May (retrieved from: http://observer.guardian.co.uk/uk_news/story/0,6903,1227962,00.html, 1–3).

Dworkin, R. (2003) Terror and the attack on civil liberties, *The New York Review of Books*, 50 (17), 1–20 (retrieved from: http://www.nybooks.com/articles/16738).

Dworkin, R. (2006) It is absurd to calculate human rights according to a cost-benefit analysis, *The Guardian*, 24 May, p. 28.

Elsworthy, S. and Rifkind, G. (2006) *Making Terrorism History*. London: Rider & Co
Epstein, B. (1996) Radical democracy and cultural politics: What about class What about political power? in D. Trend (ed.) *Radical Democracy: Identity Citizenship and the State*, pp. 127–39. London and New York: Routledge.
Equal Opportunities Commission (EOC) (2004) *Fairness for All: a New Commission for Equality and Human Rights – Response to the White Paper* (retrieved from http://www.eoc-gb.org).
Equalities Review (2007) *Fairness and Freedom: The Final Report of the Equalities Review* (retrieved from: www.theequalitiesreview.org.uk/equality_review.pdf)
Etzioni, A. (1997) *The New Golden Rule: Community and Morality in a Democratic Society*. London: Profile Books.
European Commission (2001) *Proposal for a Council Framework Decision on Combating Terrorism*, Com (2001) 521 final, 19 September (retrieved from: http://www.statewatch.org/news/2001/sep/terrorism.pdf).
European Monitoring Centre on Racism and Xenophobia (2003) *Anti-Islamic Reactions in the EU After the Terrorist Acts Against the USA (United Kingdom,* (retrieved from: http://eumc.eu.int/eumc/material/pub/112001/uk-en.pdf).
European Parliament (2006) Temporary Committee on the Alleged Use of European Countries by the CIA for the Transport and Illegal Detention of Prisoners, Working Document no. 7. http://www.statewatch.org/cia/documents/ working-doc-no-7-nov-06.pdf).
European Policy Centre (2005) *The Status of Imams in Europe*. Communication to Members S38/05.
Ewing, K.D. and Gearty, C.A. (1990) *Freedom Under Thatcher: Civil Liberties in Modern Britain*. Oxford: Clarendon Press.
Fairclough, N. (2000) *New Labour, New Language?* London and New York: Routledge.
Fairness for All: a new Commission for Equality and Human Rights (2004) White Paper (retrieved from: http://www.dti.gov.uk/access/equalitywhite paper.pdf).
Fanon, F. (1967) *Black Skins, White Mask*. London: Grove Press.
Fekete, L. (2002) All in the name of security, in P. Scraton (ed.) *Beyond September 11: An Anthology of Dissent*, pp. 102–7. London: Pluto Press.
Fekete, L. (2004) Anti-Muslim racism and the European Security State, *Race & Class*, 46 (3), 3–29.
Fekete, L. (2005a) *The Deportation Machine: Europe, Asylum and Human Rights*. London: Institute of Race Relations.
Fekete, L. (2005b) 'Speech crime' and deportation. Independent Race and Refugee News Network, 11 August (retrieved from: http://www.irr.org.uk/2005/ august/ak000012.html).
Fekete, L. (2006) 'Speech crime' and deportation, in T. Bunyan (ed.) *The War on Freedom and Democracy: Essays on Civil Liberties in Europe*, pp. 75–91. Nottingham: Spokesman Books.
Fenwick, H. (2002) The Anti-terrorism, Crime and Security Act 2001: a proportionate response to 11 September? *The Modern Law Review*, 65 (5), 724–6.

Fitzpatrick, J. (2003) Speaking law to power: the war against terrorism and human rights, *European Journal of International Law*, 14 (2), 241–64.

Fraser, N. (1992) The uses and abuses of French discourse theories for feminist politics, in N. Fraser and S.L. Bartky (eds.) *Revaluing French Feminism: Critical Essays on Difference, Agency and Culture*, pp. 177–94. Bloomington and Indianapolis: Indiana University Press.

Fraser, N. (1997) *Justice Interruptus: Critical Reflections on the 'Postsocialist' Condition.* New York and London: Routledge.

Fraser, N. and Honneth, A. (2003) *Redistribution or Recognition? A Political-philosophical Exchange.* London and New York: Verso.

Freeman, M. (2005) Order, rights and threats: terrorism and global justice, in R. Ashby Wilson (ed.) *Human Rights in the 'War on Terror'*, pp. 37–56. Cambridge: Cambridge University Press.

Furedi, F. (1997) *Culture of Fear: Risk-taking and the Morality of Low Expectations.* London: Continuum International Publishing Group.

Furedi, F. (2004) *Therapy Culture: Cultivating Vulnerability in an Uncertain Age.* London and New York: Routledge.

Gearson, J. (2002) The nature of modern terrorism, in L. Freedman (ed.) *Superterrorism: Policy Responses*, pp. 7–24. Oxford: Blackwell.

Gearty, C. (1991) *Terror.* London and Boston: Faber and Faber.

Gearty, C. (2005a) 11 September 2001, Counter-terrorism, and the Human Rights Act, *Journal of Law and Society*, 32 (1), 18–33.

Gearty, C. (2005b) *Principles of Human Rights Adjudication.* Oxford: Oxford University Press.

Gearty, C. (2006) *Can Human Rights Survive?* Cambridge: Cambridge University Press.

Giddens, A. (2006) Misunderstanding multiculturalism, *Comment is Free, The Guardian*, 14 October (retrieved from: http://commentisfree.guardian.co.uk/anthony_giddens/2006/10/tony_giddens.html).

Giddens, A. (1990) *The Consequences of Modernity.* Cambridge: Polity Press.

Giddens, A. (1994) Risk, trust, reflexivity, in U. Beck, A. Giddens and S. Lash (eds.) *Reflexive Modernization: Politics, Tradition and Aesthetics in the Modern Social Order*, pp. 184–97. Cambridge: Polity Press.

Giddens, A. (1998) *The Third Way: The Renewal of Social Democracy.* Cambridge: Polity Press.

Giddens, A. (1999) *Runaway World: How Globalization is Reshaping our Lives.* London: Profile Books.

Giddens, A. (2000) *The Third Way and its Critics.* Cambridge: Polity Press.

Gilchrist, A. (2004) *The Well-connected Community: A Networking Approach to Community Development.* Bristol: The Policy Press.

Gillborn, D. (1990) *'Race', Ethnicity and Education: Teaching and Learning in Multiethnic Schools.* London: Unwin Hyman/Routledge.

Gillborn, D. (1995) *Racism and Antiracism in Real Schools.* Buckingham: Open University Press.

Gilliat-Ray, S. (1998) Back to basics: the place of Islam in the self-identity of young British Muslims, in P.B. Clarke (ed.) *New Trends and Developments in the World of Islam*, pp. 93–103. London: Luzac Oriental.

Gil-Robles, A. (2005) *Report by Mr Alvaro Gil-Robles, Commissioner for Human Rights, on his Visit to the United Kingdom, 4–12 November 2004*, ComDH (2005) 6.

Gilroy, P. (2004) *After Empire: Melancholia or Convivial Culture*. London and New York: Routledge.

Gilroy, P. (2005) Multiculture, double consciousness and the 'war on terror', *Patterns of Prejudice*, 39 (4), 431–43.

Goldberg, D.T. (1994) Introduction: multicultural conditions, in D.T. Goldberg (ed.) *Multiculturalism: A Critical Reader*, pp. 1–44. Oxford, UK and Cambridge, USA: Blackwell.

Gordon, M. (1964) *Assimilation in American Life: The Role of Race, Religion and National Origins*. Oxford and New York: Oxford University Press.

Governance of Britain (2007) Green Paper, Cm 7170.

Government Consultation (2002) Equality and diversity: making it happen (retrieved from: http://www.womenandequalityunit.gov.uk/equality/project/making_it_happen.doc).

Government Response on Consultation (2004) Commission for Equality and Human Rights (retrieved from: http://www.womenandequalityunit.gov.uk/equality/project/consultation_govtresponse_nov2004.doc).

Graham, D. (2005) Preachers of hate could be charged with treason, *The Telegraph*, 8 August (retrieved from: http://www.telegraph.co.uk/news/main.jhtml?xml=/news/2005/08/08/nextreme08.xml-33k-).

Greaves, R. (2005) Negotiating British citizenship and Muslim identity, in T. Abbas (ed.) *Muslim Britain: Communities Under Pressure*, pp. 66–77. London: Zed Books.

Grin, J. (2005) Reflexive modernization as a governance Issue – or: designing and shaping re-structuration, in J.P. Vob, D. Bauknecht and R. Kemp (eds.) *Reflexive Governance for Sustainable Development*, pp. 46–65. Cheltenham: Edward Elgar.

Guardian Unlimited (2006) Full statement: Forest Gate raid, *The Guardian*, 2 June (retrieved from: http://www.guardian.co.uk/print/0,,329495606-111274. html).

Guardian Unlimited (Staff & Agencies) (2006) Muslim leaders call for 'partnership' in tackling terrorism, 14 August (retrieved from: http://politics.guardian.co.uk/terrorism/story/0,,1844421,00.html).

Gutman, A. (1994) Introduction, in A. Gutman (ed.) *Multiculturalism: Examining the Politics of Recognition*, pp. 3–24. New Jersey: Princeton University Press.

Habermas, J. (1994) Struggle for recognition in the democratic constitutional state, in A. Gutman (ed.) *Multiculturalism: Examining the Politics of Recognition*, pp. 107–48. New Jersey: Princeton University Press.

Hall, S. (1991) Old and new identities, old and new ethnicities, in A.D. King (ed.) *Culture, Globalization and the World System*, pp. 51–65. Basingstoke: Macmillan.

Harris, P. (2001) Race riots ignite Bradford, *The Observer*, 8 July (retrieved from: http://observer.guardian.co.uk/uk_news/story/0,6903,518610,00.html, pp. 1–4).

Harrison, M. (2005a) Introduction, in M. Harrison, D. Phillips, K. Kusminder, L. Hunt and J. Perry (eds.) *Housing, 'Race' and Community Cohesion*, pp. 1–24. Coventry: Chartered Institute of Housing.

Harrison, M. (2005b) From community cohesion to an inclusion and co-operation agenda, in M. Harrison, D. Phillips, K. Kusminder, L. Hunt and J. Perry (eds.) *Housing, 'Race' and Community Cohesion*, pp. 82–102. Coventry: Chartered Institute of Housing.

Hart, R. (2006) Towards a community-based approach to counter-terrorism. Report on the Wilton Park Conference in Association with DEMOS (retrieved from: http://www.wiltonpark.org.uk/documents/conferences/WPSO6/pdfs/WPSO6-5.pdf).

Hayes, B. (2006) There is no 'balance' between security and civil liberties – just less of each', in T. Bunyan (ed.) *The War on Freedom and Democracy: Essays on Civil Liberties in Europe*, pp. 48–61. Nottingham: Spokesman Books.

Hellyer, H.A. (2007) Ruminations and reflections on British Muslims and Islam post-7/7, in T. Abbas (ed.) *Islamic Political Radicalism: A European Perspective*, pp. 247–62. Edinburgh: Edinburgh University Press.

Hencke, D. and Muir, H. (2006) Kelly: Imams failing to deter radicals, *The Guardian*, 14 August (retrieved from: http://politics.guardian.co.uk/terrorism/story/0,,1844135,00.html).

Herzfeld, M. (1992) *The Social Production of Indifference*. Chicago and London: The University of Chicago Press.

Hewitt, P. (2004) Equality and human rights in the 21st century. Speech at launch of the White Paper on the Commission for Equality and Human Rights, 12 May (retrieved from: http://www.womenandequalityunit.gov.uk/equality/project/cehr_launch_speech%20.doc).

Hewitt, R. (2005) *White Backlash: and the Politics of Multiculturalism*. Cambridge: Cambridge University Press.

Hillyard, P. (2002) In defence of civil liberties, in P. Scraton (ed.) *Beyond September 11: An anthology of dissent*, pp. 107–12. London: Pluto Press.

Hillyard, P. (2006) The 'war on terrorism': lessons from Ireland, in T. Bunyan (ed.) *The War on Freedom and Democracy: Essays on Civil Liberties in Europe*, pp. 5–10. Nottingham: Spokesman Books.

HM Government (2006) *Countering International Terrorism: The United Kingdom's Strategy*, Cm 6888. Norwich: The Stationery Office.

Holden, M. (2006) Reid heckled during speech to Muslims, *The Scotsman*, 20 September (retrieved from: http://news.scotsman.com/latest.cfm?id=138996 2006).

Holloway, D. (2004) Identity and the Northern Ireland conflict: an overview, Community Dialogue, March (retrieved from: http://www.communitydialogue.org/identityAndTheNorthernIrelandConflict.html).

Home Office (2001) *Community Cohesion: A Report of the Independent Review Team* (chaired by Ted Cantle). London: Home Office (retrieved from: http://www.homeoffice.gov.uk/comrace).

Home Office (2002) *Secure Borders, Safe Haven: Integration with Diversity in Modern Britain*, Cm 5387. London: Home Office.

Home Office (2004a) *Counter-terrorism Powers: Reconciling Security and Liberty in an Open Society*, Cm 6147. London: The Stationery Office.

Home Office (2004b) Strength in diversity: towards a community cohesion and race equality strategy. Home Office Communication Directorate (retrieved from: http://www.homeoffice.gov.uk/comrace).

Home Office (2005a) *Improving Opportunities, Strengthening Society: The Government's Strategy to Increase Race Equality and Community Cohesion.* London: Home Office.

Home Office (2005b) *Controlling our Borders: Making Migration Work for Britain* (retrieved from: http://www.official-documents.co.uk/document/cm64/6472/6472.htm).

Home Office (2006a) 'No room for complacency' on terror threat, 9 August (retrieved from: http://www.homeoffice.gov.uk/about-us/news/security-speech-090806?version=1).

Home Office (2006b) Rebalancing the criminal justice system in favour of the law-abiding majority: cutting crime, reducing re-offending and protecting the public (retrieved from: http://www.homeoffice.gov.uk/documents/CJS-review.pdf/CJS-review-english.pdf?view=Binary).

Home Office Faith Communities Unit (2004) *Working Together: Co-operation between Government and Faith Communities.* London: Home Office (retrieved from: http://www.communities.gov.uk/index.asp?id=1502454).

Home Office Press Release (2005) Tackling terrorism-behaviours unacceptable in the UK, 24 August (retrieved from: http://press.homeoffice.gov.uk/press-releases/Tackling_Terrorism-behaviours_Un?version=1).

Home Office Press Release (2006) English language tests for those seeking to settle, 4 December (retrieved from: http://www.press.homeoffice.gov.uk/press_releases/migrants-english-tests).

Honig, B. (1996) Difference, dilemmas and the political home, in S. Benhabib (ed.) *Democracy and Difference: Contesting the Boundaries of the Political*, pp. 257–77. Princeton, New Jersey: Princeton University Press.

Honig, B. (2006) Another cosmopolitanism: law and politics in the new Europe, in R. Post (ed.) *Seyla Benhabib: Another Cosmopolitanism*, pp. 102–27. Oxford: Oxford University Press.

Honneth, A. (2003) Redistribution as recognition: a response to Nancy Fraser, in N. Fraser and A. Honneth (eds.) *Redistribution or Recognition? A Political-philosophical Exchange*, pp. 110–97. London and New York: Verso.

House of Commons (Hansard), 24 May 2007, Column 1428–33.

House of Commons (2005) Equality bill – explanatory notes (retrieved from: http://www.publications.parliament.uk).

House of Commons (2006) Explanatory notes to Equality Act 2006 (retrieved from: http://www.opsi.gov.uk/acts/en2006/2006en03.htm).

House of Commons Constitutional Affairs Committee (2005) *The Operation of the Special Immigration Appeals Commission (SIAC) and the Use of Special Advocates, Volume 1*, HC 323-1. London: The Stationery Office Limited.

House of Commons Foreign Affairs Committee (2005) *Human Rights Annual Report*, HC 109. London: The Stationery Office.

House of Commons Home Affairs Committee (2005) *Terrorism and Community Relations*, HC 156-1. London: House of Commons.

Huck, P. (2005) Collateral damage, *The Guardian*, 2 March, p. 7.

Human Rights Watch (2004) 'Empty promises:' diplomatic assurances no safeguard against torture, 16 (4 D).

Huntington, S. P. (1993) The clash of civilizations? *Foreign Affairs*, 72 (4), 22–49.

Hussain, D. (2005) Dilwar Hussain: never mind what we are against. What are we for, *The Independent*, 28 August (retrieved from: http://comment. independent.co.uk/commentators/article308565.ece).

Hussain, Y. and Bagguley, P. (2003) Citizenship, ethnicity and identity: British Pakistanis after the 2001 'social disorder'. Working paper, Department of Sociology and Social Policy, University of Leeds.

Hussain, Y. and Bagguley, P. (forthcoming) Muslim responses to the 7th July bombings in London, in D. Zimmerman (ed.) *Terrorism and Diaspora*. Zurich: Centre for Security Studies.

Huysmans, J. (2006) *The Politics of Security: Fear, Migration and Asylum in the EU*. London and New York: Routledge.

Hyland, J. (2001) British Muslims threatened with treason charges, *World Socialist Web Site*, 10 November, 1–5 (retrieved from: http:www.wsws.org/articles/ 2001/nov2001/trea-n10.shtml).

ICM (2006) *Guardian* Muslims' poll, June 2006 (retrieved from: http://www. icmresearch.co.ok/reviews/2006/guardian%20-%20muslims%20-%20june06/ guardian%20muslim%20june06.asp).

Ignatieff, M. (1993) *Blood and Belonging: Journeys into the New Nationalism*: New York: Farrar, Straus and Giroux.

Ignatieff, M. (1996) Nationalism and toleration, in R. Caplan and J. Feffer (eds.) *Europe's New Nationalism: States and Minorities in Conflict*, pp. 213–32. Oxford: Oxford University Press.

Ignatieff, M. (2005) *The Lesser Evil: Political Ethics in an Age of Terror*. Edinburgh: Edinburgh University Press.

Inside Employment Studies (2005) *Leading Faith in Management*, February, Issue 1.

Irwin, S. (2005) *Reshaping Social Life*. London and New York: Routledge.

Isin, E.F. and Wood, P.K. (1999) *Citizenship and Identity*. London: Sage Publications.

Islamic Human Rights Commission (2004) *British Muslims' Expectations of the Government*. Wembley: Islamic Human Rights Commission.

Islamic Human Rights Commission (2005) *UK: Human Rights Under Sustained*

Attack in the 'War on Terror', 2 November (retrieved from: http: //www.ihrc. org.uk/show.php?id=1777).

Jefferson, T. and Holloway, W. (1997) The risk society in the age of anxiety, *British Journal of Sociology*, 48 (2), 252–66.

Jeffery, S. (2006) Q&A: the glorification of terrorism, *Guardian Unlimited*, 15 February (retrieved from: http://www.guardian.co.uk/terrorism/story/0,,1710 370,00.html).

Johnston, P. (2005) Calls to deport 'the voice of al-Qa'eda', *The Telegraph*, 27 July (retrieved from: http://www.telegraph.co.uk/news/main.jhtml?xml=/news/ 2005/07/27/nmass.27.xml).

Joint Committee on Human Rights (2003) *Anti-terrorism, Crime and Security Act 2001, Statutory Review and Continuance of Part 4*, Sixth Report, 3 March (retrieved from: http://www.publications.parliament.uk/pa/jt200203/jtselect/ jtrights/67/6702.thm).

Joint Committee on Human Rights (2004) *Commission for Equality and Human Rights: Structure, Functions and Power*, Eleventh Report, 20 April (retrieved from: http://www.publications.parliament.uk/pa/jt200304/jtselect/jtrights/ 78/7802.htm).

Joint Committee on Human Rights (2006a) *The UN Convention against Torture*, Nineteenth Report (retrieved from: http://www.publications.parliament.uk/ pa/jt200506/jtselect/jtrights/185/18508.htm).

Joint Committee on Human Rights (2006b) *The Human Rights Act: The DCA and Home Office Reviews*, Thirty-second Report (retrieved from: http://www. publications.parliament.uk/pa/jt200506/jtselect/jtrights/278/27802.htm).

Joly, D. (2004) Introduction, in D. Joly (ed.) *International Migration in the New Millennium: Global Movements and settlement*, pp. 1–14. Aldershot: Ashgate.

Joppke, C. (2004) The retreat of multiculturalism in the liberal state: theory and policy, *British Journal of Sociology*, 55 (2), 241–50.

Kalra, V.S. (2002) Riots, race and reports: Denham, Cantle, Oldham and Burnley inquiries, *Sage Race Relations Abstracts*, 27 (4), 20–30.

Kearns, I. and Muir, R. (2006) Citizenship in a multicultural democracy, expert paper: our nation's future (retrieved from: http://www.number10.gov.uk/ output/page10557.asp).

Kelly, R. (2006a) Britain: our values, our responsibilities. Speech to Muslim organizations on Working Together to Tackle Extremism Together, 11 October (retrieved from: http://www.communities.gov.uk/index.asp?id=1503690).

Kelly, R. (2006b) Speech by Ruth Kelly at the launch of the Commission on Integration and Community Cohesion, 24 August.

Kelly, R. (2007) Speech by Ruth Kelly MP at the launch of the interim statement of the Commission in Integration and Cohesion on 21 February (retrieved from: http://www.communities.gov.uk/index.asp?id+1506358, http://www. communities. gov.uk/index.asp?id=1502280).

Kennedy, H. (2005) *Just Law: The Changing Face of Justice – and why it matters to us all*. London: Vintage.

Khan, S. (2006) Fabian Society lecture, 3 July (retrieved from: http://www.fabian.society.org.uk/press_office/news_latest_all.asp?pressid=50).

Kivisto, P. (2005a) The revival of assimilation in historical perspective, in P. Kivisto (ed.) *Incorporating Diversity: Rethinking Assimilation in a Multicultural Age*, pp. 3–32. Boulder and London: Paradign Publishers.

Kivisto, P. (2005b) Social spaces, transnational immigration communities, and the politics of incorporation, in P. Kivisto (ed.) *Incorporating Diversity: Rethinking Assimilation in a Multicultural Age*, pp. 299–319. Boulder and London: Paradign Publishers.

Klung, F. (2000) Values for a Godless Age: *The History of the Human Rights Act and its Political and Legal Consequences*. London: Penguin Books.

Kooiman, J. (2005) *Governing as Governance*. London: Sage Publications.

Kostakopoulou, D. (2006) Thick, thin and thinner patriotism: is this all there is? *Oxford Journal of Legal Studies*, 26 (1), 73–106.

Kundnani, A. (2001a) From Oldham to Bradford: the violence of the violated, *Race & Class*, 43(2), 105–31.

Kundnani, A. (2001b) In a foreign land: the new popular racism, *Race & Class*, 43 (2), 41–60.

Kundnani, A. (2006) Cant on cohesion, black information link (retrieved from: http://www.blink.org.uk/print.asp?key=12374).

Kundnani, A. (2007) *The End of Tolerance: Racism in 21st Century Britain*. London: Pluto Press.

Laclau, E. and Mouffe, C. (1985) *Hegemony and the Socialist Strategy: Towards a Radical Democratic Politics*. London: Verso.

Lash, S. (1994a) Reflexivity and its doubles: structure, aesthetics, community, in U. Beck, A. Giddens and S. Lash (eds.) *Reflexive Modernization: Politics, Tradition and Aesthetics in the Modern Social Order*, pp. 110–73. Cambridge: Polity Press.

Lash, S. (1994b) Expert-systems or situated interpretations? Culture and institutions in disorganized capitalism, in U. Beck, A. Giddens and S. Lash (eds.) *Reflexive Modernization: Politics, Tradition and Aesthetics in the Modern Social Order*, pp. 198–215. Cambridge: Polity Press.

Lash, S. (1999) *Another Modernity: A different rationality*. Oxford: Blackwell Publishers.

Laxer, G. (2003) Radical transformative nationalisms confront the US empire, *Current Sociology*, 51 (2), 133–52.

Lea, M. (2005) Murdered by Human Rights, *The Sun Online* (retrieved from: http://www.thesun.co.uk/article/0,,2-20006210534,00.html).

Leggett, W. (2005) *After New Labour: Social Theory and Centre-left Politics*. Basingstoke: Palgrave.

Leweling, T. (2005) Exploring Muslim diaspora communities in Europe through a social movement lens: some initial thoughts, *Strategic Insights*, IV (5), 1–15 (retrieved from: http://www.ccc.nps.navy.mil/si/2005/May/lewelingMay05.asp).

Liberty and Justice (2005) *UK Compliance with the UN Convention Against Torture, Joint Committee on Human Rights* (retrieved from: http://www.justice.org.uk/images/pdfs/uncatsept05.pdf).

Liberty Press Release (2005) Prime Minister threatens fundamental human rights, 5 August (retrieved from: http://www.liberty-human-rights.org.uk/press/2005/pm-threatens-human-rights-act.shtml).

Liberty Press Release (2006) New terrorism act powers will make Britain less safe, 13 April (retrieved from: http://www.liberty-human-rights.org.uk/press/2006/terrorism-act-will-make-us-less-safe.shtml).

Lichtblau, E. (2003) U.S. uses terror law to pursue crimes from drugs to swindling, *The New York Times*, 28 September, p. 2.

Life in the United Kingdom Advisory Group (2003) The new and the old, report of the life in the United Kingdom Advisory Group, Home Office (retrieved from: http://www.ind.homeoffice.gov.uk/6353/aboutus/thenewandtheold.pdf).

Local Authority Association (2004) *Community Cohesion – an Action Guide*. London: Home Office.

Local Government Association (2002) *Guidance on Community Cohesion*. London: Home Office.

Lord Falconer (2007) Human rights and terrorism. Speech to the Royal United Services Institute, 14 February (retrieved from: http://www.rusi.org/events/ref:E45740BC85792E/info:public/infoID:E45D3093433F92/).

Lord Phillips (2006) Terrorism and human rights. University of Hertfordshire Law Lecture, 19 October (retrieved from: http://www.judiciary.gov.uk/publications_media/speeches/2006/sp191006.htm).

Mac an Ghail, M. (1999) *Contemporary Racisms and Ethnicities*. Buckingham: Open University Press.

Mac an Ghail, M. (2006) Summary, *Anti-terrorism Laws: The Experience of the Irish and Muslim Communities in the UK*. Report from the Seminar held on 21 April (retrieved from: http://www.cre.gov.uk/about/birmingham_seminar.html).

MacTaggart, F. (2004) Introduction, strength in diversity: towards a community cohesion and race equality strategy. Home Office Communication Directorate (retrieved from: http://www.homeoffice.gov.uk/comrace).

Malik, A.A. (2006) The state we are in, in A.A. Malik (ed.) *The State We Are In: Identity, Terror and the Law of Jihad*, pp. 14–31. Bristol and England: Amal Press.

Mamdani, M. (2005) *Good Muslim, Bad Muslim: America, the Cold War and the Roots of Terror*. New York: Three Leaves Press.

Mantouvalou, V. (2006) Anti-terrorism measures fall short of European standards, in T. Bunyan (ed.) *The War on Freedom and Democracy: Essays on Civil Liberties in Europe*, pp. 161–6. Nottingham: Spokesman Books.

Marranci, G. (2006) *Jihad Beyond Islam*. London: Berg.

Martínez, M.M. (2003) Identities, subjectification and subject positions:

reflections on transformation in the sphere of social intervention, *International Journal of Critical Psychology*, 9, 92–106.

Mason, A. (2007) Multiculturalism and the critique of diversity, in A.S. Laden and D. Owen (eds.) *Multiculturalism and Political Theory*, pp. 219–20. Cambridge: Cambridge University Press.

Masood, E. (2006) British Muslims: ends and beginnings, open democracy (retrieved from: http://www.opendemocracy.net/globalization/british_muslims_4048.jsp).

May, S. (1999) Introduction: towards critical multiculturalism, in S. May (ed.) *Critical Multiculturalism: Rethinking Multiculturalism and Antiracist Education*, pp. 1–10. London: Falmer Press.

McAdam, D. (1994) Culture and social movements, in E. Larana, H. Johnston and J. Gusfield (eds.) *New Social Movements: From Ideology to Identity*, pp. 36–58. Philadelphia: Temple University Press.

McGhee, D. (2003) Moving to 'our' common ground – a critical examination of community cohesion discourse in twenty-first century Britain, *Sociological Review*, 51 (3), 383–411.

McGhee, D. (2005a) *Intolerant Britain: Hate, Citizenship and Difference*. Berkshire: Open University Press and McGraw-Hill.

McGhee, D. (2005b) Patriots of the future? A critical examination of community cohesion strategies in contemporary Britain, *Sociological Research Online*, 10 (3) (retrieved from: http://www.socresonline.org.uk/10/3/contents.html).

McGhee, D. (2006) Getting 'host' communities on board – finding the balance between 'managed migration' and 'managed settlement' in community cohesion strategies, *Journal of Ethnic and Migration Studies*, 32 (1), 111–27.

McLaren, E. (2006) Britain facing a new breed of fascists, warns Reid, 9 August, *Times Online* (retrieved from: http://www.timesonline.co.uk/0,,1-2-2305628-2,00.html).

Merali, A. (2006) Is the veil an obstacle to Muslim integration? 12 October (retrieved from: http://www.ihrc.org.uk/show.php?id+2172).

Metropolitan Police Service (2002) Guide to the management and prevention of critical incidents (retrieved from: http://www.newscotlandyard.police.uk/foi/pdfs/other_information/corporate/management_and_prevention_of_critical_incidents_guide.pdf).

Modood, T. (1992) British Asian Muslims and the Rushdie affair, in J. Donald and A. Rattansi (eds.) *'Race', Culture and Difference*, pp. 260–78. London: Sage Publications.

Modood, T. (2002) The power of dialogue, in Muslim Council of Britain, *The Quest for Sanity: Reflections on September 11 and the Aftermath*, pp. 112–16. Middlesex, England: Muslim Council of Britain.

Modood, T. (2005) Remaking multiculturalism after 7/7, *Open Democracy*, 29 September (retrieved from: www.opendemocracy.net).

Modood, T. (2006) British Muslims and the politics of multiculturalism, in T. Modood et al. (eds.) *Multiculturalism, Muslims and Citizenship: A European*

Approach, pp. 37–56. London and New York: Routledge.

Modood, T. (2007) *Multiculturalism (Themes for the 21st Century)*. Cambridge: Polity Press:

Mouffe, C. (1992) Feminism, citizenship and radical democratic politics, in J. Butler and J.W. Scott (eds.) *Feminists Theorize the Political*, pp. 369–84. New York and London: Routledge.

Mouffe, C. (1993) *The Return of the Political*. London: Verso.

Mouffe, C. (1995) Democratic politics and the question of identity, in J. Rajchman (ed.) *The Identity in Question*, pp. 31–42. New York: Routledge.

Mouffe, C. (2005) *On the Political*. London and New York: Routledge.

Muslim Council of Britain (2006) Voices from the minarets: MCB study of UK Imams and mosques (retrieved from: http://www.mcb.org.uk/uploads/vfm.pdf).

Muslim News (2005) MCB calls for judicial inquiry into London bombing, *Muslim News*, 17 August (retrieved from: http://www.muslimnews.co.uk/index/press'php?pr=212).

Muslim Public Affairs Committee (2006) 5 things you can do to stop terror (retrieved from: http://www.mpacuk.org/content/view/824/34/).

National Commission on Terrorist Attacks upon the United States (2004) *The 9/11 Commission Report* (retrieved from: http://www.iwar.org.uk/homesec/resources/9-11/final-report.htm).

Nellis, M. (2007) Electronic monitoring and the creation of control orders for terror suspects in Britain, in T. Abbas (ed.) *Islamic Political Radicalism: A European Perspective*, pp. 263–78. Edinburgh: Edinburgh University Press.

Number 10 Downing Street (2003) Support shown for citizenship ceremonies, 9 December (retrieved from: http://www.number10.gov.uk/output/page49 62.asp).

Number 10 Downing Street (2004) Citizenship ceremonies begin, 26 February (retrieved from: http://www.number10.gov.uk/output/page5422.asp).

Office of Deputy Prime Minister (2004) *Social Cohesion*, HC 45-1. London: House of Commons.

Oldham Independent Review (2001) *One Oldham One Future*. Oldham: Oldham Independent Review.

Oliver, M. (2005) Blair calls for task force to combat 'evil ideology', 19 July, *The Guardian* (retrieved from: http://www.guardian.co.uk/attackonlondon/story/0,16132,1531798,00.html??gusrc=rss).

O'Malley, P. (1996) Indigenous Governance, *Economy and Society*, 26, 301–26.

O'Niell, S., Rumbelow, H. and Glenhill, R. (2005) Muslim 'task force' criticized for being too established, 20 July, *The Times* (retrieved from: http://www.timesonline.co.uk/article/0,,22989-1700976,00.html).

Panja, T. (2007) Gordon Brown plans new anti-terror laws, *Guardian Unlimited*, 3 June (retrieved from: http://www.guardian.co.uk/worldlatest/story/0,,6680435,00.html).

Parekh, B. (2000a) *The Future of Multi-ethnic Britain*. London: Profile Books.

Parekh, B. (2000b) *Rethinking Multiculturalism: Cultural Diversity and Cultural*

Theory. Basingstoke: Palgrave.

Parekh, B. (2002) Terrorism or intercultural dialogue, in K. Booth and T. Dunne (eds.) *Worlds in Collision: Terror and the Future of Global Order*, pp. 270–83. Basingstoke: Palgrave Macmillan.

Parekh, B. (2006a) Europe, liberalism and 'the Muslim question', in T. Modood, A. Triandafyllidou and R. Zapata-Barrero (eds.) *Multiculturalism, Muslims and Citizenship*, pp. 179–203. London and New York: Routledge.

Parekh, B. (2006b) Where is Britain going? Expert paper, our nation's future (retrieved from: http://www.number10.gov.uk/utput/Page10559.asp).

Parker, M. (2006) Blair, backs Straw in Veil Row, 18 October, *Arab News* (retrieved from: http://www.arabnews.com/?page=4&section=0&article=88382&d=18&m=10&y=2006).

Parker, M. (2007) Chancellor Gordon Brown and UK Muslims, *Arab News*, 15 January (retrieved from: http://www.arabnews.com?page+4&section+0&article+90983&d+15&m+1&y+2007).

Patel, I.A. (2007) The scales for defining Islamic political radicalisation, in T. Abbas (ed.) *Islamic Political Radicalism: A European Perspective*, pp. 42–56. Edinburgh: Edinburgh University Press.

Pattenden, R. (2006) Admissibility in criminal proceedings of third party and real evidence obtained by methods prohibited by UNCAT, *International Journal of Evidence and Proof*, 10 E & P, 1–41 (retrieved from: http://www.uea.ac.uk/law/resources/Torture_PR_edited3.pdf).

Phelan, P. (1993) *Unmarked: The Politics of Performance*. New York and London: Routledge.

Phillips, T. (2005) After 7/7: sleepwalking into segregation. Speech to the Manchester Council for Community Relations on 22 September (retrieved from: http://83.137.212.42/sitearchive/cre/Default.aspx.LocID-0hgnew07s.ReflocID-0hg00900c002.Lang-EN.htm#top).

Political Policy News (2005) New task force to battle 'evil ideology', 19 July (retrieved from: http://www.politics.co.uk/domestic-policy/new-tasorce-battle-evil-ideology-$1500...).

Post, R. (2006) Introduction, in R. Post (ed.) *Seyla Benhabib: Another Cosmopolitanism*, pp. 1–12. Oxford: Oxford University Press.

Preventing Extremism Together Working Groups (2005) *Working Together to Prevent Extremism*. London: Home Office.

Privy Counsellor Review Committee (2003) *Anti-terrorism, Crime and Security Act 2001 Review: Report*, HC 100. London: The Stationery Office.

Putnam, R., Feldstein, L. and Cohen, D. (2003) *Better Together: Restoring the American Community*. Australia: Simon & Schuster.

Ramzy v. the Netherlands [2005] ECHR, Application No. 25424/05.

Rattansi, A. (1999) Racism, 'postmodernism' and reflexive multiculturalism, in S. May (ed.) *Critical Multiculturalism: Rethinking Multiculturalism and Anti-racist Education*. London: Falmer Press and Taylor & Francis Group, 77–112.

Reid, J. (2006) Reid addresses RUSI on '20th-century rules, 21st-century conflict', 3 April (retrieved from: http://www.mod.uk/DefenceInternet/DefenceNews/ DefencePolicyAndBusiness/ReidAddressesRusiOn20thcenturyRules21st centuryConflict.pdf).

Roberts, B. (2005) Rules Britannia: Blair reveals his 12-point plan to tackle terror, *The Mirror*, 6 August (retrieved from: http://www.mirror.co.uk/printable_ version.cfm?objectid+15825699&siteid+94762).

Robertson, G. (2005) Foreword, in G. Robertson (ed.) *Torture: Does it Make Us Safer? Is it Ever OK? A Human Rights Perspective*, pp. ix–xviii. New York and London: The New Press.

Rose, N. (1999a) Preface to the Second Edition, in N. Rose (ed.) *Governing the Soul: The Shaping of the Private Self*, Second Edition, pp. vii–xxvi. London and New York: Free Association Books.

Rose, N. (1999b) *The Powers of Freedom: Reframing Political Thought*. Cambridge: Cambridge University Press.

Ross, J. (2005) A history of torture, in G. Robertson (ed.) *Torture: Does it Make Us Safer? Is it Ever OK? A Human Rights Perspective*, pp. 3–17. New York and London: The New Press.

Roy, O. (2004) *Globalized Islam: The Search for a New Ummah*. New York: Columbia University Press.

Runnymede Trust (1997) Islamophobia (retrieved from: http://www.runnymede trust.org/meb/islamophobia).

Runnymede Trust (2002) *The Nature of Islamophobia* (retrieved from: http:// www.runnymedetrust.org/meb/islamaphobia/nature.html).

Said, E.W. (1978) *Orientalism*. London: Penguin Books.

Schuster, L. and Solomos, J. (2001) Introduction: citizenship, multiculturalism, identity, *Patterns of Prejudice*, 35 (1), 3–12.

Seddon, M.S. (2004) Muslim communities in Britain: a historiography, in M.S. Seddon, D. Hussain and N. Malik (eds.) *British Muslims: Between Assimilation and Segregation*, pp. 1–42. Markfield: The Islamic Foundation.

Seddon, M.S., Hussain, D. and Malik, N. (2004) Introduction, in M.S. Seddon, D. Hussain and N. Malik (eds.) *British Muslims: Between Assimilation and Segregation*, pp. vii–xvi. Markfield: The Islamic Foundation.

Shaw, D. (2007) Terrorism focus for the new-look Home Office, BBC News, 29 March (retrieved from: http://news.bbc.co.uk/2/hi/uk_news/6507523.stm).

Silvestri, S. (2007) Europe and political Islam: encounters of the twentieth and twenty-first centuries, in T. Abbas (ed.) *Islamic Political Radicalism: A European Perspective*, pp. 57–70. Edinburgh: Edinburgh University Press.

Singh, D. (2006) Speech by Darra Singh at the launch of the Commission on Integration and Community Cohesion (retrieved from: http://www.communities.gov.uk/index.asp?id=1502287).

Singh, D. (2007) Not speaking English is the single biggest barrier to successful integration, Commission on Integration and Community Cohesion. Speech to launch interim report (retrieved from: http://.integrationandcohesion. org.uk/news/Not_speaking_english_is_the_sigle_biggestbarrier_to_successful _integration.aspx).

Sivanandan, A. (2006) 'The rules of the game?' in T. Bunyan (ed.) *The War on Freedom and Democracy: Essays on Civil Liberties in Europe*, pp. 1–4. Nottingham: Spokesman Books.

Smith, L. (2001) Britain: Bradford is fourth city hit by riots, World Socialist Web Site, 10 July (retrieved from: http://www.wsws.org/articles/2001/jul2001/ brad-j10.shtml, pp. 1–4).

Snow, D. and Benford, R. (1988) Ideology, frame resonance, and participation mobilization, in B. Klandermans, K. Hanspeter and S. Tarrow (eds.) *International Social Movements Research*, Vol. 1, pp. 197–217. Connecticut and London: JAI Press Inc.

Snow, D., Burke Rochford, E., Worden, S. and Benford, R. (1986) Frame alignment processes, micromobilization, and movement participation, *American Sociological Review*, 51 (4), 464–82.

Solomos, J. (2001) Race, multi-culturalism and difference, in N. Stevenson (ed.) *Culture and Citizenship*, pp. 198–211. London: Sage Publications.

Spalek, B. (2007) Disconnection and exclusion: pathways to radicalization, in T. Abbas (ed.) *Islamic Political Radicalism: A European Perspective*, pp. 192–230. Edinburgh: Edinburgh University Press.

Staunœs, D. (2003) Where have all the subjects gone? Bringing together the concepts of intersectionality and subjectification, *NORA*, 11 (2), 101–10.

Stevenson, N. (2002) Cosmopolitanism, multiculturalism and citizenship, *Sociological Research Online*, 7 (1), 1–17 (retrieved from: http://www.socresonline. org.uk/7/1/stevenson.html).

Stevenson, N. (2003) Cultural citizenship in the 'cultural' society: a cosmopolitan approach, *Citizenship Studies*, 7 (3), 331–48.

Straw, J. (1999) Building a human rights culture. Address to the Civil Service College Seminar, 9 December (retrieved from: http://wwww.nationalarchives.gov.uk/ERO/records/ho415/1/hract/cscape.htm).

Straw, J. (2006) In quotes: Jack Straw on the veil, BBC News, 6 October (retrieved from: http://news.bbc.co.uk/2/hi/uk_news/politics/5413470.stm).

Sturcke, J. (2007) Libyan terror suspects win deportation appeal, *Guardian Unlimited*, 27 April (retrieved from: http://www.guardian.co.uk/print/o,, 329795457-111274,00.html).

Tarrow, S. (1994) *Power in Movement: Social Movements, Collective Action and Politics*. Cambridge and New York: Cambridge University Press.

Taylor, C. (1994) The politics of recognition, in A. Gutman (ed.) *Multiculturalism: Examining the Politics of Recognition*, pp. 25–75. New Jersey: Princeton University Press.

Temko, N. (2006) Beckett rejects links between foreign policy and terrorism, *The Observer*, 13 August (retrieved from: http://politics.guardian.co.uk/terrorism/

story/0,,1843687,00.html).

Tempelman, S. (1999) Constructions of cultural identity: multiculturalism and exclusion, *Political Studies*, XLVII, 17–29.

Tempest, M. (2004) It boils down to intolerance, *The Guardian*, 2 July (retrieved from: http://politics.guardian.co.uk/homeaffairs/story/0,,1252905,00.html, pp. 1–4).

The 1990 Trust (2006) *Muslim Views: Foreign Policy and its Effects* (retrieved from: http://www.blink.org.uk/docs/muslim_survey_report_screen.pdf).

The National Commission on the Terrorist Attacks Upon the United States (2004) *The 9/11 Commission Report: The Full Report of the National Commission on the Terrorist Attacks Upon the United States*. Washington, DC: W.W. Norton & Company.

Trend, D. (1996a) Democracy's crisis of meaning, in D. Trend (ed.) *Radical Democracy: Identity, Citizenship and the State*, pp. 7–18. London and New York: Routledge.

Trend, D. (1996b) Introduction, in D. Trend (ed.) *Radical Democracy: Identity, Citizenship and the State*, pp. 1–4. London and New York: Routledge.

Troyna, B. (1987) *Racial Inequality in Education*. London: Tavistock.

Troyna, B. (1993) *Racism and Education*. Buckingham: Open University Press.

Troyna, B. and Hatcher, R. (1992) *Racism in Children's Lives: A Study of Mainly White Primary Schools*. London: Routledge.

Turner, B.S. (2002) Cosmopolitan virtue, globalization and patriotism, *Theory, Culture & Society*, 19 (1–2), 45–63.

Ungoed-Thomas, J. (2006) The 'hearts and minds' battle for British Muslims that failed, *Times Online*, 13 August (retrieved from: http://www.timesonline.co.uk/article/0,,2087-2310565,00.html).

Verkaik, R. (2005) Religious leaders unite to defy terror, *The Independent*, 11 July, p. 14.

Wainright, M. (2006) Dangerous attack or fair point? Straw veil row deepens, *The Guardian*, 7 October (retrieved from: http://www.guardian.co.uk/religion/story/0,,1889846,00.html).

Waldron, J. (2003) Security and liberty: the image of balance, *The Journal of Political Philosophy*, 11 (2), 191–210.

Walzer, M. (2004) *Politics and Passion: Towards a More Egalitarian Liberalism*. New Haven and London: Yale University Press.

Ward, I. (2006) Shabina Begum and the headscarf girls, *Journal of Gender Studies*, 15 (2), 119–31.

Weedon, C. (1987) *Feminist Practice and Postructuralist Theory*. Oxford: Basil Blackwell.

Weir, S. (2006) Introduction, in S. Weir (ed.) *Unequal Britain: Human Rights as a Route to Social Justice*, pp. ix–xviii. London: Politico's.

Werbner, P. (2000) Divided loyalties, empowered citizenship? Muslims in Britain, *Citizenship Studies*, 4 (3), 307–24.

Werbner, P. (2002) *Imagined Diasporas Among Manchester's Muslims: The Public Performance of Pakistani Transnational Identity Politics*. Santa Fe: School of American Research Press.

Werbner, P. (2005) The translocation of culture: 'community cohesion' and the force of multiculturalism in history, *The Sociological Review*, 54 (4), 745–68.

Westminster Halls Debates (2005) *Terrorism and Community Relations* (retrieved from: http://www.theyworkforyou.com/whall/?id=2005-10-27a.141.1&s=Privy).

Wetherell, M. (2007) Introduction, community cohesion and identity dynamics: dilemmas and challenges, in M. Wetherell, M. Laflèche and R. Berkeley (eds.) *Identity, Ethnic Diversity and Community Cohesion*, pp. 1–14. London: Sage Publications.

Wintour, P. (2006) Muslims must do more, says Blair, *The Guardian*, 5 July (retrieved from: http://www.guardian.co.uk/print/o,,329521419-103685,00.html).

Women and Equality Unit (2002) *Equality and Diversity: Making it Happen* (retrieved from: http://www.womenandequalityunit.gov.uk/equality/project/making_it_happen/cons_doc.htm).

Woolf, M. (2005) 'The way to let terrorists win is to shut down free speech', *The Independent*, 11 July, p. 15.

Yaqoob, S. (2007) British Islamic political radicalisation, in T. Abbas (ed.) *Islamic Political Radicalism: A European Perspective*, pp. 279–96. Edinburgh: Edinburgh University Press.

Young, I.M. (1990) *Justice and the Politics of Difference*. Princeton: Princeton University Press.

Young, J. (1999) *The Exclusive Society: Social Exclusion, Crime and Difference*. London: Sage Publications.

Young, J. (2003) To these wet and windy shores: recent immigration policy in the UK, *Punishment & Society*, 5 (40), 449–62.

Yuval-Davis, N. (1992) Fundamentalism, multiculturalism and women in Britain, in J. Donald and A. Rattansi (eds.) *'Race', Culture and Difference*, pp. 278–92. London: Sage Publications.

Yuval-Davis, N. (1994) Women, ethnicity and empowerment, *Feminism & Psychology*, 4 (1), 179–97.

Zedner, L. (2005) Securing liberty in the face of terror: reflections from criminal justice, *Journal of Law and Society*, 32 (4), 507–33.

Zine, J. (2006) Unveiling sentiments: gendered Islamophobia and experiences of veiling among Muslim girls in a Canadian islamic school, *Equity & Excellence in Education*, 39, 239–52.

Žižek, S. (2002) *Welcome to the desert of the real*. London and New York: Verso.

Index